CAGES TO JUMP SHOTS

CAGES TO JUMP SHOTS

Pro Basketball's Early Years

ROBERT W. PETERSON

New York   Oxford
OXFORD UNIVERSITY PRESS
1990

Oxford University Press

Oxford   New York   Toronto
Delhi   Bombay   Calcutta   Madras   Karachi
Petaling Jaya   Singapore   Hong Kong   Tokyo
Nairobi   Dar es Salaam   Cape Town
Melbourne   Auckland

and associated companies in
Berlin   Ibadan

Published by Oxford University Press, Inc.,
200 Madison Avenue, New York, New York 10016

Oxford is a registered trademark of Oxford University Press

Library of Congress Cataloging-in-Publication Data
Peterson, Robert, 1925–
Cages to jump shots: pro basketball's early years / Robert W. Peterson.
p.   cm.   Includes bibliographical references.
Includes bibliographical references.
ISBN 0–19–505310–9
1. Basketball—United States—History.
2. National Basketball Association—History.   I. Title.
GV885.7.P49   1990
796.332′64′0973—dc20   90–31214

2 4 6 8 9 7 5 3 1
Printed in the United States of America
on acid-free paper

To Peg

Preface

Professional basketball has had a long and colorful past, but much of it has been obscured in the mists of time. I venture to guess that the average well-informed fan believes the pro game began with the first year of the National Basketball Association in 1949. In fact, the first professional teams had appeared fifty-three years before that, and thousands of men and a few women were paid to play during the intervening decades.

Anyone who has dipped into the copious literature on baseball's history can identify Honus Wagner, Ty Cobb, Three-Finger Brown, and Christy Mathewson. Their contemporaries and counterparts in basketball were Al Cooper, Harry Hough, Ed Wachter, and Andy Suils—hardly names that resonate in sports history. The main reason is that during the first half of this century major league baseball was by far the most popular team sport. Football was a distant second, and basketball was not even in the running. When the NBA began, even hockey, Canada's national game, got more ink than professional basketball.

A secondary reason, no doubt, is that baseball, by the nature of the game, lends itself better than other sports to contemplation and myth-making. Nothing in sports quite matches the pitcher-batter confrontation and the orderly progression of balls, strikes, outs, and innings. Basketball—and football and hockey, too—lacks that linear appeal. A basketball game may offer forty-eight minutes of furious action, culminating in a pretty jump shot that wins it at the buzzer, but the jump shot defies analysis and there are only so many ways to describe it. By contrast, a baseball fan can spend a happy hour (or unhappy hour, if his team lost) speculating that the winning run scored because an outfielder was three feet out of position, and that the runner was waved home because the third base coach knew the fielder's arm was mediocre.

So it is understandable that professional basketball's early days have not been as thoroughly explored as baseball's. A curious fan could learn a good deal by consulting the encyclopedias on the game and the works of a few authors who have touched on the pioneering players and leagues. By and large, though, it's pretty thin gruel, especially for the earliest years.

This book aims to enrich the soup. It covers more than sixty years, from the day in 1891 when James Naismith nailed up the peach baskets at Springfield College to the infancy of the NBA. The book ends with the 1954–55 season, when the NBA introduced the 24-second shot clock, the rule change that brought basketball into the modern era.

Over that span, basketball changed far more than any other team sport in its rules, techniques, and the skills required to play it at the professional level. The reader will learn how the pro game evolved from a 14-man melee in a cage, usually ending in a score on the order of 10 to 3, into the ten-man battle of wits, brawn, and agility it had become in the early years of the NBA.

More than passing attention will be given to the pioneering professional leagues, not because they were in the national eye (they were not), but because they employed the stars of their era. The early leagues are often depicted as fly-by-night affairs. Most of the leagues that operated between 1898, when the first was started in the Philadelphia-Trenton, N.J., area, and the formation of the National Basketball Association were indeed shaky. Only a couple of them lasted more than six years. But as early as 1910 the six teams in the Central League completed a schedule of seventy games—just twelve fewer than the regular season schedule of the NBA today. That's fly-by-night?

Furthermore, a star professional could earn as much as the average major league baseball player, the darling of the sporting crowd at the time, by selling his services to the highest bidder and playing almost every night. In a nutshell, professional basketball has had a far richer and more extensive past than is readily apparent.

Hundreds of players, teams, and leagues are mentioned, but this book is not encyclopedic. It may be more social history than sports history because I am less interested in knowing that the Trenton Tigers won the Eastern League championship in 1912 than I am in the kind of men they were, how they played the game, and what their victory meant to them and Trenton's fans. Nevertheless, to satisfy readers who crave details and statistics, an appendix gives the results of all major leagues from 1898 to 1954.

The word "major" requires definition in this context. All of the early leagues were local or regional, covering a metropolitan area, one or two states, or—at most—cities in the Northeast and Midwest. If they attracted many of the best professional players of their time, they are "major," even if the teams represented small cities. In 1910 the Central League, for example, had a team in Pittsburgh, but its other members were McKeesport, Johnstown, Greensburg, Homestead, and Uniontown, Pa. For my purposes it was a major league because its player rosters included such pioneer stars as Andy Sears, Joe Fogarty, Jimmy Kane, Bill

Keenan, and Dutch Wohlfarth. If my definition of major is too broad for the reader's taste, I ask indulgence.

There is a strong temptation to dismiss these early players and teams as small potatoes. That temptation will be resisted in this book. The professional game *was* small potatoes by the standards of today's NBA, but the players were not. They were skilled athletes during a period when their game was a backwater on the national sports scene. As we explore their world, it is well to remember that they were the best of their times.

In compiling this history, I have relied chiefly on several basketball guides, yearbooks, and magazines, and the skimpy newspaper and magazine coverage of the professional game in its first forty-odd years. The story has been enriched by the recollections of players, referees, team owners, and managers who patiently sat with me and talked for hours about the game and the lives they led as professional basketball men before the game was of much consequence on the nation's sports pages.

Four of the men who gave freely of their time are in Basketball's Hall of Fame, and perhaps others should be, but no effort was made to seek out only former stars. Rather, I sought to interview a representative sample of men covering various eras and sections of the country. Most had passed the biblical three score years and ten, and one, Joe Schwarzer, was a sprightly ninety-two-year-old who had no difficulty recalling what it was like to play in the New York State League in 1919.

I am deeply indebted to the following men for their courtesy and willingness to dredge their memories for my enlightenment: Gerry Archibald, Scott Armstrong, Frank A. Baird, Carl B. Bennett, Robert J. Calihan, Alfred (Al) Cervi, Charles H. (Chuck) Chuckovits, Haskell Cohen, Albert Cooper, Jr., Hans Dienelt, J. Emmett (Flip) Dowling, William (Pop) Gates, Sidney Goldberg, Moe Goldman, Joel S. (Shikey) Gotthoffer, Lester Harrison, Roy Hurley, Harry E. (Buddy) Jeannette, Sam (Sammy) Kaplan, Andrew (Fuzzy) Levane, Nathan (Nat) Militzok, Emmett Morrison, Harry (Jammy) Moskowitz, John P. Nucatola, John J. O'Brien, Jr., Herman C. (Chick) Passon, Gene Scholz, Joseph K. Schwarzer, and Dr. Moe C. Spahn. I am also grateful to the following, whom I interviewed by telephone: Roosevelt (Roosie) Hudson, Johnny Jordan, Orwell Moore, owner of the All-American Red Heads; Bernard (Bernie) Price, and Paul Sokody.

This book would have been a considerably more difficult undertaking without the help of William F. Himmelman, the NBA's historian. Bill Himmelman is, to put it crudely but accurately, a basketball nut and a demon for data. His passion for the last fifteen years has been collecting information about professional players, teams and leagues going back to the nineteenth century, and no doubt he knows more about them than any living soul.

Bill contributed in several ways. To find my interviewees, I turned to his card-indexed file with the names, addresses, and basketball records of some four thousand players for the period covered by this book. He is responsible for the appendixes listing major league standings and the results of the World Tournaments which were held from 1939 to 1948. He also read the manuscript in an effort to catch any egregious errors and mistakes in emphasis. He is not to be blamed for any errors that remain; they are my own. Bill Himmelman's colleague in statistical research, Karel deVere, also contributed useful data.

For a project like this book the author always owes a debt to librarians. I should mention particularly Wayne R. Patterson, research specialist at the Basketball Hall of Fame library, who went far beyond the call of duty to locate materials for me. June Steitz, the Hall's retired librarian, was also most obliging.

In addition, I am grateful to the following persons who filled in gaps in the story or assisted in some other way in the research: Bonnie Askenase and Michael Cardozo of Proskauer, Rose, Goetz & Mendelsohn, counsel to the National Basketball Association; Sheldon Basloe and Jerry Levin of the family of pioneer promoter Frank J. Basloe; author Ocania Chalk, Mildred Cooper, daughter of one of the first professional players; H. Thomas Dewhirst, Morris (Moe) Dubilier, Abe Gerchick, Mary Hedge, director of archives at the YMCA of Greater New York; Andrea Hinding, archivist at the YMCA of the USA Archives; Sister Martin Joseph Jones, director of archives at the State University College at Buffalo; Peter Levine, historian at Michigan State University; Cynthia McLane of the McKeesport, Pa., Heritage Center; Sue Merighi, reference librarian at the Millville, N.J., Public Library; John V. Miller, director of Archival Services at the University of Akron; Buffalo baseball historian Joseph M. Overfield, Donna L. Richardson, research librarian of the Society of Actuaries; author Wayne O. Rumlow, the late Bus Saidt, sports editor of the Trenton, N.J., *Times;* Sharon B. Shrieves, junior library assistant at the Trenton Free Public Library; and Lee Williams, director emeritus of the Basketball Hall of Fame.

Finally, I would be an ungrateful wretch if I did not express my gratitude to my wife, Peg. She does not know a slam dunk from a point guard and has minimal interest in learning the difference. But Peg willingly helped with the dreary task of typing manuscript and was of good cheer during the many hours when I was engrossed in the world of seventy years ago. If there is no special place in Valhalla for authors' spouses, there should be.

Ramsey, N.J.   Robert Peterson

Contents

CAGES TO JUMP SHOTS

1

The Old Pros Remember

In twenty-five cities across America, 324 very large young men in short pants and sneakers spend eight months each year stuffing a 9.55-inch ball through an 18-inch hoop. For their labors they earn the admiration of a national audience and salaries averaging about $775,000 a year.

Their vineyard is the National Basketball Association, the pinnacle of a sport that attracts more spectators on the high school, college, and professional levels than baseball and football combined. Baseball may be the national pastime and football the national mania, but basketball is the national game. The NBA is its Mecca. For young athletes growing up in big-city ghettoes, the rural heartland, and many parts of suburbia, professional basketball offers the dream of fame and wealth.

It was not always so. For fifty years after its beginnings in the last years of the nineteenth century, basketball was a stepchild on the national sports scene. It had its local heroes in such hotbeds as Brooklyn, Trenton, N.J., Troy, N.Y., Philadelphia, Indianapolis and Fort Wayne, Ind., Oshkosh and Sheboygan, Wis., and Akron, Ohio, but their fame rarely penetrated the offices of sports editors on major newspapers and magazines.

During the 1920s—often called the Golden Age of Sport—the Original Celtics dominated professional basketball as no team has in any other sport, but their stars are never mentioned in the same breath with Babe Ruth, Red Grange, Dempsey and Tunney, Bill Tilden, and Bobby Jones. Another measure of the comparative obscurity of pro basketball in its early years may be seen in the fact that Paul Gallico, publishing a hugely entertaining memoir titled *Farewell to Sport* in 1937 after retiring as sports editor of the New York *Daily News,* managed only one paragraph on basketball in 341 pages of reminiscence. And that snippet was about college basketball, which he called a "brisk, mildly exciting game to watch, with plenty of skill, speed, and hard body-contact."

Professional basketball began in gaslit social halls and National Guard armories in the Northeast. The early pros became hometown icons. Their

3

victories were celebrated in reams of fervent prose in the local press. As early as 1910 some professional stars could, by playing with different teams four or five nights a week, earn as much as major league baseball players, then the elite of the sports world. To be sure, their income was modest by today's standards—perhaps $2400 a year—but at a time when a skilled laborer made $800 for a year's work, professional basketball was already an attractive alternative to the workaday world.

Their game was not the race-horse, slam-dunking ballet of the modern NBA. It was slow, almost stately by comparison, with crisp passing but little all-out running, careful shot selection, and only two approved shooting methods—the one-hand layup near the basket and the two-hand set shot.

A major league baseball player of today who was caught in a 1915 time warp would feel right at home on John McGraw's New York Giants. Oh, the uniforms and gloves would look primitive and the ball would have less rabbit in it than the modern ball, but the game would be three strikes, four balls, three outs, and nine innings. With due allowance for the dead ball and the consequent rarity of home runs, strategy in McGraw's era was much the same as it is today. Similarly, football in 1915 would look familiar to today's player, although the equipment was much cruder, the players on average were much smaller (and played both offense and defense), and offensive formations were designed primarily for running plays.

In contrast, a modern NBA player who stepped onto a 1915 basketball court would be at sea. He would find himself a giant among pygmies. Most early pros were barely above the average height for adult males, and several pioneer stars stood only a few inches above five feet. It was not until the 1940s that big men began to dominate professional basketball.

The court itself would confound today's professional. It was likely to be only 65 feet long and 35 feet wide—roughly two-thirds the size of the regulation NBA court. It was also likely to be enclosed in a cage with wire or rope netting walls from 10 to 35 feet high. The basket might have a backboard—but it might not, depending on the league. The ball would feel decidedly strange, too: a leather-encased pumpkin somewhat larger than today's molded ball, with laces along one side creating a bulge that made shooting and dribbling an adventure. In most leagues double dribbling was permitted; that is, a player could bounce the ball any number of times, catch it, and resume dribbling. One player might shoot all foul shots for his team, and free throws were given for such violations as running with the ball or kicking it, as well as for charging and hacking. The game lasted 40 minutes—eight minutes less than today's NBA contests.

Because in a cage the ball was never out of bounds, a typical game was over in not much more than an hour. There were no 24-second shot clock, no midcourt 10-second line, and no 3-second restriction on offensive players in the foul lane.

The jump shot and dunk were unimagined. Layups near the basket were

An early basketball. The player is holding it in proper form to launch a two-hand set shot. *Basketball Hall of Fame Photo.*

performed with one hand as they are today, although the shot required a much more delicate touch in leagues in which backboards were not used. The other accepted shot—the two-hand set—might be launched underhand, from the chest level, or overhead. After every field goal and successful free throw, the teams lined up at center court for a center jump, which today is used only to start the game.

Offensive play was extremely conservative. Often a team would while away several minutes by passing and dribbling until a man broke free under the basket or its ace set-shooter had time to fire a high-percentage shot. The result was that typical scores were 14 to 7 and 23 to 21 in those early days. Even in the late 1930s, when the game was beginning to evolve into modern basketball, scores tended to be in the 30s and 40s.

Still, the pioneering pros were laying the foundation stones for the National Basketball Association. What kind of men were they? How did a boy learn the game and turn professional? What did basketball mean in their lives?

The earliest professionals are long in their graves, and so we must look for answers to a few letters and newspaper clips in which they spoke about the game. But many men who played professionally between the two World Wars, when the pro game was in its adolescence, are still alive. Let us hear from five of them.

J. Emmett (Flip) Dowling, born in Albany, N.Y., in 1899, was a high school star as a 6-foot 1-inch center at Cathedral Academy before and during World War I. At the same time, he was playing for semipro teams under an assumed name. After graduation he joined Cohoes in the New York State League, one of four professional circuits struggling for existence in the postwar years. He later became a basketball referee and an outstanding high school basketball and football coach in Albany.

Here Flip Dowling speaks about his introduction to play-for-pay:

> When I was in high school, I was playing outside basketball, let's put it that way. A group of fellows who called themselves the Elm Club used to run dances in the Catholic Union Hall, which had been an armory. They decided they wanted a basketball team, but they were a little older and had not played much athletics, you see, so they got a group of basketball players together, and every Friday night they'd have a basketball game and a dance. We drew pretty good crowds.
>
> And we used to play all the towns around here. We'd get all the fellows and their girls in a bus and go out and play Voorheesville, Castleton and Mechanicville, little towns around Albany.
>
> Then one night when we were playing at Catholic Union Hall, a couple of thugs—fellows the Elm Club members knew, but they were ruffians—after the game was over they raided the box office and stole all the proceeds. There was a brawl and some people got arrested and had to go to police court. So the next year the Elm Club didn't take up basketball because they didn't want to get involved—it was too much of a headache.
>
> But an alderman by the name of Dolan—he ran a saloon—got interested and backed us and we called the team the Dolans. I graduated from high school that year—in 1918—but I was still playing under an assumed name because I was also playing for Albany State Teachers' College. The Dolans were a pretty good team. World War I ended during the course of that season, and a fellow by the name of Brownie Hepinstall, from Rensselaer, who had had a team in the Army in France, brought a team called the Minesweepers to Albany. With the Minesweepers, we just packed the place. Ordinarily, after we'd paid the band we'd split up the proceeds and we might have gotten four or five dollars apiece

for playing. But when the Minesweepers were there we got something like eight or ten dollars.

So Brownie Hepinstall started playing with us. He was a promoter and he kind of took over as manager. We made more money under him then we ever did before, although we weren't looking for money, we just wanted to play basketball.

William H. (Brownie) Hepinstall, Jr., was an organizer as well as a promoter. Under his direction the New York State League, which had been dormant since 1916, was reorganized for the 1919–20 season with franchises in Mohawk Valley cities and Pittsfield, Mass. Flip Dowling and his youthful teammates were eager to play as full-fledged pros. "We were still kids, and we thought it was great that we were going to play in this league," Dowling said. "But Brownie had other ideas. He wanted to have a championship team, and he wanted us to sit on the bench." So when Hepinstall brought in Barney Sedran, Max (Marty) Friedman, and Harry Riconda, all established stars in the New York metropolitan area, for his Albany franchise, Flip Dowling and his teammates looked elsewhere for action. Dowling was signed by Cohoes of the New York State League. Here he recalls the professional game in 1919:

> Nearly all the teams in the New York State League played in armories. I guess whoever ran the armory got in on the split of the gate, even though he did not run the club. I remember that later on, when I played for All-Syracuse, which was not in a league, we actually had to join the National Guard to play in the armory. We never went to drills or anything like that, and when the season was over they gave us a discharge.
>
> In the New York State League, all the clubs had cages. The cage was made of fish net that ran from the ceiling down to the floor. It was attached to the floor with hooks. In Albany, the net went up only so high—35 feet or something like that—and they had stringers the rest of the way up to the girders.
>
> The league did not use backboards. A piece of iron rod was suspended from the ceiling and came through the net to hold the basket.
>
> In the cage, it was common practice if the man with the ball was near the net, you would grab the net on both sides of him and press him into the net so he couldn't pass the ball and they'd have a jump ball. Otherwise, the cage didn't make much difference in how the game was played.
>
> But there was one fellow who played down in Catskill by the name of Toby Matthews. Catskill had the best net in the business—real strong—and he had developed a one-hand shot where he could roll the ball off that net into the basket. That one-hand shot was unusual because in those days most of the players used a two-hand shot.
>
> We only had one official. There was an awful lot of picking off—blocking. The official couldn't cover everything, and when he had his back to you there were a lot of pick-offs—that kind of roughness. And when your man went in to the basket, you'd take him into the net pretty hard, but as far as other types of

A typical rope net cage. This one was used in the armory at Paterson, New Jersey. *Basketball Hall of Fame Photo.*

roughness are concerned, I can't remember much—maybe a little more contact on rebounds. But I refereed college basketball for 25 years after that, and, as I remember, the college game wasn't any rougher, or tamer, than the pros'.

Joel S. (Shikey) Gotthoffer starred for the Philadelphia Sphas, one of the nation's best teams during the 1920s and '30s. Born in New York City, January 1, 1911, he grew up playing basketball on a boy-built court behind tenement houses in the Bronx. After playing on three consecutive city championship teams at James Monroe High School, Gotthoffer graduated in 1928 and was offered basketball scholarships by six eastern universities.

Over the next couple of years, he enrolled in three of them, but each time, a college coach with whom he had played on pickup semipro teams in New York revealed that Gotthoffer had been a "professional" and thus was ineligible for college play. So Gotthoffer attended New York University, paying his own way and assisting basketball coach Howard Cann. "What struck me as strange," he remembered, "was that some of the NYU ballplayers were playing for money on the side at the time. I never said anything to Cann; I doubt that he knew it because he was a very strait-laced type of guy."

In the 1932–33 season, Gotthoffer joined the Yonkers Knights of Columbus team of the Metropolitan Basketball League, which was hoping to enter the American Basketball League, the major professional circuit then. His salary was

$15 a game, no trifling sum in the depths of the Great Depression when that was a workman's wage for a week's labor.

Gotthoffer recalls how he joined the Philadelphia Sphas and played on the side in the Penn State League:

> The American Basketball League was going into high gear in 1934. Max Posnack of St. John's Wonder Five (a famous college team) was playing with the Sphas, and he wanted to go with the New York Jewels, who were made up of the old Wonder Five. So Eddie Gottlieb, who owned the Sphas, told John J. O'Brien, the president of the league, "Fine, they can have Posnack if I can have Gotthoffer from Yonkers." So he ended up paying $2,500 for me. That was big, big, *big* bucks, and I joined the Sphas.
>
> Gottlieb paid me $35 a game at first, but my salary grew as the years went on. By 1942, when I left the Sphas, I was close to a hundred dollars a game. I was voted the team's most valuable player six years consecutively. I'm only speculating, but if you took my salary today and put it in the category of the monies they're fooling around with—with television and everything—it would be in the million-dollar class.
>
> I was also what they called an import in the Penn State League. Even though I was under contract to the Sphas, Gottlieb gave me permission, when the Sphas weren't playing, to play twice a week in Nanticoke, a real mining town. I got $150 a ballgame. The owner of the ball club also owned a big gin mill and money didn't mean anything to him.
>
> I played the first few games in a cage at Nanticoke, and I came home with the cage's markings on me. You could play tick-tack-toe on everybody after a game because the cage marked you up; sometimes you were bleeding and sometimes not. You were like a gladiator, and if you didn't get rid of the ball, you could get killed.
>
> The miners came to the games with coal dust on their faces and hands, and they'd sit in the bleachers and scream for blood.
>
> But the miners were just verbal. They never became physical with you, they never really wanted to kill you. Doc Sugarman, who had played and refereed in the Penn State League, told me that he was so incensed with these miners hollering for blood that one day he bought a piece of meat and put it in his jacket before he went into the cage. And when they started to holler, he took the meat out and threw it into the bleachers and said, "Here, you wolves, here's meat!"
>
> Whenever he came into Nanticoke after that, they used to holler, "Give us meat!"

From the beginnings of basketball, it was realized that a tall man had an advantage over a short one simply because he was closer to the basket. Despite this understanding, very few of the early professionals were men of inordinate size. Joe Lapchick, center for the Original Celtics, the most famous team in basketball's first half-century, was considered a giant at 6-foot-5. Although no statistics are available on average heights of early players, it is likely that the average during basketball's first fifty years was under six feet.

By the late 1930s that was beginning to change. It was no longer unusual to see a team trot onto the floor with two or three players 6-foot-4 and over. The day of the big man was coming. It arrived for good in the mid-1940s when 6-10, 240-pound George Mikan demonstrated that a really big man could handle the ball, pass, shoot, rebound, and generally dominate the game of basketball.

After that, players like Harry (Buddy) Jeannette, one of the brightest stars in the pro game over the previous decade, were no longer so eagerly sought. Jeannette was a prolific scorer, a tenacious defender and rebounder, and an excellent ball handler, but at 5-11 he was overmatched near the basket. He had played on three teams that won World Tournaments, emblematic of the world's championship during the 1940s, and by the 1947–48 season, when he was player-coach of the Baltimore Bullets, champions of the Basketball Association of America, he was probably the highest paid player in the country at $15,000 a year.

Jeannette started in professional basketball in the 1938–39 season with the Warren, Pa., Penns of the National Basketball League. His career as player, coach, and general manager spanned nearly forty years—the four decades when the game was developing into a major spectator sport.

Here Buddy Jeannette speaks about the advent of the big man:

> When I first started there were no big guys in the game. Hell, in those days if you were 6-feet-5 your parents hid you in the closet; they were ashamed of you.
>
> Not until I was playing for Detroit in 1940–41 did the big guys start coming in. We had Slim Wintermute, who was 6-9, but he was skinny, a beanpole. The Akron Goodyears had the first real big guy—John Pelkington. He was about 6-6 and wide. Then came big Ed Sadowski. I'll never forget walking into practice with the Detroit Eagles and here was Sadowski. He had this suit with stars on it because he had just come from Chicago where he had played with the College All-Stars that beat the Harlem Globetrotters; the Globetrotters had won the World Tournament that year. Sadowski was about 6-6 and really wide—he had a set of shoulders—but he could run and move.
>
> We had a few big guys when I played with the Rochester Eber-Seagrams the next year. The next time I ran into any big guys was when I went to play with the Fort Wayne Zollner Pistons. They had Pelkington then, and Jerry Bush, about 6-foot-3, and Carlisle Towery, 6-5. I was the midget again—I never made it to 6 feet.
>
> George Mikan was the first real big guy that actually dominated the game. He was 6-10 and *strong*. But when he was coming in, I was going out.
>
> The big guys always have it over the little guys. Can you imagine me playing in today's game? Hell, I'd only come up to the navel of most of the players in the NBA.
>
> No way could I play in today's NBA. I was never an outside shot. I did my

scoring by penetrating and laying them up or getting rebounds and putting them in. I was never a Bobby McDermott who could stand out there 25 feet away and pop it in. There's very few guys my size playing in the league today—and if they are, they can jump over the damn hoop. I was a jumper in those days, but I couldn't jump that high.

Could I shoot with them? Did you ever see Larry Bird play? Unreal the way they shoot. You know what we shot? If we got 33 percent it was real good. No, they're much better today. They're bigger, they're faster, and they're rougher.

During professional basketball's first half-century, America was two societies, one black and one white. In 1896, the year the first professional teams began playing, the Supreme Court, in *Plessy vs. Ferguson,* wrote segregation into the national law. The decision permitted southern states to enforce statutes separating the races in schools and such public accommodations as railroads, hotels, swimming pools, parks, and other amenities. Most northern states did not maintain separate schools for blacks or segregate them by law in public accommodations, but blacks were second-class citizens in the North, too, by custom if not legislative fiat.

So it is not surprising that, like the larger society, professional sports were segregated. (As we shall see, though, a handful of blacks played on white professional teams before World War II.) What *is* surprising today, when upwards of 75 percent of the NBA's players are black, is that there were only two nationally known black teams in the first fifty years. One was the Renaissance Big Five of New York. The other was the Harlem Globetrotters, who are still entertaining millions after sixty years on the road.

William (Pop) Gates starred for both teams in a career spanning the years from 1938 to 1956. He also played on integrated teams after World War II when the unwritten color line in sports was beginning to waver. Born August 30, 1917, in Decatur, Ala., Pop Gates grew up in Harlem and learned to play basketball in the Harlem YMCA and New York City's playgrounds. After playing on an integrated city championship team at Benjamin Franklin High School, he joined the Renaissance for the 1938–39 season. The barnstorming Rens capped Gates's first professional season by winning the first World Tournament in Chicago.

Pop Gates remembers those days with the Renaissance:

We played every day in the week, sometimes twice on Saturdays and Sundays. We'd get in the bus and ride anywhere from 100 to 300 miles to get to the ball game. In certain areas, we had to ride another few hundred miles to find a place to sleep, due to the conditions in the country at that particular time.

We barnstormed between New York and Chicago, and then we'd set up a base of operations in Chicago and cover the area within 300 or 400 miles, maybe further. We'd play in Kansas City, St. Louis, Milwaukee, into Minnesota. We played all the big arenas of the Middle West at that time. We had to play in small cities, too, because of the fact that you couldn't play in big cities all the time; to

William (Pop) Gates, a Renaissance star and
one of the first black players in a professional
league after World War II.

keep the money coming in, you had to play the small towns—wherever we could
get to in time to make the ball game.

We had no particular problems playing in the eastern part of the country,
even though certain areas of the East were just as prejudiced at that time as the
South. They wanted to see the Renaissance play because of the popularity of the
team, and I guess you could say we were accepted because they wanted to see us.

We found prejudice all over the South—and not just the South. Take
Illinois, Indiana and Ohio—those states border on the South and there was
prejudice there also as far as staying in hotels and eating is concerned.

So we would do what we called eating out of a grocery store bag. You buy your
stuff in a grocery store and make your own sandwiches. That was automatic
when we left a big town to barnstorm through small towns. Even when I was
with the Globetrotters in the middle 1950s we had to stay in private homes in
Negro areas in the South and even in some places in the Middle West.

A few blacks played in the white National Basketball League during World War II, but they had made no lasting impact. After the war, though, times were changing. Jackie Robinson had crossed organized baseball's color line in 1946 with the Montreal Royals, the top farm team in the Brooklyn Dodgers chain. The National Basketball League followed baseball's lead that fall when the Rochester Royals signed black star Dolly King, and Pop Gates joined the Buffalo Bisons. The Bisons became the Tri-Cities Blackhawks in January, representing Moline and Rock Island, Ill., and Davenport, Iowa.

Pop Gates recalls his experience with Tri-Cities:

> As far as the team was concerned, I had no problems. But our home base was Moline, and they were used to keeping blacks out of hotels. I did stay in a hotel two days. Then came one of the team's owners—Cliff Ferris or Leo Ferris—and we had a very heated discussion about pulling me out of there. I said, "I want to stay with the team. I'm part of the team, I think I should stay with them." However, they prevailed and I wound up being shunted to a YMCA there.
>
> Later on that season, a guy in Rock Island—he was reputed to be one of the mob people operating out of Chicago—said I could stay in a hotel he had. A certain number of ballplayers on the team said, "We're going to stay with Pop over at the Rock Island hotel." I've forgotten the name of it. There was Wilbur Schu, Don Otten and other ballplayers, maybe five of us.

Tri-Cities did not offer Pop Gates a contract for the 1947–48 season.

The career of Alfred (Al) Cervi links professional basketball's distant past with the modern game. His first coach as a professional during the 1937–38 season was Allie Heerdt, who had been captain of the Buffalo Germans, the most famous team in the early years of the century. And in 1954–55, when the NBA ushered in the modern era by adopting the 24-second shot clock, Cervi coached the Syracuse Nationals to the league championship.

Born in Buffalo, February 12, 1917, Al Cervi learned to play basketball and baseball in the city's municipal leagues. He was an all-city selection in both sports and in football when he graduated from East High School in 1936. While playing for the Adam Hat team in the Downtown YMCA Basketball League (for $7 a game and a hat once a month), Cervi was invited by Allie Heerdt to join the Buffalo Bisons in the National Basketball League. "I remember that I got $15 a game," he said. "That was a lot of money in those days. But we loved the game. We wanted to play, and we played for love of the game."

In the post-World War II years, Cervi was a perennial all-star in the NBL as a guard for the Rochester Royals. Later he was a mainstay of the Syracuse Nats in the NBA until his final playing season in 1952–53. He continued coaching in the NBA until 1957.

Cervi was a fierce competitor, a playmaker, scorer, and an advocate of unrelenting defense, as both player and coach. At 5 feet 11½ inches, he starred in an era that prized backcourt men in the 5-10 to 6-2 range like Bobby Davies, Red Holzman, Dick McGuire, Bobby Wanzer, Bob Cousy, and Slater Martin.

Here Al Cervi remembers the years after World War II and the infancy of the National Basketball Association:

> I have often said that in my opinion the 1945–55 era was the best basketball ever played. There was good defense. There was no 24-second clock until 1954. You can disguise any weakness in 24 seconds. If I were a coach today, I would stress strong defense for the first 14 seconds. I would play you so that you would have a hell of a time getting the ball over the midcourt line, and that only leaves you four or five seconds to get ready to shoot, so you're forcing the team to take bad shots.
>
> I don't know what they're talking about today when they talk defense. Your hand has to be in your man's face. You don't let him get the ball. The first thing in good defense is to keep the ball from your man. You've got to stay with him. You've got to be able to backtrack and side shuffle. You've got to know when to call the switch and when to reswitch. These are vital, vital things in defense. Never turn your head. Call for help. Your eyes are all over the place, and your hands are going like snakes all the time. You're throwing defensive fakes, too; I see defensive fakes once a year in pro ball play today.
>
> Defense was much better in those days. And you had to take good shots. If you took the shots they take today, you'd be sitting on the bench. Possession was of such an essence then. Two, three, four bad shots and you could lose a ball game. Today each team takes 20 bad shots. I think they go on the premise that if Team A makes 12 mistakes, Team B can make 12 mistakes.
>
> In the '45–'55 era, you had to take a better shot because the defense was better. They switched better and blocked out on rebounds tremendously. If a man blocks out properly, there's no way the offensive man can get the rebound unless the defender slips or the ball bounces over his head.
>
> The backcourt handled the ball better. We had better playmakers. The ballplayers today should be, without question, better shooters. But if you take the best shooters of that period under the conditions today, they could do equally well because the defense isn't that good.

Flip Dowling, Shikey Gotthoffer, Buddy Jeannette, Pop Gates, and Al Cervi had a part in the evolution of professional basketball into the multi-million-dollar spectacle it is today. In their day the financial stakes were not so high, although a good player could earn a decent living at basketball, and they played as much for the love of the game as for money. "Oh, yes, I'd do it all over again," Al Cervi said. "I loved to play. I'd give anything, give you back my 70 years to start over again. I enjoyed it all—especially as a player and player-coach. Of course, I liked to win so much that sometimes it took some of the pleasure away."

2

The Birth of Basketball

Like the other major professional team sports in the United States, basketball was originally played for fun, not money. Unlike the others, basketball was born out of the fertile brain of one man to meet a particular need. Sports historians agree that baseball evolved out of the English game of rounders and a variant called town ball which was played by boys in Colonial America. Football grew out of English rugby, and the progenitor of today's hockey was a game played in Canada in the mid-nineteenth century.

The origin of basketball was different. It sprang full-blown from the mind of James Naismith, a versatile athlete who, in the fall of 1891, was a physical instructor at the School for Christian Workers in Springfield, Mass. Naismith, a thirty-year-old Canadian, had played soccer, rugby, and lacrosse and had been on the track and tumbling teams at Montreal's McGill University. Twice he was selected as McGill's best all-around athlete. He also played professional lacrosse with the Montreal Shamrocks.

After graduating from McGill in 1887, Naismith stayed on as a physical instructor while studying theology at Presbyterian College in Montreal. He received his theology degree in 1890 (although he was not ordained until 1915), but his thoughts were turning to physical training as a vehicle for promoting Christianity among young men. The most promising avenue was the Young Men's Christian Association, which was gradually developing physical training programs to supplement its primary interests in Bible study, education, and social welfare. The first course for YMCA physical directors was given in 1887 at the School for Christian Workers (later the International YMCA Training School, now Springfield College). James Naismith, apparently planning to become a physical director, went to Springfield for the academic year of 1890–91 and completed the course. He was obviously a superior student because he was asked to stay on for 1891–92 as an instructor. Had Naismith followed the normal

James Naismith, basketball's inventor, as he looked at the time
the game was born. *Basketball Hall of Fame Photo.*

course of assignment to a local YMCA as physical director, there might be no
basketball today.

In the fall of 1891, James Naismith was happily teaching boxing, wrestling,
swimming, and canoeing. He was fulfilled. Naismith was an exemplar of what
was called "muscular Christianity" and was fully in sympathy with the YMCA's
growing emphasis on a sound mind in a sound body. Besides, he had an outlet for
his competitive spirit; under the relaxed standards of that day for intercollegiate
athletics, the 5-foot 10-inch, 160-pound Naismith played center on the school's
football team. (He devised the first football helmet, a set of muffs to protect his
ears in scrimmages.) Among his teammates was Amos Alonzo Stagg, who went
on to become the most famous football coach of the early years of the twentieth
century.

Naismith's pleasure in his work was short-lived. Midway through the fall
term, the Physical Department faculty faced a problem with a class of eighteen
prospective YMCA general secretaries. They were all mature men, not callow
students, and they were required to take an hour of gym class every day. During
the early fall and late spring, there was no problem because the instructor could
take them outside and start a game of football or baseball. Springfield's winters,

The gymnasium at the School for Christian Workers in Springfield, Massachusetts, where basketball was first played in December 1891. Peach baskets were hung on a beam below the overhead running track. *Basketball Hall of Fame Photo.*

though, are not conducive to outdoor play and the class was increasingly bored and irritated by the winter regimen of calisthenics, gymnastics, and such children's games as Prisoner's Base that were the staples of the YMCA's gymnasium programs. The general secretaries class had already driven two instructors to distraction when the department's chairman, Dr. Luther H. Gulick, dumped the problem in Naismith's lap.

Naismith had made the mistake of telling his colleagues at faculty meetings, "The trouble is not with the men but with the system we are using. The kind of work for this particular class should be of a recreative nature, something that would appeal to their play instincts." He had also told Gulick that it should be possible to invent a new game that would be "interesting, easy to learn, and easy to play in the winter and by artificial light."

Gulick directed him to go to it. Reluctantly, Naismith took over the class of "incorrigibles," as he soon dubbed the secretarial candidates. He immediately ended the calisthenics and heavy work on the horse, parallel bars, and other apparatus and tried holding their interest with a series of simple games. They didn't buy in. Next Naismith introduced modifications of rugby, soccer, and lacrosse, but they turned out to be either too tame or too rough.

Recalling his dilemma many years later, Naismith wrote that after two weeks of working with the incorrigibles, he was thoroughly discouraged. With only a day remaining before he was to report to the faculty on his success or failure, James Naismith, his Scots' stubborness aroused, sat down to study popular sports systematically. He first decided that the new game must use a ball, since all popular team sports had one. A large ball or small? Sports that used a small ball required intermediate equipment—bat, stick, or racket—and Naismith was striving for simplicity. The choice was easy: it would be a large ball.

Naismith believed that the most interesting game in those days was rugby, which was gradually evolving into American football, but it could not be played in a gymnasium because tackling was essential to the game. What was the alternative to running with the ball? Passing it, of course. Naismith wrote, "I can still recall how I snapped my fingers and shouted, 'I've got it!'"

All that remained now was to decide how scores would be made. Since Naismith did not want rough play in the gym, he rejected the idea of having ground-level goals as in hockey, lacrosse, soccer, and football; he did not want his incorrigibles driving the ball with all their force. He thought back to his Canadian boyhood and the game of Duck on the Rock and remembered that the most effective way of knocking off the duck was to throw one's own rock in an arc so that it would not go far if it missed the guard's rock. So, he reasoned, if the goal in his new game were horizontal, finesse rather than force would be desirable. Furthermore, if the goal were above the players' heads, the opponents could not mass around the goal to prevent a score. James Naismith went to bed that night with an untroubled heart for the first time in two weeks.

The next morning, he asked the school janitor for two boxes about 18 inches square. The janitor said he had no boxes, but added, "I have two old peach baskets down in the store room, if they will do you any good." Thus did the game miss being called boxball.

Naismith mounted a ladder and tacked the peach baskets to the lower rail of the balcony around the gym. It happened that the height of the rail was ten feet, which established the basket's height for the ages, although there have been sporadic attempts to raise it.

Finally, he wrote out the rules, had them typed, and posted them on the gym's bulletin board for the incorrigibles to read. The rules were:

> The ball to be an ordinary Association football (soccer ball).
> 1. The ball may be thrown in any direction with one or both hands.
> 2. The ball may be batted in any direction with one or both hands (never with the fist).
> 3. A player cannot run with the ball. The player must throw it from the spot on which he catches it, allowance to be made for a man who catches the ball when running at a good speed if he tries to stop.

4. The ball must be held in or between the hands, the arms or body must not be used for holding it.

5. No shouldering, holding, pushing, tripping or striking in any way the person of an opponent shall be allowed; the first infringement of this rule by any person shall count as a foul, the second shall disqualify him until the next goal is made, or, if there is evident intent to injure the person, for the whole of the game, no substitute allowed.

6. A foul is striking at the ball with the fist, violation of rules 3, 4, and such as described in rule 5.

7. If either side makes three consecutive fouls, it shall count a goal for the opponents. (Consecutive means without the opponents in the meantime making a foul.)

8. A goal shall be made when the ball is thrown or batted from the grounds into the basket and stays there, providing those defending the goal do not touch or disturb the goal. If the ball rests on the edge and the opponent moves the basket, it shall count as a goal.

9. When the ball goes out of bounds, it shall be thrown into the field of play by the person first touching it. In case of a dispute, the umpire shall throw it straight into the field. The thrower-on is allowed five seconds; if he holds it longer, it shall go to the opponent. If any side persists in delaying the game, the umpire shall call a foul on that side.

10. The umpire shall be the judge of the men and shall note the fouls and notify the referee when three consecutive fouls have been made. He shall have the power to disqualify men according to Rule 5.

11. The referee shall be the judge of the ball and shall decide when the ball is in play, in bounds, to which side it belongs, and shall keep the time. He shall decide when a goal has been made, and keep account of the goals, with any other duties that are usually performed by a referee.

12. The time shall be two fifteen-minute halves, with five minutes' rest between.

13. The side making the most goals in that time shall be declared the winner. In case of a draw, the game may, by agreement of the captains, be continued until another goal is made.

When the prospective YMCA secretaries reported for gym class that morning, Naismith was ready. He promised that if the new game did not please them, he would try no further experiments. He read the rules, divided the eighteen class members into two teams, and put the soccer ball into play by throwing it up between two men selected as centers. "It was the start of the first basketball game and the finish of the trouble with that class," Naismith said.

Neither Naismith nor the players left detailed descriptions of that first game. The inventor said that a great many fouls were made, as was to be expected. Since the penalty for second fouls (including such infractions as running with the ball and holding it against the body) was temporary expulsion, Naismith said that sometimes half of a team would be in the penalty area. "It was simply a case of no one knowing just what to do," he wrote. "There was no team work, but each man did his best."

Naismith's account (written, remember, long after the event) implies that several goals were scored that morning, but some reports have it that either Lyman W. Archibald, one of seven Canadians in the class, or W. H. Davis scored the only goal and the game ended 1–0. Whatever the final score, the new game captivated the players. Within a couple of weeks, 200 people were lining the gallery for the daily noon-hour games.

The exact date of that first game is uncertain, but it must have been in early December 1891. By the time the school's Christmas break began, the secretaries were hooked on the new game and many apparently introduced it in YMCAs back home during their vacation. Naismith wrote that when they returned to school, the ringleader of the incorrigibles, a North Carolinian named Frank Mahan, suggested that the game be called Naismith ball. "I laughed and told him that I thought that name would kill any game," Naismith wrote, so Mahan said, "Why not call it basketball?"

The school's newspaper, *The Triangle,* which went to YMCAs around the country, carried the first report of the new game on January 15, 1892. It was an article titled "Basket Ball," signed by Jas. Naismith and illustrated with a line drawing of players in action. Modest James Naismith did not mention that he had invented basketball. (Later claims that others fathered the game are discussed in Appendix A.) Naismith began his article in laconic fashion: "We present to our readers a new game of ball, which seems to have those elements in it which ought to make it popular among the Associations."

He included the rules and some sketchy advice about the court. Teams might have from three to forty players, depending on the size of the floor. "The fewer players down to three, the more scientific it may be made, but the more players the more fun, and the more exercise for quick judgment," Naismith wrote.

All things considered, he opined that nine men was best for a team. Three would be defenders called a goalkeeper and two guards. Three were center men and three were offensive men—two "wings" and a "home man"—who were expected to do most of the scoring.

It is likely that despite Naismith's intention to keep roughness out of his new game, it had already appeared among his incorrigibles because he had much to say about rough play in the article:

> The very men who are rough in playing will be the very first ones to oppose the game on this account, for there is that in man's nature which will retaliate, and the rough player generally gets the worst of the roughness. If there is need for such a game, let it be played as any other game of science and skill, then men will value it. But there is neither science nor skill in taking a man unawares, and

The first organized basketball team. Representing the YMCA training school at Springfield, Massachusetts, the team played match games in early 1892. Note the wire baskets at left and right, which had supplanted the original peach baskets. *Front row, left to right:* Finlay G. MacDonald, William H. Davis, and Lyman W. Archibald. *Center:* Frank Mahan and James Naismith, basketball's inventor. *Top:* John G. Thompson, Eugene S. Libby, Edwin P. Ruggles, William R. Chase, and T. Duncan Patton. *Basketball Hall of Fame Photo.*

shoving him, or catching his arm and pulling him away, when he is about to catch the ball. A dog could do as much as that.

Naismith had already thought of a free throw as a possible penalty for rough play, but he dismissed it since "after a little practice, a good thrower could convert it into a goal almost every time, because of the limits of the ordinary gymnasium." He urged physical directors to keep a "good, firm grasp" on the game to make sure players did not get out of hand. "If men will not be gentlemanly in their play, it is our place to encourage games that may be played by gentlemen in a manly way, and show them that science is superior to brute force with a disregard for the feelings of others," Naismith wrote.

Nine players from Naismith's secretaries class organized a team and played other teams at the school in Springfield during the late winter and early spring of 1892. They may also have demonstrated the game at YMCAs in New England

and upstate New York. In May, *Physical Education*, the YMCA's monthly for physical directors, published the team's picture and reported that it had never lost a game. The peach baskets used in the earliest games had apparently already been abandoned because the photo shows two wire mesh baskets which look to be about 15 inches in diameter and 30 inches deep.

With the impetus furnished by Naismith's *Triangle* article and the missionary work of Springfield's students, basketball quickly became the rage in YMCA gymnasiums. (There were fewer than 200 gyms in Ys around the country at that time.) Physical directors found basketball the perfect recreation to end an evening class largely devoted to calisthenics, gymnastics, and work with weights. The young business and professional men who frequented the gym also welcomed the game and kept coming back for more.

Those early YMCA basketball games were long on enthusiasm, short on skill. In fact, they often resembled pitched battles. Thirty years after the 1892 event, a veteran Trenton, N.J., newspaperman named Marvin A. Riley remembered the first game at the Trenton YMCA this way:

> Just prior to this night I had been in Boston, where I had witnessed several games of what was then called basket ball, and was familiar with the few simple rules that governed the play. Professor William J. Davidson came from the Springfield Training School of Springfield, Massachusetts, to be the physical director of the then new YMCA. He had learned and played the game at the Training School.
>
> Davidson and I talked the matter over and decided to put on a basketball game as the feature of the opening of the YMCA gymnasium. You will bear in mind that no one else in Trenton knew anything at all about the game with the exception of Davidson and myself.
>
> The preliminary arrangements for that first game were very simple. Basketballs and basketball goals had not yet arrived in Trenton, because the game was practically local to Boston. Our goals for that first game were the old-fashioned, two-handled, round bushel baskets, and were lashed by ropes to the gymnasium gallery. The ball was a regulation oval football. Can any of the basketball players of today imagine dribbling an oval football? And could any of the crack goal shooters of today miss tossing the ball into a bushel basket?
>
> There were about eighty young men on the floor of the YMCA gymnasium that opening night, and in order that no one should feel slighted, it was decided that Davidson and I would "choose sides." This we did, the result being that each of us had a fighting force of forty good men and true. Dave mobilized his regiment in one end of the gym, and I got mine in the other, and he gave his battlers his ideas as to how the game was played; and I gave my bunch of "huskies" what I had gathered from witnessing the games in Boston.
>
> I do not know what Dave told his bunch, but I told mine that the sole object of the gentle pastime was to toss the ball in the basket of the other team, and stop

An outdoor basketball game in 1892. *Basketball Hall of Fame Photo.*

them from tossing the ball in our basket—not to trip if it could be avoided—not to hold unless absolutely necessary, and not to slug excepting as a final resort in extreme emergency.

A referee was selected, who was told to blow a whistle to begin the contest and at any and all other times he might deem necessary or advisable for the safety of the players or the good name of the Association.

Both teams lined up at opposite ends of the hall, presenting the appearance of shock-absorbing regiments. The referee blew the whistle and we never saw nor heard of him again until an armistice was finally declared, with about one-third of those who went over the top still on their feet.

That first game was surely the "cat's meow." Very few of the eighty who started in with nice new gym uniforms came out with their shirts on their backs, and most of us were artistically tattooed with fingernail scratches. Frequently there were twenty or more fairly good wrestling matches going on simultaneously, and occasional scientific sparring exhibitions took place without in any slightest way interfering with the progress of the game. I cannot recall the scoring of any goals because the defensive work was so remarkable that no one of the eighty players engaged secured an open shot for the bushel basket. If any player did get his hands on the ball it took several minutes to dig him out from under the mob that immediately hopped him.

The game was not stopped—it ran down of its own accord. It was all played in one period of about one hour and a half duration. Unless my memory fails me, I had nineteen survivors and Dave seventeen, and on this basis we claimed the fight. Later Davidson figured it out that under a strict interpretation of the rules the game was a tie, because neither side had tossed the oval into the bushel basket. One of my gang sarcastically remarked that as no other rules had been enforced during the festivities, it was not fair to enforce that one. However, Dave won his point, and it went on record as a tie basketball game.

Even allowing for the hyperbole that is bound to creep into an account of a memorable night recalled thirty years later, it is clear that James Naismith's ideal of a non-contact game was already waning. It is also clear that the players' level of skill in passing and shooting was such that a good junior high school team of today would have trounced the best five athletes among the eighty stalwarts who played Trenton's first basketball game.

That game was not, however, typical of basketball during the first couple of years when the game was taking YMCAs by storm. More often, teams were made up of nine men, as Naismith originally recommended. In 1893, the official Y rules suggested that teams be made up of five men when the gymnasium was small, nine if the playing space was larger. A year later the number was established at five per team when the playing space was less than 1800 square feet, seven if the floor was up to 3000 square feet, and nine if it was bigger than that. It was not until 1897 that teams were fixed at five men.

Within a year of basketball's invention, organized teams began forming to play match games in YMCAs; the first probably were in Brooklyn, N.Y. The game appeared in college gyms, too, first at Geneva College in Beaver Falls, Pa., and the University of Iowa. The soccer ball was still used, but peach baskets had given way to 15-inch cylindrical wire baskets introduced by Lew Allen of Hartford, Conn. If the gym had a gallery, as most YMCA facilities did, the baskets were screwed to the rail at a height approximating ten feet. If there was no gallery, the baskets were attached to the end walls. After each score, a long pole was used to punch the ball out of the basket or someone climbed a ladder to retrieve it. (Open-bottom baskets were introduced about 1912.)

By the 1894–95 season, a well-appointed gymnasium had 18-inch iron hoops with braided cord netting. The manufacturer, the Narragansett Machine Co., of Providence, R.I., made it easy for the referee to retrieve the ball by providing a long hanging cord which, when pulled, lifted the net, causing the ball to roll out the top. The first official basketball was in use, too. It was about four inches larger in diameter than the soccer ball. The rules specified that the ball should be a rubber bladder covered with a leather case, and not less than 30 nor more than

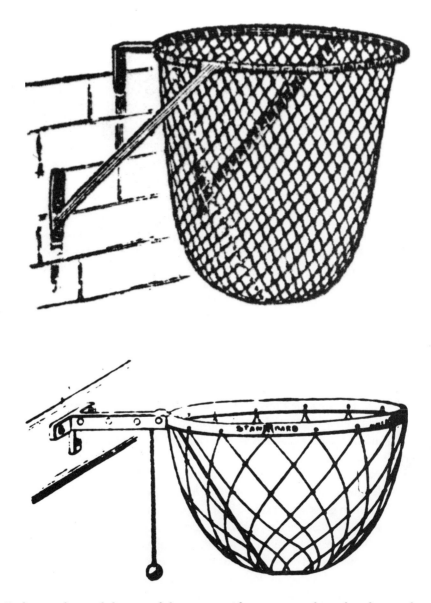

Baskets used around the turn of the century. After a score in the goal at the top, the referee climbed a ladder to retrieve the ball or punched it out with a long pole. In the basket at the bottom, the referee pulled the hanging cord, which lifted the net and made the ball roll out.

32 inches in circumference, making the average ball slightly larger than the modern ball.

Backboards were authorized for the following season, not to aid shooters but to inhibit spectators. Basketball games were already drawing partisan crowds and when they were played in gyms with galleries for the spectators, it was easy for a fervid spectator to reach over the rail and guide the shots of his favorites into the basket or deflect those of the opponents. So for 1895–96, the rules called for a 4-by-6-foot wire or wood screen behind the basket to keep fans from interfering. Wire screens were soon dented by repeated rebounds, giving the home team an advantage because the players knew the peculiarities of their own backboards, and so gradually wood supplanted the wire mesh boards.

The rules were evolving, too. At first, field goals counted one point and there were no foul shots; offenders were penalized by temporary removal from the game. Then free throws were introduced as penalties for fouling, including such violations as running with the ball or kicking it. Free throws were shot from 20 feet until 1894–95 when the distance was reduced to 15 feet. The rule-makers tinkered with scoring, too, setting the value of a field goal at three points and penalizing fouls by awarding a point to the opponents. Finally, for the 1895–96 season, they settled on two points for a field goal, one for a successful foul shot.

A basketball game during these formative years would look decidedly strange to a present-day player, although its essential elements were in place—a ball roughly the size of today's ball though much less easily handled, and a basket with an 18-inch diameter and a backboard behind it. The players' uniforms were motley, varying from the trousers, tights, and short-sleeved jerseys used in the gymnasium to track suits and even football pads.

To start each half of play and after each score, the referee threw up the ball between opposing centers, but he did it from the sidelines. Both referee and umpire ranged along the sidelines during the game; the referee followed the ball and made rulings on out-of-bounds balls, which team had the ball, when it was in play, and when goals were made. He also kept the time. The umpire called all fouls, including what are now called violations.

On a jump ball, the referee threw the ball up from the sideline and the opposing centers could either tap it to a teammate or catch it themselves. Their objective was to get it to their forwards, who were often called "attacks," or, in the case of a nine-man team, to the "home man" under the basket.

For a brief period, the court was marked off into three equal segments, and forwards, centers, and guards were restricted to their sector. But even when all players could go anywhere on the court, it was common for the defensive players, the guards or backs (and, in a nine-man team, the goalkeeper), to spend most of the game near their opponents' goal. The dribble was developing, but more as a way to escape an opponent than to advance the ball. A player with the ball who was trapped by his guard in a corner would roll or bounce the ball a short distance away and race to get it before the defender could. Skillful players realized that it was possible to control the ball and move with it by bouncing it on the floor. Others dribbled by tapping the ball in the air. Good athletes soon were racing downcourt while tapping the ball just a few inches above their hands until a new rule required them to tap it above the head.

Defense was entirely man-to-man in the early years, and defenders took pride in denying shots to their opponent. Often several minutes went by before either team had a shot at the basket. One-hand shots were rare, except when a player was right under the basket.

Here is how one of the early experts described shooting methods and team play:

> The two best methods of throwing for the goal are the underhand toss, giving a reverse rotation to the ball, and the overhand shot from the chest, in which the ball is pushed or shot upward and outward toward the goal.
>
> A favorite method of scoring is for one attack to throw to the basket. Should the ball fail to enter, another attack quickly places himself under the basket, catches the ball as it descends and pushes it into the basket. The tallest attack should always play under the basket, as the shorter the space between his outstretched hand and the goal the better for him.
>
> The centre men are so placed as to assist the forwards or help the backs, and, as the strain comes on each of these divisions, they should be able to make a good shot for goal and be quick enough to stop a good play of an opponent. Their aim should be to keep feeding the ball forward to their own men and keep them in a position to score goals.
>
> The backs, to whom the defense is entrusted, should be the biggest and heaviest men on the team. They should not be so big nor so heavy, though, as to be clumsy and slow, for quickness of the foot and eye is indispensable in basketball, and no other qualities can make up for its lack. It is exceedingly difficult for an attack to make a goal if the defense sticks closely to him and plays him well, so that the first and most frequent thought in the mind of a back should be to stick to his opponent like glue and he should follow these tactics without varying. In fact, if a back should prevent his opponent from throwing a goal, and yet during the whole game has not once touched the ball himself, he has a right to think he has played a good game.

When the ball went out of bounds, there was a scramble to get it because James Naismith's rules stated that the first team to touch it could throw it back in. "It was not uncommon," Naismith wrote in his reminiscences, "to see a player who was anxious to secure the ball make a football dive for it, regardless of whether he went into the apparatus that was stored around the gym or into the spectators in the bleachers." Naismith recalled an instance in which the ball flew up into the gallery: "Immediately the players from one team scrambled for the narrow stairway, crowding it so that they could make little speed. Two of the players on the other team boosted one of their mates up until he could catch the lower part of the balcony, swing himself up, and regain the out-of-bounds ball."

Many of the pioneering players bore scars from those skirmishes out of bounds. When a player got the ball and was returning it to play from the sideline or endline, he had five seconds to pass or roll it to a teammate or bounce it in bounds and get it himself.

James Naismith, naturally, was *the* authority on basketball for the first three years. His articles on how to organize teams, officiating, and other aspects of the game were regularly seen in YMCA publications. Just as naturally, his influence waned when he left basketball's Springfield birthplace in 1895 to become physical director of the YMCA in Denver and study medicine at Gross Medical College there. Naismith earned his medical degree in 1898, but instead of hanging out a doctor's shingle, he went to the University of Kansas to begin a thirty-nine-year career as professor of physical education and chapel director.

After his ordination as a Presbyterian minister in 1915, he also preached for several years at a church in Vinland, Kansas. Naismith was chaplain of the First Kansas Infantry and went with them to the Mexican border in 1916. During World War I, he took leave from the university and spent nineteen months in France with a YMCA unit serving American doughboys.

Naismith was as surprised as anyone at basketball's burgeoning popularity. Until his death, November 28, 1939, Naismith was a regular at University of Kansas basketball games (he had "taught" the team for a few years around the turn of the century), but he kept the game in perspective. When his good friend Forrest C. (Phog) Allen, one of the premier college coaches of the early years, said he was going to coach a college basketball team, Naismith was disbelieving. "Why Forrest," he said, "basketball is just a game to play. You don't coach it."

After Naismith left Springfield, Dr. Luther Gulick, his old mentor despite the fact that Gulick was four years younger, took over as basketball's guide and arbiter of rules. Gulick was well suited to the task; the official *History of the Y.M.C.A. in North America* credits him with developing the physical training philosophy and methods that brought the YMCA's programs from the days when gymnasium superintendents were retired boxers and circus acrobats into the age of professional physical directors who aimed to "Christianize" the gym. Gulick, the son of missionaries in Hawaii, had been a Y gymnasium superintendent himself and had earned a medical degree from New York University before going to Springfield in 1887 to spend thirteen years leading the Y's physical training program into the modern era.

He faced plenty of problems, not so much with the game itself as with the love-hate relationship YMCA general secretaries and physical directors had for basketball. On the one hand, basketball was attracting new members to YMCA gymnasiums and was enhancing interest in the community in the wider work of the local Y. As an article in *Physical Education* noted in the summer of 1894,

Dr. Luther H. Gulick, the YMCA's authority on basketball after James Naismith left Springfield. *Basketball Hall of Fame Photo.*

"One of the best solutions to the difficulty of maintaining the interest of the members has been the judicious introduction of the play element into the work; and in this line nothing has been so peculiarly and generally satisfactory as Basket Ball." In addition, the article said, basketball leagues stimulated community interest; thus inter-YMCA competition was valuable, even though it required charging a nominal entrance fee for games to pay traveling expenses of visiting teams and other costs.

On the other hand, physical directors were asking, "Is Basket Ball a Danger?" That was the title of an article in *Young Men's Era* that same summer in which five physical directors gave their views. Their consensus was, "No, not necessarily," although all expressed the worry that basketball might be permitted to push dumbbell drills out of gym activities and monopolize the floor for too much time.

In a typical reply, Thomas Cornelius, physical director of the Baltimore YMCA, advised:

> The new game of basket-ball, which is the most popular of all gymnastic games, and deservedly so, takes nearly an hour to play, and very little else can be done the same evening. It is an all-around game, decidedly more so than any other game I know. It emphasizes very nearly all the points of class work and some that it does not.
>
> It is also recreative, which class work generally is not, but it was never intended to take the place of regular systematic classwork, and should be kept well under control: never allowing it to crowd out the other.
>
> It should be played at stated times: say, once a week for afternoon classes and once a week for night classes, and the ball religiously kept off the floor at all other times. Properly managed it is an aid to our work and a drawing card, improperly managed it will do harm.

Two years later, a survey of twenty-six YMCAs around the country found basketball to be beneficial to most Associations. Attendance was up in most of their gyms, and the majority described inter-Y play and games with colleges and National Guard units as "helpful" to the aims of the YMCA. A minority reported too much roughness, incompetent officials, and bad feeling between teams, particularly in games outside the local gym.

Rough play and unsportsmanlike conduct continued to be frequent complaints against the game and, in January 1897, Luther Gulick had strong words about it in *Association Men*. Reporting on a game between two YMCA teams, he said that the umpire, appointed by the home team, called no fouls and did nothing when one of the home boys took a swing at an opponent. He wrote:

> *The game must be kept clean.* It is a perfect outrage for an institution that stands for Christian work in the community to tolerate not merely discourteous and ungentlemanly treatment of guests, but slugging and that which violates the elementary principles of morals. It hurts the religious life of the Association; it hurts the influence of the Association in the community; it hurts the personal influence of the general secretary and physical director of the Association; it injures the character of the men who play. If the fact were generally known, it would influence the financial support of the Association. It would have a large measure of influence in determining the amount of credence that the young men should give to the claims of the Association that it aims to lead men into a high Christian life.

In subsequent issues, other YMCA leaders suggested that perhaps basketball should be ousted from the gym. "Is basketball of such vital importance that it must be included in our instruction?" asked H. L. Chadwick of Philadelphia.

"Our apparatus has not grown rusty, neither do we see any loss in our attendance, or in the legitimate work of the gymnasium, since we refused to allow any game to usurp the whole of the gymnasium for hours at a time, and finally to usurp our time. The few who considered the game of paramount value deserted the gymnasium and hired outside places to play, but the business and professional men, the students, clerks and mechanics go on steadily with their exercises and are not crazed over games of basketball."

Turning to rough play, Chadwick said that if roughness could not be controlled, that was another reason to ban basketball. (At least one YMCA—in Camden, N.J.—did forbid basketball in its gym that year.) Chadwick's attack generated defenses of basketball in the pages of *Association Men,* reflecting the game's soaring popularity in the YMCA. But by this time, basketball had outgrown the YMCA's ability to control it.

While the debate over the game's value simmered in YMCA publications during the late winter of 1896–97, the first professionals were on the court.

3

The Earliest
Professionals

It cannot be said with certainty that professional basketball began in Trenton, N.J., but virtually all historians of the game give the distinction to that city. (A claim that Herkimer, N.Y., was first is discussed in Appendix A.)

What *is* known is that the players of the Trenton Basketball Team were paid to play during the season of 1896–97. No irrefutable testimony has been found for an earlier professional team, so Trenton it must be. The uncertainty should not be surprising because at the time basketball was merely a blip on the sports horizon and historians were not paying attention. The game was enjoying great popularity in YMCAs and a few colleges, but it was far behind baseball in the public eye and also trailed horse racing, bicycling, college football, track and field, and even cricket in the favor of sports fans.

The Trenton Basketball Team was one of the YMCA teams mentioned by H. L. Chadwick which had deserted Y gyms and found other places to play. The team may have been ousted; the record is unclear. The minutes of the Trenton YMCA's board of directors for the period make no mention of the basketball team, although there is a cryptic note in the minutes for November 1895 that a two-man committee was appointed "to investigate the reported trouble in the gymnasium." We may speculate that the trouble concerned basketball.

The Trenton YMCA had fielded a team for match games since the 1892–93 season and by 1896 claimed the mythical national championship after beating YMCA and college teams in the New York-Philadelphia corridor. They also ventured as far west as Nanticoke in the Pennsylvania coal regions and as far north as Hartford and Waterbury, Conn.

In its October 31, 1896, issue, Trenton's *Daily True American* reported that the YMCA's players "are no longer sailing under the colors of the YMCA but have organized independently this year, through some difficulties." The team, the paper said, would play its home games at the Masonic Temple. The "difficulties" must have caused hard feelings because twenty-six years later Trenton basketball historian Marvin A. Riley was loath to talk about them. He wrote that at the end of the 1895–96 season "considerable friction developed between the YMCA team and the secretary. Little things, perhaps, of no great importance when taken singly but in total sufficient to create a breach which resulted in the YMCA team leaving the old home and going up to Masonic Temple." That was as far as Riley would go.

A ten-man roster was announced for the Trenton Basketball Team, headed by Fred Cooper, captain, and Albert Bratton, the YMCA team's stars during the three previous seasons. Two local sportsmen, Fred Padderatz and W. S. Saunderson, were to handle the team's business affairs.

What was probably the first advertisement for a basketball game appeared in the *True American*, November 4. It was a one-column, two-inch ad among the notices for public sales and church bazaars and announced the "Grand Opening of the Season of the National Champions" Saturday, November 7, at Masonic Temple. Their opponent would be the Brooklyn YMCA, "champions of New York." Seats were priced at 25 cents, standing room at 15 cents.

The Masonic Temple was a huge, three-story building in downtown Trenton, with stores on the ground level, the Masonic lodge rooms on the second floor, and a large social hall with a high ceiling on the third. The hall may have had electric lights; most public buildings of the period were illuminated by gaslight, but Trenton's downtown was being wired for electricity around that time. The third-floor hall was fitted out with portable baskets and with the game's first cage enclosing the court.

The cage was literally that—a 12-foot wire mesh fence set on the sidelines and end lines. Doors at both ends allowed access. In reporting on this innovation, the *True American* said its purpose was "so that the ball will never go among the spectators." This is a reasonable explanation because the rule giving an out-of-bounds ball to the first player to touch it was still in effect, and it would have been bad for business to have players wrestling in the laps of paying customers for possession of the ball. With the cage the ball was never out of bounds.

In his reminiscences, Marvin A. Riley put a slightly different twist on the cage's origin. He wrote, "The Trentons conceived the idea that the cage would make the game faster by stopping all out-of-bounds delays." And, he reported, the cage "did make the game faster and more enjoyable for the spectators. . . ."

A third explanation was given in 1945 by Fred Cooper, then the Trenton city recreation director, in recalling the early days. He said that Peter E. Wurfflein, the *True American*'s sports editor, commented after watching the Trentons in practice, "They played like a lot of monkeys and should be put in a cage." No sooner said than done. Manager Fred Padderatz, a carpenter by trade, promptly built a cage and put the Trentons in it.

The cage was not copied quickly by other independent teams; in fact, they derided it as "Trenton's monkey cage." But the first professional league, formed in 1898, made use of the cage mandatory, and it was not long before almost all

A typical wire mesh cage with a wooden frame about 1910. This was the home court of Pittsburgh South Side.

independents in the East had cages on their home courts, many of them made of rope netting rather than wire mesh. Cages were rarely used in the Midwest and West—and never by colleges and high schools—but they continued in vogue among eastern pros until the early 1930s, long after the YMCA, the Amateur Athletic Union, and colleges and high schools had changed their rules to eliminate scrimmages on out-of-bounds balls. The cage lived on in the nation's sports pages for two generations after its disappearance from the court because sports editors found "cagers" and "cage game" were fitted more easily into headlines than "basketball players" and "basketball."

On November 7, 1896, the Trenton Basketball Team, smartly clad in new uniforms of red, sleeveless jerseys, black padded knickers and wool stockings, opened their season by trouncing the Brooklyn YMCA, 16–1, a fairly typical score for that era. The *True American* reported that the game drew a "large and fashionable audience" of seven hundred. Padderatz and Saunderson had thoughtfully built risers in the hall so that spectators in seats well back from the court could see over those at courtside.

Seven men were on each team—two forwards, two "defense," a center, and two "side centers." The game had seen seven minutes of "fierce playing" before the first field goal was scored by Trenton's Newt Bugbee, a side center,

The first professionals, the Trenton Basketball Team of 1896–97. *On floor:* Captain Fred Cooper, *left,* and Al Bratton. *Seated, from left:* Bill Harrison, Tommy Cook, Frank Buckley, Albert Mellick, Harry Bates. *Standing:* Marvin A. Riley (referee), Spencer Clayton, Bill Clayton, Newton Bugbee, Fred Padderatz (manager). *Courtesy of Frank J. Basloe family.*

according to the *True American,* Captain Fred Cooper, a forward, led the scoring with six points on three baskets, and a player named Simonson scored Brooklyn's only point on a free throw with three minutes left in the game. Trenton's starting seven played all forty minutes, and Brooklyn had only one substitution.

In accord with the usual practice, the home team named the referee and the visitors the umpire. The Trentons selected Marvin A. Riley to referee, giving the historian a first-hand view of what is presumed to be the first professional game. The qualifier "presumed to be" is necessary because neither Riley nor any of the other participants ever pinpointed the first play-for-pay game, except to say that it happened that season, but it seems probable that when the Trentons left the YMCA for the Masonic Hall, they did so with profit in mind.

After the game, Padderatz, Saunderson, and Marvin Riley hosted both teams for supper at the Alhambra Restaurant. Legend has it that Trenton's players earned $15 each for the game, with Cooper receiving an extra dollar as captain and, in effect, coach, although the term was not used. The amount seems improbably high, even if 700 people were jammed into the hall and the box office took in $150. The team would have had to pay the hall rental, fees for the referee and umpire, and traveling costs for the Brooklyn team before dividing what remained. Unless Padderatz, Saunderson, and the Trenton players who did not get into the game received nothing, it seems unlikely that each man's share would have been more than $5.

The Trenton Basketball Team played nineteen more games that season and finished with a record of 19–1. Their only loss was an 8–0 shutout at Millville, a small town in southern New Jersey with a strong YMCA team whose court was a onetime roller skating rink. The Trentons later revenged that defeat by blanking Millville, 14–0, in their cage. Among the Trentons' conquests, presumably all simon-pure amateurs, were several YMCA teams, Central High School and the Manual Training School of Philadelphia, Temple College, and the University of Pennsylvania. In their season finale, the Trentons whipped their amateur successors of the Trenton YMCA, 14–2. (Earlier in the season, the YMCA's directors had forbidden their team to play a scheduled game against the professionals.) The star of the YMCA team was Fred Cooper's younger brother Albert, who would develop into a set-shot artist and become a standout in the first professional league.

The Cooper brothers were natives of England, sons of a family of pottery workers in the village of Henley, near Stoke-on-Trent. Fred was eleven years old and Albert seven when the family came to the United States in 1885 to work in the flourishing potteries in Trenton. Both became excellent athletes, starring in soccer, baseball, and foot-racing.

Fred had joined the YMCA as a young man and found a kindred spirit in Al Bratton, another accomplished soccer player, when they began playing with the YMCA's basketball team for the season of 1893–94. Marvin A. Riley credited them with leading the YMCA's team into championship ranks by introducing soccer's passing patterns and thus bringing systematic play to basketball. Riley's descriptions of their passing are not really specific, but they suggest that Cooper and Bratton were the first to make a fast series of short, snappy passes on the run toward the basket. "The Trenton system of passing was definite," he wrote. "It meant to carry the ball to the opponent's basket in order that a goal might be scored, and time and again I have seen Cooper and Bratton in those early days, pass the ball back and forth between them—no one else touching it—and score against the efforts of an entire opposing team. I have seen them do this trick away from home and witnessed the spectators rise en masse and cheer the brilliant exhibition in spite of the fact that it was being done by invading players." Their skill at moving the ball left their opponents "pass drunk" and "cross-eyed" in Marvin Riley's admiring prose.

He did not give similarly glowing descriptions of their shooting methods, but it is safe to assume that nearly all shots were taken with two hands from a set position, except when a player was in position for a layup. Contemporary accounts of Trenton's games were rich with adjectives like "pretty" and "beautiful" in reporting field goals, but shooting methods were not explained. Dribbling was never mentioned, either, so probably the dribble was still chiefly a defensive measure employed only to escape close guarding in a corner. The method of dribbling would be a violation in today's game: the ball was caught with both hands after each bounce.

When the YMCA changed its rules to bar the two-hand dribble in 1898, Luther Gulick wrote, "The object of the rule is to largely do away with dribbling. To give definite illustration: A man cannot dribble the ball down the floor even with one hand and then throw for goal. He must pass it. One man cannot make star plays in this style. The game must remain for what it was originally intended to be—a passing game. Dribbling has introduced all of the objectionable features that are hurting the game. It gives the advantage to heavy men and to rough play."

In the early years of professional basketball, the pros went along with most YMCA rules, but not this one. Many pro leagues continued the two-hand dribble well into the 1930s, putting a premium on the strong, heavy player who could bull his way downcourt, double-dribbling with two hands and backing into any opponent who got in the way.

The Trenton Basketball Team's success in making basketball a paying proposition was soon emulated by other independent teams, and evidently by a few renegades in the YMCA, too. The YMCA's Athletic League, formed in 1896 to govern all of the organization's sports programs, was soon reporting instances of local YMCA's paying membership fees for basketball players and of others forming leagues with "unregulated" teams. The Athletic League's monthly letters urged physical directors to uphold the principles of "clean sport." "Much of the outlaw basketball could be eliminated by an explanation of the aims and purposes of registering the men and the necessity of upholding pure amateurism," the league advised physical directors.

The Amateur Athletic Union, established in 1888 to control amateur sports, included the YMCA in its membership, and so the Y teams followed AAU rules in dealing with outside teams, at least in theory. In fact, the Trentons and other professional teams had played YMCA teams regularly long before the AAU decided in 1899 that a pro team could play amateurs so long as the pros were registered as such. The Y's Athletic League Letter advised that "associations desiring to play registered professional teams should, when arranging for games, get a written statement from the team to the effect that they are professionals." The statement was to be forwarded to the Athletic League's office for filing "to prevent their playing at one time as amateurs and another as professionals. A man that knowingly becomes a professional cannot be reinstated, so such action prevents him from entering amateur sports again."

The New York Wanderers, originally the 23rd Street YMCA club, one of
the best of the early professional teams. *Seated, from left:* William C. Reed,
John H. Wendelken, player-manager Bob Abadie. *Standing:* Alexander
(Sandy) Shields, "Kid" Abadie, William H. Reed, Walter Grief. *Courtesy of
Frank J. Basloe family.*

The AAU held the first national basketball championship tournament in 1897
in New York City. Twelve amateur teams were entered, most of them from New
York, and the 23rd Street YMCA team won the title and the gold medals that
went with it. The team promptly decided to turn professional, and, honest to a
fault, informed the AAU. The team was quickly suspended by the 23rd Street
YMCA and barred from its gym. For the next dozen years, the team was without
a home court and gained renown as the New York "Wanderers," the first of
several famed barnstorming teams.

Recalling the Wanderers' peregrinations many years later, player John H.
Wendelken wrote: "With our reputation established, Bob Abadie, who was
named Manager, had no difficulty in dating teams in New England, New Jersey,
Pennsylvania, and Hudson (Valley) and Mohawk Valley clubs (in upstate New
York). The remuneration for these games averaged $12 to $15 above expenses per
player, depending on the number making the trip. We always kept it at a
minimum," he added drily.

Unlike later barnstorming teams which would hit the road for a week or more, the Wanderers scheduled midweek games in towns within easy railroad travel of New York so that they could return home after a game for their regular jobs or studies. (Wendelken and another player were medical students.) On weekends, they would venture farther afield, and over the Thanksgiving, Christmas, New Year's, and Easter holidays, the Wanderers would be on the road for three or four days. Their most exhausting trip, over the New Year's holiday in 1901, found them playing four games within a 24-hour period in western Pennsylvania and East Liverpool, Ohio. They whipped Pittsburgh South Side on New Year's Eve and then played morning, afternoon, and evening games on January 1. The Wanderers were sufficiently well known by this time that they were asked to endorse a spring tonic manufactured by Hood's Laboratories in Lowell, Mass. They did, and each player got $5 and a complimentary bottle. They came to regret this bonanza because, said John Wendelken, they were subjected to "endless kidding" by other teams who had seen their endorsement in the company's advertisements.

By the late 1890s there were scores of professional teams in the Philadelphia-New York area, southern New England, the Hudson River Valley of New York State, and eastern and southwestern Pennsylvania. They were not pros in today's meaning—only in the sense that the players were paid. There were no contracts, and pay was by the game. Sometimes a visiting professional team had a guarantee; other times they played for a percentage of the gate receipts and divided the take. Occasionally, according to John Wendelken's recollections, there might also be a side bet between the teams. In one memorable game he cited, the New York Wanderers' claim to the national championship was disputed by the Webster, Mass., club, champions of the Massachusetts League, and Webster offered the Wanderers a guarantee of $150 with a side wager for the same amount. The Wanderers beat Webster, 29–10, for a payday of $300. (Wendelken also recalled that a "slick-looking gent" visited the Wanderers in their hotel and offered $500 if they would throw the game. "We threw him out," said Wendelken, thus ending the first recorded bribe attempt in pro basketball's annals.)

The game was changing during this period. The most notable change was reduction in the number of players on a team to five for the 1897–98 season, which led to faster, more open play and a little less emphasis on brute strength. Because the typical court in the early days was small, cutting the number of players from fourteen to ten put more value on speed, quickness, and effective passing and less on sheer strength.

Still, the professional game was no place for shrinking violets. Marvin A. Riley was a busy referee in the early professional era. He had this to say about what was allowed:

In those days you must know that when a guard met forward, or any other player, head-on—no hipping or shouldering—just plain front to front—it was not called a foul. All that was necessary was to make the play on the ball, just as you make the play in football on the man who is carrying the ball—excepting, of course, you could not hold or use your hands—but you could play the ball and put all you wanted in back of your play. If the player who was dribbling happened to be right in back of the ball—that was his fault. Chris [Stinger of the Trentons] used to throw enough into these dribbling plays to separate the dribbler from the ball, and then either [George] Cartlidge, [Newt] Bugbee or whoever was playing the opposite guard, would amble along and pick up the loose ball. As a buster, Stinger was an ace. He was built like a wood-shed—broad and square—if he had been a college football player the sports writers would have said they couldn't figure out how he kept his feet . . .

In one game I recall, "Sandy" Shields of the New Yorks—one of the game's greatest exponents—was coming down on Trenton's basket like a cyclone. Sandy had a lot of weight, too, and enough speed to qualify for the sprints. Chris stepped on the accelerator for all the speed there was in the Stinger motor. Sandy did not put on the brakes, neither did Chris; consequently, they met and it was Sandy who went backwards to a squat on the floor. Chris picked up the ball, passed it up the floor and then calmly went back to his guard position to wait for the next attack. He took Charlie Bossert, of Camden, the same way one night in Camden. I was behind the whistle. Bossert got up and came after me demanding to know why I had not called a foul.

"Did he trip you?" I asked.

"No," replied Bossert.

"Did he hold you?"

"No."

"Did he slug you?"

"No."

"What did he do?"

"You saw him—he sat on my back."

"Well," I said, "you big truck horse, if you let him do that, don't come crying to me. Get in there and play ball."

Marvin Riley also recalled seeing a game between Trenton and Millville in which by agreement no fouls were called. It was the finale of Trenton's season in 1897–98. Trenton had already beaten Millville in three hotly contested games that season, and Millville blamed its losses on foul calling. Riley reported:

You can tell the whole wide world that there was SOME ACTION in that merry little melee. The referee tossed up the ball and immediately sought a place of refuge and did not show his head until the time came again to toss up the ball. A scrimmage (jump ball) occurred only when the players became so hopelessly locked together that they could not be separated except by the aid of the referee and the referee was not at all enthusiastic about giving the assistance, either. [Trenton won the no-foul game, 8–4.]

Despite the ample allowance for rough play, basketball was no longer just a massed battle for the ball. Many teams were copying the Trentons' short passing game, and the first designed plays were appearing. Originally, all plays were off the center jump. A center who could get the tap was all-important because there was a jump ball after every score, and many teams had an awkward center whose ability to get the tap was his only value. The center (or occasionally the team captain) would indicate by a slight movement of the head or hand the direction the ball would be tapped. "Guards down" was the most common play off a jump; the center would tap the ball to one of his forwards and one of the guards would race past, take a pass from the forward, and dribble near the basket to pass off to the other guard coming from the opposite side for the shot. (The rules prohibited the dribbling guard from shooting.)

The pivot play was appearing, too, according to John Wendelken of the Wanderers. The play is usually credited to Dutch Dehnert of the Original Celtics, who perfected it in the 1920s. But Wendelken said the Wanderers used a similar play called the "double-cross," around the turn of the century. In the Wanderers' version of the pivot, one of the players would dart to the foul line and crouch with his back to the basket. Taking a pass, he would juggle the ball from hand to hand or roll it on the floor in front of him until the two guards criss-crossed past him. The pivot man would either bounce it to one of the criss-crossers or come out of his crouch, pivot, and shoot.

The most important part of a basketball player's equipment—his shoes—was evolving, too. The earliest pros used the high-topped leather shoe with a soft leather sole that was standard in the gym. In the late 1890s, many teams had adopted the tennis sneaker, and by 1900 the first shoe designed for basketball—canvas high-top with a rubber sole pitted with holes for better traction—was in use.

In pro basketball's infancy, there were, of course, no modern arenas specially designed for basketball and hockey. Even the gymnasiums of YMCAs, colleges, and high schools were far from ideal because they predated the game's beginnings. The YMCA gym in Trenton, for instance, where the first professionals learned the game, had two steel pillars in the middle of the floor, leading to the first "post" plays. In other Y gyms, shots from the corners were impossible because an oval gallery with a running track overhung the court.

In his reminiscences, Fred Cooper remembered that Temple College's court in Philadelphia was long and narrow with a big boiler at one end, and, Cooper said, "if the ball did not drop, we knew we had scored." At Nanticoke, Pa., hot steam pipes lined the walls at courtside, inflicting severe burns on hapless players who were pushed against them. A similar hot time was in store for visitors in Wilmington, Del., because the hall was heated by a potbelly coal stove at courtside.

A top-of-the-line basketball shoe sold by A.G. Spalding &
Bros. in 1904. It cost $4.00 a pair; shoes of lesser quality
cost $1.00. *Basketball Hall of Fame Photo.*

Not all of the early basketball arenas were quite so confining. Many teams,
especially in upstate New York and New England, rented National Guard
armories. They were barnlike halls capable of seating 1500 or more people
around a big playing area. (To Marvin Riley, the court in the New Britain,
Conn., armory seemed a mile-and-a-half long after Trenton's Masonic Temple.)
Other teams played in large social halls and in public auditoriums with seats that
could be removed to accommodate the court. John Wendelken said most of the
arenas the New York Wanderers visited offered "excellent playing conditions."
Sometimes, though, they found that their hosts' baskets were 16 inches in
diameter instead of the regulation 18 inches; often, especially in upstate New
York, the baskets were set out a foot from the wood, glass, or wire backboards,
making it advisable to shoot "clean" rather than use the board.

The first professional basketball league emerged from this chaotic picture in 1898. It was grandly called the National Basketball League, despite the fact that no team's home city was farther than 70 miles from any other.

The league was organized chiefly through the efforts of sporting editors in Philadelphia and Trenton. Marvin A. Riley, who had a hand in it as sports editor of the *Trenton Times,* gave most of the credit to Peter E. Wurfflein, sports editor of the *True American,* who was elected secretary-treasurer of the league. The president was Horace Fogel, sports editor of the Philadelphia *Public Ledger.* Benjamin Rumpf of Millville, N.J., was named vice-president.

Franchises were awarded to Trenton, Millville, Camden, N.J., Germantown, Pa. (then a suburb of Philadelphia, now part of the city), and two Philadelphia teams—the Clover Wheelmen and the Hancock Athletic Association. Formation of the league was not without disputes. For one thing, it was hard to make a schedule because all teams wanted home dates on Saturdays. For another, Trenton, which still had the only cage in the country, evidently insisted on making it mandatory (it was), and a couple of teams procrastinated in building cages on their courts. But the league became a reality in August 1898, for championship play to start in December.

The National League rules specified a court of 65 by 35 feet with a wire cage at least 10 feet high and having rounded corners. Some teams must have had gaslights on their courts because the rules required that illumination must be satisfactory to the referee. Backboards were to be 4-by-4-foot wire screens, and the basket's rim was to extend 12 inches from the board.

Not more than eight men per team could play in any game. Players must have been on a team's roster at least five days before playing in a game, and, the rules said: "If a player of a League team should play with any other team, whether under an assumed name or not, he shall be suspended from competing on any League team for one month." The league had a reserve clause similar to organized baseball's in that era: "Players signed one year stand reserved for the next year."

Apparently no limit was placed on players' salaries, but in his reminiscences Marvin A. Riley said that Trenton's players got $2.50 each for a home game, $1.25 for road games. Since they played a league game at home and one away each week and carried ten players, the team payroll was $37.50 a week. The league paid its four referees, including Marvin Riley, $3 a game.

Even with such modest costs, three teams ran into financial trouble early in the season. Germantown, the Clover Wheelmen, and the Hancock A.A. dropped out in January, having played only five or six games of their 20-game schedule. A Philadelphia team was organized out of the wreckage and finished in last place in the four-club circuit. Trenton won the league championship with an 18–2–1 record; runner-up was Millville with 14–6–2.

An attempt was made that same season to start a league in New York, but it survived only a month. Members were the New York Wanderers (still called the 23rd Street YMCA), Cook's All New Yorks, Brooklyn Signal Corps, the Fourteenth Separate (National Guard) Company of Yonkers, the Bay Ridge Athletic Club, and a team in Flushing (then a Long Island village, now a part of New York City). The short-lived circuit called itself the New York District of the National League, but it had no affiliation with the Philadelphia–southern New Jersey league.

The National League lasted for five more seasons, although with several franchise shifts. Trenton won the first two championships. The New York Wanderers took the third pennant, and Bristol, Pa., and Camden won the last two. During the league's second season, it was challenged by the Interstate League, which was organized by Peter E. Wurfflein after he left the National League in a dispute over franchises. The Interstate League took Millville from the National's ranks and had four clubs in Philadelphia, plus Conshohocken, Pa., a Philadelphia suburb. The Interstate did not pose a serious threat to the older circuit and died early in 1900 when Millville defected to rejoin the National League.

Again in the 1901–02 season, a rival league was organized. It was called the American League and had teams in Trenton (but not the Trenton Basketball Team, which stayed with the National), Wilmington, Del., Burlington, N.J., Camden, two Philadelphia clubs, and Norristown and Chester, Pa. Also that year a New England league was in operation. The National League's supremacy was upheld when its champion, Bristol, Pa., beat Wilmington, the American League winner, and Manchester, N.H., champions of New England, in post-season play.

If Marvin A. Riley's recollections are to be believed, that 1901–02 season may have seen the first jump shooter. The jump shot, which revolutionized basketball fifty years later, did not appear regularly in the pro game until the late 1940s, when Jumping Joe Fulks began setting scoring records. But in Riley's reminiscences, he described a jump shooter. Calling Jack (Snake) Deal of Camden the "greatest goal tosser" in the game's first twenty-five years, Riley wrote, "Deal never set for a shot—he took them on the jump—and landed them too." Deal's example was not followed by other players, though; the standard shooting methods continued to be the two-hand shot from a stationary position and the layup under the basket.

Riley himself apparently set a record for earnings from a single game that same year, and he did it as a referee. He was in considerable demand as an official and worked college and high school games as well as crucial games for professional teams. Riley was called upon to referee a game between bitter rivals and took the job for 10 percent of the gate receipts. The box office took in $1200, so Riley earned $120. "I think that is a record price even in this day of high finance basketball," he said. (He was writing in 1923.)

> I think I earned the money, too, for if there was ever a dog fight in a basketball cage between two teams, it was this particular game. I ran myself flat-footed to prevent fights, and once I caught a swing meant for a player that gave me as beautiful a black eye as ever adorned the map of a prize fighter . . . It was my luck, too, that the game should go into an extra period.
>
> Imagine, if you can, what that extra period was for me. Three thousand wild-eyed fans with money bet on the result of the game, and playing an extra period. I had so much excitement that night that nothing in the world could have given me a thrill for a month. The following night I almost went to sleep refereeing a game at Ithaca between Cornell and Harvard.

The National League began to come apart at the seams during 1903 when other teams, especially those in the New England League, lured away many stars. Among the defectors was John H. Wendelken of the New York Wanderers, who recalled that he got $50 a game and expenses with Springfield, Mass., for two or three games a week. Other National League stars were playing under several names for non-league clubs, and fan interest dropped off. The league was reorganized for the 1903–04 season, but it had to battle not only fan apathy but another rival called the American League in the same Philadelphia–southern New Jersey territory. Both circuits died in December 1903.

4

Fumbling, Faltering, Failing

Basketball made remarkable strides during the first two decades of the twentieth century. By 1910, nearly two hundred colleges were fielding teams for intercollegiate play, although some had dropped the sport after an early trial. Westminster, Pa., College, for example, which would become a power in the 1930s, did not have a team in 1910–11 because the faculty believed the game "interfered with good scholarship."

Teams were proliferating in high schools and settlement houses, too. Although basketball still trailed football and baseball in the affections of high school sports fans, it was gaining favor because it had certain advantages over the older sports. One was that a basketball team could be equipped for much less money. Shortly after the turn of the century, a basketball player could be outfitted with jersey, knee-length pants, long stockings, canvas shoes with rubber soles, and a warm-up sweater for as little as $4.35. A top-of-the-line outfit in the A. G. Spalding Bros. catalogue went for $14.35.

Another advantage was that small rural high schools, which would be hard put to find enough athletes for a football or baseball team, could usually round up the six or seven required for basketball. By 1920 virtually all high schools in the cities and a majority in small towns had basketball teams.

Most of the early professional players came out of the YMCAs, high schools, and club and settlement house teams. It was not until well after World War I that college players began turning professional in appreciable numbers. One reason was that, while a professional career could be lucrative, it was also precarious. There were no no-cut contracts (in most cases, no contracts at all) and no payday for an injured player. In addition, there was still a stigma attached to professionalism in sports. The view of many gentlemen sportsmen was voiced in 1904 by the YMCA's Luther Gulick, who wrote that professionalism "has ruined every branch of athletics to which it has come. When men commence to make money out of sport, it degenerates with most tremendous speed, so that those who love sport have come to set their faces like a flint against every tendency toward professionalism in athletics. It has in the past inevitably resulted in men of lower character going into the game, for, on the average, men of serious purposes in life do not care to go into that kind of thing."

This elitist view of professionalism was not aimed only at basketball players. Major league baseball players, too, were looked down on by a segment of the public in that era as men of low character and behavior. This perception must have been a lingering residue of the Puritan ethic because, while it is true that most professional athletes in the early years of this century were not well educated, there is no evidence that they had any more character deficiencies than their fellow citizens. They were, by and large, sons of the working class who happened to be athletically gifted.

An aspiring young basketball player had at least as much chance of earning a living from basketball as he does today although no chance at all of becoming rich and nationally famous. From 1900 to World War I, there was always at least one professional league in operation and often three or four. A few teams barnstormed all season long, and many cities and small towns had semipro clubs on which a player could supplement his income from a regular job.

The professional leagues were confined to the Northeast, partly because that region was the prime breeding ground for basketball and also because population centers were close enough together to make league play practicable. The age of air travel, which brought the possibility of transcontinental leagues, was far in the future. Most teams traveled by railroad and interurban trolley; a few of the clubs used the newfangled automobile for short trips.

All of the early leagues were unstable, only one surviving more than six seasons. That was the Eastern League, which operated from 1909 to 1923 except for a suspension during World War I.

Following is a list of all early "major leagues" through 1922. (They were major only in the sense that they attracted the best players, not in having widespread attention.) For season-by-season standings, see Appendix B.

- *National League*—1898–1904. Teams in southern New Jersey, southeastern Pennsylvania, and Delaware.
- *New England League*—1902–05. Teams in Massachusetts and New Hampshire.
- *Central Massachusetts League*—1902–03. Teams in Massachusetts and Connecticut.
- *Philadelphia League*—1903–09.
- *Western Massachusetts League*—1903–04. Teams in Massachusetts and Connecticut.
- *Central League*—1906–12. Teams in western Pennsylvania and eastern Ohio.
- *Eastern League*—1909–23. Teams in southeastern Pennsylvania, New Jersey, and New York. (Suspended operations in 1918–19 because of the war.)

- *Hudson River League*—1909–12. Teams in eastern New York State and New Jersey.
- *New York State League*—1911–15, 1916–17, and 1919–23. Teams in eastern and central New York, Massachusetts, and New Jersey.
- *Pennsylvania State League*—1914–21. Teams in the coal region of eastern Pennsylvania and Paterson, N.J.
- *Interstate League*—1915–17 and 1919–20. Teams in New York, New Jersey, and Connecticut.
- *Connecticut State League*—1917–18 and 1920–21. Teams in Connecticut and New Jersey.

None of these leagues attracted national attention. Not until the mid-1920s did reports of professional basketball begin appearing with any regularity in major newspapers, and even then the stories tended to be sketchy at best, deprecatory at worst.

All of the pioneer leagues had frequent shifts of franchises as fan support waned and players sought greener pastures. There were no interleague agreements to prevent teams from jumping where they wished, and it was not uncommon for teams to cancel a league game if they had the prospect of a better payday for a game outside the league.

Even the rules of the game were not uniform. During basketball's infancy, five separate sets of rules were in use: the National rules, which called for a cage and were used by most professional teams; the intercollegiate code; the YMCA rules used by AAU teams; women's rules; and a hybrid code in effect in the New York State League. A few professional teams, especially in the Midwest, followed the AAU rules, but when they played other professionals, it was common to play the first half under National rules, the second with the AAU code.

The most significant differences between the National and amateur rules were that doubling dribbling was permitted by the professionals but not by the amateurs; the baskets for the pro game extended 12 inches from the backboard as against 6 inches for the amateurs (no backboards were used in the New York State League), and cages were used by most professional teams but not by amateurs.

Until 1915, most professional leagues followed the AAU code in allowing the best foul-shooter to take all of his team's free throws. In 1910 the New York State League, under the urging of Ed and Lew Wachter of the Troy Trojans, adopted the rule that the man who was fouled must shoot the free throw. The other leagues were slow to adopt this innovation, their argument being that it would lead to more rough play because a team would not hesitate to foul a poor free-throw shooter. When the other leagues came around five years later, their fears proved to be baseless; the pro game was no rougher than before. (The colleges continued to allow one man to shoot all free throws until 1924.)

While the free-throw specialists were in their heyday, they invariably led their leagues in scoring. In the 1911–12 season, for example, Bill Kummer of Connellsville, Pa., topped the Central League scoring race with a total of 1,404 points in 62 games. That gave Kummer an average of nearly 23 points a game at a time when team totals were mostly in the 20s and 30s. Of that remarkable total, 938 points were made on free throws. Kummer had 233 field goals for the season. So did Dutch Wohlfarth of Johnstown, Pa., who was known as the blind dribbler because he could dribble without looking at the ball, an unusual skill at the time. But Wohlfarth did not have a single free throw in 58 games, so he finished sixth in the scoring race behind Kummer and four other free-throw specialists.

The best of the early free-throw specialists would be considered mediocre today. In the Central League's 1909–10 season, for example, the best free-throw shooting percentage was achieved by Joe Fogarty of Johnstown. He hit 736 foul shots in 1,114 tries for a .660 percentage. Today the NBA's best foul shooters hover in the .900 range.

Foul shots were thrown with both hands, either underhand or with a push shot from the chest. Undoubtedly the reason for their failure to net as many as two out of three was the ball, which after a few minutes of fast action was rarely a true sphere.

Joe Schwarzer, who began playing professionally in the New York State League in 1919, remembers:

> The ball was four pieces of leather sewn together, with a slit in the center where they put the bladder in and laces over that. When you shot the ball, you could see it going up by leaps and bounds depending on how the air would hit the laces. And of course because it didn't bounce as well as today's ball, it was harder to dribble.
>
> It was a lot harder to shoot. When you were shooting fouls, for example, you could almost tell when the ball went up what was going to happen by watching the laces. If it hits the rim on the laces, God knows what would happen. So when you shot, you wanted the ball to rotate just once, and you didn't want the laces to hit the rim.

Several of the early leagues had teams in Philadelphia, New York, and Pittsburgh, but most professional teams were in smaller cities; some were *much* smaller. The strongest team in the 1906–07 season, for instance, represented East Liverpool, Ohio, a pottery manufacturing city of 17,000 on the Ohio River 40 miles west of Pittsburgh. Team manager William Hocking scoured the eastern cities where professional basketball had been thriving for a decade and secured the services of Joe Fogarty, Snake Deal, Ed Ferat, Bill Keenan, Winnie Kincaide, and John Pennino, all established stars in the New York–Philadelphia corridor.

The East Liverpool Potters were entered in the new Central League, which

The East Liverpool (Ohio) Potters, champions of the Central League in 1907–08. *Seated, in front:* William Kinkaide (captain), and Tommy Cartwright. *Middle row:* Ed Ferat, William Hocking (manager); and Joe Fogarty. *Rear:* John Pennino, Hudson (trainer); William Keenan, Tarr (trainer), and Snake Deal.

was organized by a sportswriter on the Pittsburgh *Dispatch* and included the South Side club of Pittsburgh, Greensburg, Homestead, Butler, and McKeesport, Pa., as well as East Liverpool. The Potters' home games were played in a cage in a theater with movable seats and drew from 500 to 1000 spectators. Their opening game was preceded by a brief speech by Mayor Blake, who was roundly cheered by the throng. East Liverpool's *Evening Review* reported, "Acknowledging the ovation given him, he stated that the house management proposed to run it as a first-class theater, which would necessitate the ladies removing their hats and take from the male contingent the privilege of expectorating on the floor."

East Liverpool fans were loyal, vocal, and boisterous and brought cowbells, tin whistles, and sleigh bells to add to the din. They were prepared to back the Potters with hard cash, and sometimes up to $2000 was bet on an important game.

The Potters had competition for the favor of East Liverpool's sports fans from a professional roller polo team that fall and winter. Roller polo, a game similar to hockey which was played on roller skates by five-man teams, was at the height of its popularity in the early years of the century. Fortunately for the basketball Potters, the roller polo team did not do well in a league made up of teams in eastern Ohio and western Pennsylvania. If it had, the cagers might have been in trouble at the box office. One night when there were both basketball and roller polo games, each attracted 500 fans, according to the *Review*.

By early December 1906, the basketball Potters were entrenched as local favorites. For a game in Pittsburgh, 400 East Liverpudlians rode a special train to the big city to see the Potters play South Side. Their victory was celebrated the next day in the lead story on Page One of the *Review,* which reported that when the rooters got home at 2:00 a.m., "they were joined by a hundred more at the station. Rockets were sent up, redfire was burned, and cowbells and horns awoke the town."

The league's original schedule called for thirty games. The East Liverpool Potters led by five games at the end and were given a silver cup by the Pittsburgh *Dispatch*. It was now early March, but the league decided to play a second half, with twenty games, to meet the demands of the fans. Pittsburgh South Side won the post-season series. East Liverpool refused to have a playoff because of a dispute over game officials.

For the following season, the Central League expanded its schedule to 72 games, and the Potters, with a 53–19 record, walked off with their second championship.

Disaster struck East Liverpool in the 1908–09 season when all their stars deserted for other teams in the Central League. Joe Fogarty, Snake Deal, and Bill Keenan joined Johnstown, and Winnie Kincaide, Ed Ferat, and John Pennino went to Uniontown. The Potters were under new management and found it impossible to replace such stars; they finished with a record of 4–67, 44½ games behind the pennant-winning Homestead Young Americans. That was the end of East Liverpool's day in the pale sun of professional basketball.

The Central League continued to operate through the 1911–12 season and vied with the Eastern and Hudson River leagues for players and regional prestige. Central Leaguers earned salaries as high as $400 a month, so scores of eastern stars continued to go west. The McKeesport Tubers won the league title in 1910 and 1911 with Andy Sears (the most noted free-throw shooter in the game) and such eastern stars as Alois Getzinger, Charlie O'Donnell, Mio Boggio, and Walter Swenson. The Tubers played home games in a skating rink (and, incidentally, were using glass backboards in 1910).

In 1911, having edged out Harry Hough's Pittsburgh South Siders for the Central League title, the Tubers challenged the DeNeri club, Eastern League winners, to basketball's first "world series." If there was any doubt of the

Central League's strength, it was dispelled when the Tubers routed DeNeri four straight games in a best-of-seven series. The first two games, played in Philadelphia, drew crowds of 2000 to the American Club hall. The final two games were played at Pittsburgh's Duquesne Gardens, but because McKeesport had demonstrated its mastery over DeNeri, they attracted small crowds. The series was arranged by the managers of the teams, not by their leagues, and McKeesport's claim to be world champions rang hollow because no series was played against Troy, champions of the Hudson River League.

By this time the Central League had been running for five years and patronage was dropping off, even in McKeesport. During the "world series," sportswriter M. F. Bowers of *The Daily News* of McKeesport reported that the team might be broken up. "Just now McKeesport is getting much beneficial advertising because of its fine basketball team," he wrote, "but if it gets away the reverse will be the case. Basketball in this city should be more liberally patronized. . . ."

Bowers's fears were well founded. McKeesport was not in the Central League for what proved to be the league's final season, 1911–12. The Tubers' old heroes went to Uniontown and finished second to Johnstown, which was led by the ubiquitous Joe Fogarty. The league started with six teams but finished with only four; one of the drop-outs was Washington, Pa., which lost all 30 games the team played. The other was Pittsburgh South Side, the only team which had been in the league each year of its existence.

The McKeesport-DeNeri "world series" in 1911 was not the only interleague test in the early years. In 1913 the only two circuits operating—the Eastern and New York State Leagues—sanctioned a series. Reading, Pa., of the Eastern League won three of five games from Troy of the New York League. Reading's title was suspect because all three of its victories came on its own court in games played under Eastern League rules. In the two games played without backboards at Troy, the Trojans demolished Reading by 28–14 and 47–13. Reading won the flip of a coin to decide the site of the fifth game and eked out a 31–29 victory at home.

Another "world" title was contested that season in Fond du Lac, Wis., one of the seedbeds of professional basketball in the Midwest. Fond du Lac's Company E of the National Guard defeated the touring New York Nationals in what the *New York Times* described as the "so-called professional basket ball championship of the United States."

Again at the end of the 1915–16 season, winners of the three operating leagues planned a world series, though without the sanction of league officials. Greystock of Philadelphia, Eastern League champions, split two games with the Paterson Crescents of the Interstate League and claimed the third game by forfeit. The Penn State League champion Wilkes-Barre Barons also bested Paterson in two straight games, but by the time they finished that series it was too late to have a playoff between Greystock and Wilkes-Barre.

Several reasons were given for the instability of the early leagues. The demise of the Central League was blamed on its long schedule by the most knowledgeable observer of the professional game. He was William J. Scheffer of the *Philadelphia Inquirer,* who edited *The Reach Official Basket Ball Guide.* The *Reach Guide* was published annually from 1901 through 1926 and covered college and independent amateur teams and leagues as well as the professionals. Its pages included a lot of self-serving articles by team managers claiming the mythical championship of a region, a state, or the world. But the *Reach Guide* also carried league standings, some statistical data, and commentary by William Scheffer on the previous season and the state of basketball. Scheffer was, by the way, the organizer and president of the Philadelphia League and the Eastern League as well as the chief chronicler of professional basketball's infancy.

Writing in the 1913 *Reach Guide,* William Scheffer decried the long schedule of the Central League. (Except in its first season, the Central's teams played from 60 to 72 games, twice the number in most of the other circuits.) "Basket ball can never be played every day like base ball," he said, "because the same set of men meet too often. This is not the case in base ball where the pitcher and catcher, a large part of the game, are changed daily . . . It is better to play exhibition games on the side, in other cities, than to have your own patrons become tired of looking at too many games."

Scheffer blamed rowdyism by players for the death of his Philadelphia League in 1909. He wrote that when league officials ordered severe penalties against players, "the managers fail to back up the censure." He noted, "If the officials are not backed up, the games become regular indoor foot ball contests, players being injured and spectators becoming disgusted. The latter are the ones to look after, as without public support, no sport will last."

The Hudson River League died midway through the 1911–12 season after early-season disputes over the presidency of the circuit had led to the desertion of four teams, including the Troy Trojans, winners of the first two pennants. Troy joined the new New York State League and won the pennant, there, too. The New York State League fell victim to World War I when it lost its playing arenas early in 1918. The U.S. Army closed its National Guard armories to outside use on February 3, effectively killing the league because all its teams played in armories. In other seasons, William Scheffer blamed economic conditions and failure of the fans to support their teams for the demise of various leagues.

Without doubt, though, the most frequent cause of trouble for the pioneer leagues was the jumping of players from team to team and sometimes the desertion of whole teams. Each league operated as a separate entity, and there was no serious effort to reach agreement among them until after World War I. The result was that players and teams were able to follow the lure of the dollar wherever it led. As noted in Chapter 3, players were drawn from the National

William J. Scheffer, organizer of the Philadelphia and Eastern
Leagues and editor of the *Official Reach Basket Ball Guide* from
1901 to 1926.

League to the New England League by higher salaries as early as 1901. The same
problem plagued those leagues' successors.

By 1909 some players were carrying the colors of five or more teams each
season. William Scheffer wrote in the *Reach Guide* that year that he had been
told by a manager in New Jersey that just twenty men represented the ten teams
he had booked for home games the previous season.

A decade later, stars were earning as much as $7500 for a season's work by
dickering for the top dollar. Joe Lapchick of the Original Celtics recalled that
when he was a budding nineteen-year-old star in 1919, he played for Holyoke,

Mass., Schenectady, N.Y., and the Brooklyn Visitations and would pit one owner against another for his services.

Lapchick remembered that he earned $40 a game in Holyoke and:

> Sometimes there were important games in Schenectady or Brooklyn. I'd make a phone call and tell the Holyoke manager I had a chance to play for $45 in Schenectady.
>
> "Don't let a few dollars stand in your way. I'll pay you $50," he'd say. That would lead to several more phone calls and the first thing I knew I was selling myself to the highest bidder for $75 a game. Like the rest of the fellows, I'd play where the money was.

Naturally, William Scheffer of the Eastern League and the presidents of other leagues decried this state of affairs. Scheffer had been calling for formation of a national commission, patterned after the body that then kept the peace in organized baseball. By 1920 the time was ripe for a national agreement. The presidents of the four existing professional leagues met in New York City and agreed to set up a three-man National Commission to make rules and settle disputes between leagues. Thomas J. Brislin of the Penn State League was elected chairman and secretary, and Scheffer was named treasurer. The third commission member was J. B. McDonagh of the New York State League.

The National Agreement aimed to restrict players to one league, forbid exhibition games with independent teams in the territory of teams in the four leagues, and set up a round-robin "world series" among the league champions. William Scheffer predicted that the Agreement would end jumping.

He was wrong. In part because the Interstate League backed out of the agreement, the National Commission never became effective. Scheffer gave fans the bad news in the 1921 *Reach Guide*:

> Because certain managers thought they were getting a little the worst of it in the distribution of players, there came a kick. If certain teams were up in the race, the fellow down at the other end became desperate and tried to land certain players. The players did not take kindly to the National Agreement. No! Why? Because they did not have the managers by the throat. Show up when they please to or to the team that offered the most money. Whose fault was this, the promoters of the commission? No! The managers themselves. How long would professional base ball live if the players were permitted to jump around to suit themselves?

Scheffer had much more to say along this line. He was aggrieved especially because his own Eastern League was unable to restrict its players to league play. In fact, no "world series" could be played as planned because several players of the Eastern League also played for Scranton, champions of the Penn State League. So the National Commission died aborning.

Among the most overworked words in sportswriting are "legendary" and "fabled." If ever they are apt, it is when they are applied to the Buffalo Germans, the first basketball team to earn a modicum of national fame and one of four full teams enshrined in basketball's Hall of Fame. (The others are the first team at Springfield, the Original Celtics, and the Renaissance Big Five.)

While the pioneer professional leagues were operating during the first two decades of the century, the Buffalo Germans were playing independently and ran up an impressive victory record. Over a span of twenty-nine years, including nine in the amateur ranks, the Germans won 761 and lost 85. In one three-year stretch, from 1908 to 1911, they had 111 consecutive victories, a string that seems safe for eternity. The vast majority of their conquests were YMCAs, college teams, semipro clubs playing under National Guard colors, and town teams, some of them from crossroads villages. During the 111-game streak, the Germans did not meet a single team from the professional Central, Eastern, and Hudson River Leagues. Their string was finally snapped in early 1911 when they did meet a good professional team representing the 31st Separate National Guard of Herkimer, N.Y.

It is fair to say that while the Buffalo Germans were an accomplished basketball team, even in their prime around 1909 they were probably not the best of their time. (In the Germans' defense, it should be noted that the reason they did not join a professional league probably had more to do with geography than fear of competition; Buffalo is far from the cities that were represented by league teams and so transportation costs would have been prohibitive had they joined a league.)

The Buffalo Germans began as a team for boys under fourteen years of age in 1895 at the German YMCA on Genesee Street in Buffalo. The organizer was Fred Burkhardt, the Y's physical director, who had learned the game under James Naismith at Springfield. By the turn of the century, the youngsters had won 87 games and lost only six and were claiming the championship of western New York.

In 1901, Buffalo hosted the Pan-American Exposition, a summer-long festival of international flora, fauna, crafts, and entertainment, including four weeks of nightly concerts by the famed John Philip Sousa's band. The Amateur Athletic Union held its all-around championships, including a basketball tournament, at the Exposition. The Buffalo Germans, now mostly eighteen and nineteen years old, entered the tourney along with seven other teams from the Northeast. The others were St. Joseph's Literary Institute of Cambridge, Mass., the Entre Nous Athletic Club of Paterson, N.J., later to become famous as the Paterson Crescents; St. Joseph's, also of Paterson; the National Athletic Club of Brooklyn; the 17th Separate Company of Flushing, N.Y., the Institute Athletic Club of Newark, N.J., and St. John's School of Manlius, N.Y.

The three-day round-robin tournament was played outdoors on grass. The

The Buffalo Germans after winning the 1901 Amateur Athletic Union championship at the Pan-American Exposition. The Germans turned professional in 1904 and became for a time the nation's best-known team. *Seated in front:* George Redlein, *left,* and William Rohde. *Center:* Henry Faust, Al Heerdt (captain), and Ed Miller. *Rear:* John Maier and Fred Burkhardt (coach). *Basketball Hall of Fame Photo.*

youthful Germans won all seven of their games by scores ranging from 16–3 to 9–3. If the scores seem unusually low, even for the period, it was because the games were only 20 minutes long, half the regulation time. Placing second was Paterson's Entre Nous Club, who lost to the Germans, 16–5, on the first day.

On the tournament's third day, the Germans were scheduled for their final two games. One had been booked for morning, but because several of the German players had school examinations that day, their captain, Alfred (Allie) Heerdt, got the agreement of their opponent, St. John's of Manlius, to shift the game to 4:00 p.m. "This agreement nearly cost them the banner and gold medals," the *Buffalo Express* reported. Said the *Express:*

> Capt. Heerdt evidently overlooked the fact that his team was scheduled to play St. Joseph's of Paterson at an earlier hour and the latter seeing a chance to help out Entre Nous, also of Paterson, declined to wait for the Buffalo players longer than the rules allowed. At the end of the stipulated fifteen min-

utes, only three German Y.M.C.A. representatives were on hand—[William] Rohde, [Hank] Faust and [Johnny] Maier—but rather than see a game go by default they determined to make a fight against the other team. . . . They did nobly and their determination to play was cheered on all sides. For nearly five minutes of the first half they held their own against the great odds, playing all around their opponents, who undoubtedly felt very cheap about putting the only blur on the three-day sport. Each side had scored a goal from a foul when (Eddie) Miller was seen to enter the Stadium . . . A united shout brought him to a realization of the situation of things his team was placed in. Throwing off his outer garments as he ran, Miller was soon in the thickest of the mixup and the St. Joseph's chances dropped 50 per cent. Miller had no sooner warmed up than Capt. Heerdt had arrived upon the grounds. Heerdt's face denoted that he was both surprised and indignant that his team had been caught in a trap, but without waiting for explanation, he followed Miller's plan . . . During the intermission Miller and Heerdt donned their uniforms and the way they sailed into St. Joseph's was delightful, running up a score of nine against a blank for the others.

That dramatic victory (the final score was 10–1) laid the foundation for the Germans' legend. Continuing to play as amateurs, they closed out the 1903–04 season with a cumulative record of more than 100 victories and fewer than ten defeats over eight seasons. Coming up in the summer of 1904 were the Olympic Games at the St. Louis World's Fair, and Allie Heerdt determined to enter his team in the basketball tournament to be held in conjunction with the Games.

By the standards of modern Olympic Games, the IIIrd Olympiad in St. Louis was a most informal affair. The games ran from May through November and featured a host of contests not usually thought of as Olympian, including handicap races, a track meet for thirteen-year-old lads, and athletic competitions for aborigines from several continents who were on exhibit at the adjacent World's Fair commemorating the Louisiana Purchase. All told, some 9000 persons took part in competitions at the Games; only about 1500 of them competed in recognized Olympics sports. Basketball was what today is called a demonstration sport; it was not recognized as Olympian until the 1936 Games in Berlin.

Nevertheless, the basketball tournament was the first truly national tourney. Entered besides the Germans were the West Side and Central YMCAs of Chicago, Turner's Tigers of San Francisco, the Missouri Athletic Club and Central YMCA of St. Louis, and the Xavier Athletic Club of New York.

Each team played five games in two days. The Buffalo Germans outclassed three opponents, running up high scores against San Francisco (78–6), the Central Y of St. Louis (87–35), and the Missouri A.C. (97–8). The New York Xavier Club went down harder, 38–29. For their last game, the Buffalo Germans faced the Central Y of Chicago, the YMCA's national champions, who had also won their first four games in the tournament. The Germans beat Chicago in a comparative breeze, 39–28.* Writing eighteen years later, Herb Reynolds, a Chicagoan who later became a well-known coach and referee, was still lamenting the loss:

> For two months previous to the scheduled date for the game, we had been practicing with a special shoe, which we had invented for outdoor play, knowing that the game was to be played in the open. We had shoes similar to baseball shoes made, and put cleats, such as football shoes are equipped with, on the soles to prevent slipping. Before the championship game we ran into a heavy rain and on the clay surface which had been selected for the game it was impossible to play, so we had to get out and hustle gym shoes for ourselves, to play the game in the Washington University Gymnasium. Our two months in heavy footwear had slowed us up, our team-work went glimmering, and we were fairly beaten. That didn't make it any easier to take the defeat when we knew that we were not playing our game, and that at our top speed we should have run away with our opponents as they played on that occasion.

Sour grapes, no doubt. But Reynolds's account suggests that the Germans were not held in awe by good teams despite their won-lost record. On the strength of their victories at the Pan-American Exposition (1901) and the Olympic Games (1904), the Germans began billing themselves as world's champions, and, indeed, they had every right to the amateur title. Back home in Buffalo, they were paraded in triumph through the downtown streets in a coach drawn by four horses and were tendered a reception by local dignitaries.

The Buffalo Germans took to the road, presumably as full-fledged professionals, for the season of 1904–05. Touring from Portsmouth, N.H., to Kansas City, Kan., they won 69 and lost 19. (The Germans reported in the *Reach Guide* later that only six men were on the roster, so that "injuries played an important part, for they lost seven straight games on two different trips when the players were in poor condition.")

For the following twenty seasons, the Germans were primarily barnstormers, although they never took another extended trip. There was talk of a world tour in 1913 but it did not materialize, and for the most part the Germans stuck fairly close to home. During their halcyon years as professionals from 1904 through 1916, the Germans played most of their games in western New York and northwestern Pennsylvania, about 80 percent of them as visitors on foreign courts. All of the players had jobs in Buffalo, so they rarely traveled far except when they took vacations in February and ventured into Ohio and northeastern New York for two weeks.

---

*Scores given here were reported by the *Buffalo Express*. Other reports gave somewhat different scores, although all agreed that the Germans' games with New York and Chicago were the closest. In some accounts, Turner's Tigers were said to be from Los Angeles rather than from San Francisco. Given the haphazard nature of the 1904 Olympics, the confusion is not surprising.

The Germans' 111-game winning streak began after a rocky start in the 1907–08 season. Their first four games were easy victories, but then, their report in the 1908–09 *Reach Guide* said, "for four weeks the team had no practice as three of the players were unable to report on account of their business engagements. With but one practice they went to Gloversville (N.Y.) and played the fast soldier team of that place. Up to the last six minutes the score was a tie, when the Germans' condition began to show and their opponents nosed out a victory. The fast pace of the afternoon game was too much for the Germans in the evening contest, and after holding the soldiers to a no-score for eight minutes they were just about able to move around, with the result that the home team ran up a one-sided score." Scores of the doubleheader were 51–33 and 56–13.

Although the "soldier team" represented Company G of the National Guard in Gloversville, they were no more military than the Germans were. They were, in fact, Ed Wachter and company, later the Troy Trojans of the Hudson River and New York State leagues, arguably the best team in the early years. More about them later.

After the debacle in Gloversville, the Germans won eleven more games before they were stopped by the Climbers of Buffalo, 27–20, on March 4, 1908. The remarkable winning streak began then with a 96–8 laugher over Ellicottville, a hamlet in southwestern New York, and a 43–18 trimming of the Climbers back in Buffalo. They closed out the 1907–08 campaign with six more victories, then went undefeated in the next two seasons, winning 74 games.

After adding twenty-six victories to the string in the 1910-11 season, they were finally stopped by the 31st Separate Co. of Herkimer in a packed state Armory in Mohawk, N.Y. The score was variously reported as 26–21 and 18–16. Their conquerers were managed by Frank J. Basloe, the most colorful manager and promoter during the game's early years. More about him later, too.

The Germans averaged 54 points to their opponents' 18 during the long winning streak. They had only five close games in that span, winning four by three points and one by four. The Germans gave no quarter to outmatched teams, running up scores like 111–17, 111–24, 104–8, and 104–13. (In 1901, while they were still amateurs, the Germans had annihilated Hobart College, 134–0.)

Despite their record, the Germans were not huge attractions at home in Buffalo's Convention Hall and Elmwood Music Hall. Their puff piece in the *Reach Guide* of 1910–11 said, "It is perhaps not surprising that the Buffalo sporting public has not supported the Germans in great numbers. The game has attained great prominence among school boys as a standard indoor winter sport, but the people at large didn't understand or appreciate what a strenuous and scientific game it is when played by men who are experts." By that time, they had the backing of Buffalo's Rambler Bicycle Club and were styled as the German Ramblers. In February 1913, they switched allegiance, becoming the Orioles in honor of their new sponsor, Nest No. 1 of the Fraternal Order of Orioles. To basketball aficionadoes, though, they remained the Buffalo Germans.

The Germans were a remarkably cohesive and long-tenured team. Of the men who had played on the AAU winners at the Pan-Am Exposition in 1901, three—Allie Heerdt, Hank Faust, and Ed Miller—were still on the team in 1915. Like all of the early teams, the Germans lacked height. It was not until 1907 that they got their first player over six feet—6-foot-3 Harry Miller, Ed's younger brother.

The Germans continued barnstorming into the mid-1920s. Their last gasp came in the 1925–26 season when for the first time the Germans—now in their second generation—entered a league, the new American Basketball League, as the Buffalo Bisons. Allie Heerdt was still the manager. The Bisons finished last among nine teams in the first half and sixth among eight in the second half. Thus the Germans' legend came to a close.

The Buffalo Germans billed themselves as "world champions" practically in perpetuity after their victory at the 1904 Olympic Games, even though they were bested in series more than once—both when they were still playing as amateurs and later as professionals. The rationale seemed to be that until an open tournament was played in which the Germans were entered, they were entitled to the world championship.

Other teams also claimed the world title at various times because it was useful for advertising purposes. The team with the best claim probably was the "fast soldier team" of Gloversville, N.Y., which licked the Germans in the afternoon-evening doubleheader just weeks before they started on the 111-game streak. Four young men who had learned basketball at the Troy, N.Y., YMCA—Ed and Lew Wachter, Bill Hardman, and Jimmy Williamson—were the nucleus of the team. From 1905 through the 1915–16 season they won the unofficial AAU title once and took four pennants in five years of play in professional leagues. Their leader was 6-foot 1-inch Edward A. Wachter, who is usually regarded as the best center of the 1900–1920 period. His brother, Louis W. (Lew) Wachter, and Hardman and Williamson were not quite in his class, but when they were joined by sharp-shooting Jack Inglis and Charles (Chief) Muller, they clearly were a formidable team.

Ed Wachter was twenty when he first played professionally in 1903 with Ware in the Western Massachusetts League. Later that year he was sold for $100 to Haverhill, Mass., in the New England League, reputedly the first sale of a basketball player. For the 1904–05 season, he joined Lew, Williamson, Hardman, and two other friends, Ray Snow and Jim Kennedy, to represent Company E of the Schenectady National Guard.

The line between amateurs and professionals was exceedingly fuzzy, and Company E apparently qualified as amateur despite Ed Wachter's pro experi-

Ed Wachter in the uniform of the Troy Trojans about 1912. A 6-foot
1-inch center, Wachter was among the brightest stars in the pioneer
period. *Basketball Hall of Fame Photo.*

ence, because the team challenged the best AAU club in the Midwest, the Blue
Diamonds of the Kansas City Athletic Club, to a series for the unofficial AAU
championship. (The AAU held no official national tournaments between 1905
and 1909 but Kansas City had defeated the Germans on their tour in 1904–05.)
Company E defeated Kansas City three straight at Kansas City's Conventional
Hall to win the series billed as the world's championship. The first two games
were donnybrooks, so rough that the second contest had to be called off with four
minutes left to play after a Blue Diamond player decked Bill Hardman.

The Troy (N.Y.) Trojans of 1912. *From left:* Bill Hardman, Jimmy Williamson, Ed Wachter, mascot John J. Casey, Jr., Chief Muller, Jack Inglis, Lew Wachter. *Basketball Hall of Fame Photo.*

For the next two seasons, Ed Wachter and company wore the colors of Company G of Gloversville. There was no league in their locale and so they played independently throughout the Northeast. In 1909 the Wachter brothers, Williamson, and Hardman went back home to Troy to play as the Troy Trojans in the new Hudson River League. The Trojans won the pennant by one game over the Paterson, N.J., Crescents, who also represented Princeton in the Eastern League. In the league's second and final season, the Trojans again edged out the Crescents and the Kingston Colonials for the title.

All of the Hudson River League teams played in large armories, and crowds of several thousand were not uncommon; Troy was averaging 3000 at home. Despite the general prosperity, there was turmoil over the leadership of the Hudson River League. Before the 1911–12 season began, Troy and three other clubs withdrew from the circuit because the remaining teams would not agree to re-elect Maj. Albert Saulpaugh, Jr., to the presidency. The league limped partway through the season before disbanding. Meanwhile, the Trojans joined the newly organized New York State League in the Mohawk Valley and won the title in its first two years. Thus Troy became the only team in professional basketball's pioneer years to win league championships in four consecutive years.

Their secret was teamwork. Throughout the ten years when the Trojans were probably the best professional team, the Wachter brothers, Bill Hardman, and Jimmy Williamson stayed together. Ed Wachter, Hardman, and the later additions of Chief Muller and Jack Inglis were always among league scoring leaders, but there were many other stars whose individual talents equalled theirs. The difference seems to have been that, while other stars flitted from team to team in pursuit of the highest wage, Wachter et al. were loyal to one another, if not necessarily to Schenectady, Gloversville, or Troy.

Lew Wachter was business manager as well as player and was one of the organizers of the Hudson River League. He was often identified also as the Trojans' captain. But the real leader was Ed Wachter, who appears to have functioned as coach. He is sometimes credited with having invented the bounce pass and fast break. It seems more likely that both had been used before he arrived in major competition, but no doubt he incorporated them into the Trojans' game. Wachter took much pride in team play and crisp passing, both as a player and later as coach at Williams College and Harvard University. Writing many years after the fact, he recalled with pleasure that James Naismith had visited the dressing room after Wachter's Schenectady team had beaten the Kansas City Blue Diamonds in 1905. He wrote that Naismith told the team, "You boys play the game of basketball as it was intended to be played, by passing the ball from one player to another until a player reaches an advantageous position to make a try for the basket."

Barnstorming trips by major teams were fairly common during the early years, especially when a league died in mid-season or when a team found it could make more money in independent play. When the New York State League broke up because of poor attendance midway through the 1914–15 season, for example, the Wachter brothers took the Troy Trojans west. They wandered through Wisconsin, Minnesota, and into Montana, then east again through North Dakota, Minnesota, Wisconsin, and Illinois, playing 29 games in 49 days and winning them all. Back home in the East, they wound up the season by taking nine straight from independent teams in New York and Massachusetts. In that same season, a team called the New York Nationals, made up of players from the Rockaways on Long Island, went all the way to the West Coast and claimed 44 victories in 45 games.

By all odds the most traveled and most successful of the early barnstorming teams was a club from New York State's Mohawk Valley which was known at various times as the 31st Separate Company of Herkimer, the Oswego Indians, and Basloe's Globe Trotters. The team was the creation of Frank J. Basloe of Herkimer, a sometime basketball player, vaudeville comedian, promoter of marathon runs, motorcycle racing, and prize-fighting and easily the best ambassador of professional basketball at the time. Basloe, whose formal education ended with sixth grade, later became a prosperous real estate and insurance man and one of Herkimer's leading citizens.

Born in Budapest in 1887, Frank Basloe came with his family to the United States when he was four years old. He first played basketball with a ball made of rags, and a wooden flour barrel hoop tacked to a barn behind the family home.

Basloe's promotional instincts flowered early. In 1903, when he was sixteen, he decided to organize a professional basketball team. Putting first things first, the young entrepreneur ordered fancy stationery with a letterhead reading "Herkimer—Champions of the Mohawk Valley," paying for it with savings from his paper route and sales of Tanglefoot flypaper. He wrote to teams in northern New York State and soon had nine games lined up.

Now it was time to sign up his "champions." Lew Wachter and Jimmy Williamson of Troy, both then in their late teens, and two youngsters from Herkimer agreed to play for $5 a game. Basloe himself was the fifth player. Borrowing $10 from his mother for the team's railroad fares to the first game in Ogdensburg, Frank Basloe took off on his first barnstorming tour. He returned home with nine victories and nearly $300 in his pocket.

From that day until the end of the 1922–23 season, Frank Basloe put a team on the road every season except 1917–18, the height of America's involvement in World War I. Over those nineteen seasons, his teams won 1,324 games, lost 127, and traveled 95,000 miles at a time when most Americans rarely left their home county.

From 1904 through the 1913–14 season, Basloe's teams barnstormed mostly in northern New York and New England and played two seasons in the minor Mohawk Valley League, winning the championship both times. The highlight of those years was the victory of his 31st Separate Company team which snapped the Buffalo Germans' 111-game winning streak before 2800 fans at the Mohawk Armory in February 1911. Two weeks later the Germans got revenge at Buffalo, beating the 31st by 30–18. Frank Basloe and Allie Heerdt of the Germans traded challenges in the newspapers for a rubber game with a side bet of $1000 on a neutral court at either Rochester or Oswego, but nothing came of it. Playing as the Oswego Indians in 1913–14, however, Basloe's team beat the Germans in both games of an afternoon-evening doubleheader at Oswego and played a third game at Tonawanda in which both teams claimed victory by two points. They tangled again the following season, with Oswego winning three out of four in a home-and-home series.

Basloe did not duck other good teams. During those years, his clubs played, and often defeated, such teams as McKeesport and Pittsburgh South Side of the Central League, and Kingston and Yonkers of the Hudson River League.

Fortified by his successes against the Buffalo Germans, Basloe appropriated their title of "world's champions" and set his sights on the Midwest in early 1914. Basketball was slower in developing in the Midwest than in the East, but by this

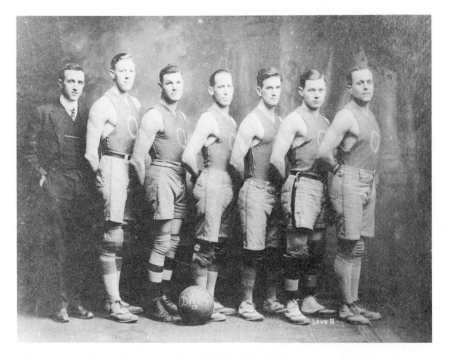

The Oswego Indians of 1912–13, also called Basloe's Globe Trotters, the most peripatetic team among the pioneers. *From left:* Manager Frank J. Basloe, Oscar (Swede) Grimstead, Jack LaCasse, Jim Murnane, Johnny Murphy, Blubs Alberding, and Mike Roberts. The team also included Jack Nolls, a Troy Trojans star. *Courtesy of Frank J. Basloe family.*

time many small towns and cities had independent teams. A few of them were fully professional in that the players devoted full time to the game in season. There were strong teams, and avid fans, in such places as Fond du Lac, Wis., Red Wing and Chaska, Minn., Muscatine, Iowa, and Fort Wayne, Ind. By 1914 it was easy for Frank Basloe to schedule between 100 and 130 games by playing through western New York, Pennsylvania, Ohio, Indiana, Illinois, and the upper Midwest.

The Globe Trotters crisscrossed these states, playing wherever and whenever they could get a guarantee of $100 and up a game. On occasion, Basloe would negotiate for a higher guarantee while the game was in progress. Once, for example, he had agreed to play a three-game series with Fond du Lac for $300. When the Globe Trotters took the floor for the first game, they saw 3500 people jammed into the armory, a lovely sight for a pioneer basketball promoter. So while the game was going on, Basloe went up into the stands, pretending to be a local fan. "Those New Yorkers think that we Fond du Lac people are a bunch of farmers," he shouted. "I wish I had an armful of garbage—I would let them have it for sure."

It happened that many fans *did* have garbage on hand—the remainder of their lunches—and they happily heaved it onto the floor. After the subsequent riot, the Fond du Lac manager found Basloe and asked, "Now what's the hold-up, Basloe? How much is it going to cost me for the next two games?"

Basloe demanded $1200 more—and he got it. At the end of the series, he also was given a cowboy suit and gun and the title of "Holdup Manager" by the fans and management of Fond du Lac.

All had been forgiven two years later. Company E of Fond du Lac was unable to field a team, so Basloe was offered a chance to play under their colors for one game a week. Ever the opportunist, he accepted, and for the rest of the 1916 season, his team had reversible jerseys. When Company E was a box office attraction, the players wore white wool jerseys with a big "E" on the front. When a New York team would be a better draw, they turned their jerseys inside out, showing O for Oswego.

The Fond du Lac armory court was perhaps the best in the Midwest during this period. It was one of the few with a cage—a three-foot wooden fence festooned with advertising posters and a net rising from the fence to the rafters—and glass backboards.

Elsewhere in the Midwest, the Globe Trotters played in various types of halls and armories; in small towns, the court might be a large community room lit by kerosene lamps. Once they played in a schoolroom before a full house—40 spectators. The Globe Trotters traveled mostly by train and trolley, but in a pinch they resorted to horse-drawn sleigh and even the caboose of a freight train. Frank Basloe kept the fans back home in central New York apprised of the Trotters' travels and travails with frequent letters to the sports editor of the *Utica Press*.

Basloe wasted no opportunities for fun and profit. Spotting a banner in a dimestore window bearing the legend, "Philadelphia Athletics, World Championship," he bought a dozen copies and scraped off the baseball team's name.

Thereafter, when his Globe Trotters were beaten on the road, Basloe would approach the victors' manager with mournful demeanor and begin this dialogue:

Basloe: "I suppose you want the banner."

Manager: "What banner is that?"

Basloe, displaying it: "The World Championship banner, of course."

Manager, with eyes alight: "You mean we get that?"

Basloe: "Well, you won it." Pause for effect. "But there's a small charge. It's $75."

After some dickering, Basloe would surrender the banner for from $30 to $50. The profitable scheme foundered when an innocent nineteen-year-old joined the

Globe Trotters and played his heart out because he couldn't bear to part with any more championship banners. In his entertaining book entitled *I Grew Up with Basketball*, Basloe sadly reported that he returned home at the end of that season with eight banners still in his suitcase.

Like William Scheffer, the organizer of leagues and chronicler of professional basketball's infancy, Frank Basloe is virtually forgotten today. But his missionary work did much to lay the foundations for the pro game's popularity west of the Alleghenies.

5

The Rise of
the Original Celtics

The 1920s are sometimes called the "era of wonderful nonsense." It seems as good a phrase as any to capture the essence of the post-World War I age when America was feeling its oats as a victor in war and the coming industrial power of the world.

Most Americans were prospering and the bonds of the old proprieties were loosening. It was the Jazz Age as well as the Golden Age of Sports. The stock market was soaring; so were hemlines. Flappers with short skirts, bobbed hair, painted faces, and dangling cigarettes were the glamour girls of the time. The glamour boys were secular icons named Babe Ruth, Red Grange, Jack Dempsey, Bobby Jones, and Bill Tilden.

In professional basketball the 1920s was the age of the Original Celtics. The Celtics were hardly a household word in the way that Babe Ruth was, but by the middle of the decade they were well enough known that they could compete for newspaper space with fencing, amateur boxing, and small-college football. Pro basketball was beginning to stir.

Although the Original Celtics spent all or parts of four seasons in leagues, they were primarily barnstormers. No team—not even Basloe's Globe Trotters—had traveled as extensively as the Original Celtics did during the twenties and thirties. In most seasons they were on the road from late September to April, playing upwards of 100 games in the East, Midwest, and South. Without doubt they were the dominant team of the 1920s, although they were not quite so dominant as later legend had it. It is sometimes said that they never lost a season series to any team. Not true. It is also said that they broke up every league they entered because they were too good. Also not true. Still, it must be said that their overall success rate was the best of the time.

The Celtics had their origins in 1914 as a team for teenagers in a settlement house in the Chelsea district of Manhattan's West Side. The first Celtics justified the name with players named Morrisey, McArdle, and Barry. By the

1916–17 season, they had moved into the semipro ranks as the New York Celtics. Playing home games at the Amsterdam Opera House on West 44th Street, the Celtics won 31, lost 10, and tied one against metropolitan area semipros. In their one game against full professionals, the Celtics were drubbed, 29–17, by the Newark Turners of the Interstate League.

When World War I ended in November 1918, the Celtics were taken over by a promoter named James A. Furey. Their first manager, Frank (Tip) McCormack, declined to allow use of the name New York Celtics, so Furey changed it to Original Celtics and booked games with metropolitan teams. For the season, they won 65 and lost only four. Their home games in the Central Opera House attracted crowds of 4000; one game, against the touring Edison Indians of New London, Wis., drew 5600 fans.

Emboldened by the Celtics' success, Jim Furey strengthened his already strong team. He added a trio of veteran professionals, and the Original Celtics began their march to fame. The newcomers were Johnny Beckman, a 5-foot 8-inch, high-scoring forward who had been sparkling for New York State, Eastern, and Penn State League teams since 1913; Oscar (Swede) Grimstead, a pro since 1911, including a season with the well-traveled Basloe Globe Trotters, and Henry G. (Dutch) Dehnert, a sturdy, 5-foot-11 guard who, at twenty-two years of age, already had four years of professional experience under his belt. Also on the squad were Mike Smolick, a nine-year professional, and Ernie Reich, another veteran. Of the *real* Originals, only Pete Barry and player-manager John J. Whitty remained.

The Celtics were challenged for dominance in the New York region by a new team organized by Tex Rickard, a boxing promoter, who planned to bring professional basketball into Madison Square Garden. His team was called the New York Whirlwinds and opened the season by beating Camden, the Eastern League champions, before 1428 spectators at the Garden. The small crowd in the cavernous Garden prompted Rickard to exile his Whirlwinds to armories around the city.

The Whirlwinds were worthy of better quarters. Their scoring leader was 5-foot 4-inch Barney Sedran, who had played for City College of New York from 1908 to 1911 and was the first professional star to come from the college ranks. He had once scored the astonishing total of 17 field goals in a New York State League game. His running mate at forward was another college man, Nat Holman, an all-around athlete who had graduated from the Savage School of Physical Education in New York in 1917 and had already made a name in the pro game as a floor general and set-shot artist. At center was Chris Leonard, a five-year professional. The guards were Max (Marty) Friedman, 5-foot-8 and a pro since 1910, and Harry Riconda, 5-foot-10, an experienced cager who later spent six years as a big league infielder.

In the spring of 1921 a three-game series was arranged between the Original

The New York Whirlwinds, whose two games with the Original Celtics in April 1921 drew a record 19,000 fans. *Seated, from left:* Marty Friedman, Chris Leonard. *Standing:* Barney Sedran, Ray Kennedy, Harry Riconda, Nat Holman.

Celtics and the Whirlwinds to decide the unofficial championship of the metropolitan region. The first game drew 11,000 fans to the 71st Regiment Armory, a record crowd for basketball except for the throng of soldiers who had seen Marty Friedman's U.S. Army team win the Inter-Allied championship tournament on an outdoor court in France in 1918.

In the first game, the Whirlwinds buried the Celtics, 40–27, in a contest played by amateur rules with plenty of whistle blowing and no double dribbling. Twenty-eight personal fouls were called against the Whirlwinds and twenty-five against the Celtics in 40 minutes of action. One player was permitted to shoot all foul shots (the amateurs did not change that rule until 1924) and so Nat Holman led the Whirlwind attack with 22 points, all on free throws. For the Celtics, Johnny Beckman scored 25 points—all but two of them on free throws.

The second game was played under professional rules at the 69th Regiment Armory before a crowd of 8000. The Celtics won a seesaw battle, 26–24. Johnny Beckman got all three Celtic baskets and added eleven of the Celtics' free-throw points. The Whirlwinds had three baskets but only 12 foul-shot points.

The third game was not played. *The Reach Guide* said the reason was not known. "Player Holman, acting for the New York Whirlwinds, had charge of arranging the deciding game with Manager Jim Furey of the Celtics, and why the game was never played can only be answered by those two men," the *Reach Guide* reported. The answer may lie in another note in the *Reach Guide*: "The series created so much interest that certain gamblers tried to connect in the fixing of one of the games. Thanks to two of the games' star players, a basket ball Black Sox scandal was averted." (The reference is to the fixing of the 1919 baseball World Series by Chicago White Sox players.)

Basketball's place on the sports totem pole of the time may be seen in the fact that although 19,000 people witnessed the two games that were played, the *New York Times*—even then the paper of record—did not carry a line of type on the games.

Two weeks after the inconclusive test of strength between the Celtics and Whirlwinds, Jim Furey signed Whirlwind stars Nat Holman and Chris Leonard for the 1921–22 season. He also added George (Horse) Haggerty, a 6-4, 220-pound bruiser, to his roster. On the strength of those additions and the Celtics' showing against the Whirlwinds, Furey began billing his team as "national champions," even though they had never ventured out of the metropolitan area.

Furey apparently intended to have his champions play independently, with Madison Square Garden as their home court. Because during the previous season most of his players had performed in organized leagues as well as with the Celtics and Whirlwinds, the leagues claimed that the players belonged to league teams and forbade teams in their circuits to play the Celtics. Eastern League president William Scheffer said that Johnny Beckman was the property of the Scranton Miners; Nat Holman, Horse Haggerty, and Ernie Reich belonged to Reading; and Dutch Dehnert and Chris Leonard were on Wilkes-Barre's roster. The Eastern League had a working agreement with the New York State League and so both leagues banned the "outlaw" Celtics. The upshot was that the Celtics could find only weak opposition for games at the Garden and attendance dropped drastically.

Acting on the wise old saw, "If you can't beat 'em, join 'em," Jim Furey made a bid for a vacant franchise in the Eastern League in early December. He was a day too late. New York Whirlwinds' manager Charlie Brickley had already won the franchise for his weakened club, now called the New York Giants. Furey was also rebuffed in an attempt to take over the Albany franchise in the New York State League.

So the Original Celtics continued to play weak sisters and bided their time. It came as the Eastern League neared the end of its first half. Brickley's New York Giants, even with the "heavenly twins," Barney Sedran and Marty Friedman, were outclassed in the Eastern League and dropped out with several games still remaining in the first half. Furey promptly took the franchise. His Celtics won the second-half championship, edging the Trenton Royal Bengals and Camden

Skeeters by one game. The Celtics then beat first-half champion Trenton two games out of three for the pennant.

The Eastern League had been in dire straits even before the Celtics' arrival (it died the following season) and their coming did little to help. Because the Celtics were playing most home games at Madison Square Garden, the other owners had visions of big-time operations and swelling coffers. They were disappointed.

"But for a city the size of New York and playing quarters that were large enough to accommodate good crowds, the season was not a financial success to the owners," William Scheffer reported in the *Reach Guide*. "In the third and deciding game of the playoff series, which was contested at Camden, the attendance figures were larger than the combined crowds that attended the games in New York and Trenton," he wrote. Scheffer, an advocate of the wire cage, complained that the cage used in the Garden was of rope netting. "Basketball is seen at its best when played in a wire cage of regulation size and the fans of New York have not witnessed basketball at its best," he said.

The Eastern League was tottering as the 1922–23 season began, and so Jim Furey entered his Celtics in the Metropolitan League. He found the financial pickings no better during five weeks in that league, and so the Celtics, who had won all twelve of their league games, dropped out and hit the barnstorming trail. In a campaign beginning in September and ending in late April, the Celtics played the astounding total of 205 games, claiming 193 victories, 11 defeats, and one tie. It was estimated that a half-million spectators saw the Celtics in their tours through thirteen states of the Northeast and Midwest that year. They even spent a couple of weeks as the Atlantic City franchise in the Eastern League before that circuit died in January 1923.

The Celtics' march through the Midwest was not entirely a triumphal tour. They were stopped in Fort Wayne, later to become one of the mainstays of the early days of the National Basketball League, by the Knights of Columbus team. Homer Stonebraker, an underhand shooter who often let fly from midcourt, scored five of the Caseys' six field goals as they beat the Celtics, 21–17. The New Yorkers gained revenge the following night, drubbing the Caseys by 48–23. Evidently they solved the defensive problem posed by Stonebraker's long heaves because all of his nine points came from the foul line.

Among the Celtics' ten other defeats that year were three to Kingston, N.Y., in five matches over the course of the season. Kingston, managed by Frank Morgenweck, who had been in professional basketball since the turn of the century, had a banner year. They won the pennant in the New York State League and also, playing as the Paterson Legionnaires, took the title in the Metropolitan League. The Celtics had split four games with Morgenweck's club, including a doubleheader, when they met for the final time at Kingston April 6. Led by Benny Borgmann, a 5-foot 9-inch, high-scoring forward who got 14 points, Kingston claimed the mythical world title by whipping the Celts, 24–19.

The Kingston Colonials of 1923. The bulky knee guards and heavy warmup sweaters were typical of the time. *From left:* Frank Morgenweck (manager), Fitzgerald (assistant manager); Charles Powers, George Artus, Carl Husta, Mickey Husta, Benny Borgmann, and Nick Harvey. *Basketball Hall of Fame Photo.*

Another of the Celtics' defeats came at the hands of the Trenton Royal Bengals, who won the first-half championship in the Eastern League before it disbanded. It was the only game the two clubs played that year, and so William Scheffer, Eastern League president, said that Trenton was the national champion of '22–'23. Scheffer blamed the Celtics in part for the demise of his league. "Not that the Celtics have been a success financially," he wrote, "but seven good men have been taken away from the league clubs that would have bolstered up the Eastern in such a way that the organization would positively have been continued."

With the death of the Eastern and New York State leagues during the 1922–23 season, professional league basketball was moribund. Of the major circuits that had flourished after a fashion before and immediately after World War I, only the Metropolitan League remained in operation. The Met League was a compact circuit made up of the Brooklyn Visitations, Kingston, Yonkers, the Greenpoint Knights of Brooklyn, and Paterson and Trenton, N.J., William Scheffer reorganized the Philadelphia League, but it was regarded as a minor league. It permitted only three established professionals on each club's roster.

hardly invincible. As mentioned earlier, they lost three out of five to Kingston in 1922–23. In the 1925–26 season they split six games with the all-black Renaissance Big Five. They also lost three out of five to the Nonpareils of Brooklyn and two of three to the Philadelphia Sphas. Still, during their glory years from 1921 to 1928, the Original Celtics were the most consistently successful team.

Their secret, like that of the old Buffalo Germans and Troy Trojans, seems to have been excellent teamwork based on long acquaintance, as well as the brilliance of their players. Nat Holman, Johnny Beckman, Joe Lapchick, Chris Leonard, Dutch Dehnert, and Davey Banks—the best-known Celtics—were all regarded as among the best of their time as shooters and team players.

Their game was ball possession, short passes, and high-percentage shots, just as it was for other eastern professional teams of the period. They played a tenacious man-to-man defense and may have originated switching on defense. Until their time each defender was expected to stick with his opponent, but the Celtics perfected the art of switching defenders when they were blocked by an offensive player or when an opponent got free of the Celtic assigned to him.

On offense, the Celtics favored constant movement with and without the ball. They are sometimes credited with inventing the give and go in which a player passes to a teammate and immediately cuts for the basket and takes a return pass. It seems improbable that this tactic was first used by the Celtics since it is an almost instinctive move and surely would have been common before their era.

In many historical accounts, Dutch Dehnert is said to have originated the pivot play. The story is that during 1925–26 while they were touring the South, the Celtics' attack was frustrated by the Chattanooga Rail-Lites, who used a "standing guard" as a purely defensive player. He rarely ventured into the forecourt; his sole task was to foil easy baskets by the opposition.

Dehnert is said to have volunteered to position himself in front of the standing guard with his back to the basket, receive passes from his teammates, and return the ball to them as they cut for the basket. If the standing guard tried to go around Dehnert and intercept the ball, he pivoted to the opposite side and laid up a field goal.

But John Wendelken recalled that the New York Wanderers were using a similar play around the turn of the century. And Nat Holman, in his *Scientific Basketball,* published in 1922, said his Germantown team, which won the Eastern League pennant in 1921, occasionally used their center as a pivot. Even earlier, around 1910, newspaper stories often referred to centers as pivots.

Nat Holman, in a later book called *Winning Basketball,* gave this account of the pivot play's origin:

> The play was not an amazing overnight discovery, but came about through a long process of evolutionary change, though the final result was of itself both startling and original. The Celtics made constant and important use of the play

in which one man moved slowly across the foul-line territory near his own basket, received a pass, and made a quick return play. However, the player moving across the court, either by accident or through an economy of unnecessary movement, finally came to a stop at the foul line, where he stationed himself firmly, received passes from his teammates, and made himself the central point in the offensive orbit. Thus was introduced the pivot play. The Original Celtics, with "Dutch" Dehnert in the pivot position, developed this into the most damaging scoring play ever devised and did much to bring the play to its present state of comparative success.

That's it. The Celtics formalized an offensive movement that was already evolving as players became more expert at the game and made it a fixture in their offense. It was not long before every team had at least one good ball-handler and passer who could play the pivot.

Like most professional teams of their time, the Original Celtics had no coach in the sense that the term is used today. Their passing patterns, the give and go, the pivot play and their strong defense grew out of familiarity with each other's strengths, long experience in the game, and pride in being "world's champions." At a time when most stars jumped from team to team almost weekly, or played with two or more teams on a regular basis, the Celtics were exclusively Celtics and were nourished by team play and team success, as well as salaries that were well above average.

Most of their games were on foreign courts with referees of varying competence, some of them "homers." If it was apparent that an official was inclined to favor the home side, the Celtics quickly made it plain that that was unacceptable by "sandwiching" the official between two onrushing Celtics on the ensuing center jump. As a rule that cured the official of any desire to please the local fans.

Any team that beat the Celtics was almost certain to claim the "world's championship" because their claim to the title was recognized by most of their contemporaries. This can be seen in an article in the 1923–24 *Reach Guide*. Many of the articles in the *Guide* were self-serving pieces written by promoters and officers of teams and leagues. But this one was written by John J. Murray, who had managed the New York Whirlwinds when they played the Celtics for the metropolitan area title in 1921. Murray wrote:

> . . . there is no one that can gainsay the fact that the remarkable record of the Original Celtics of New York is the greatest record achieved by any combination the game has yet produced. The mere fact that this team has shown before more people in one season than the majority of teams have played before during their entire existence and the fact that at times they have received as high as $5,000 for their appearance should be enough to convince any fair-minded fan or person connected with basketball that the Original Celtics are truly the wonder team of basketball.

The Celtics did not receive $5000 very often—perhaps only once when they played a day-night doubleheader in Cleveland that drew 23,000 fans to Public Auditorium. More often they played before audiences in the hundreds rather than thousands for a guarantee and percentage worth perhaps $400. But they were not called the greatest team of the first half-century without reason.

6

Coming Out of the Cage

While the Original Celtics were making their mark in the early 1920s, professional leagues were in the doldrums, even in the game's eastern cradle. Only one major league, the Metropolitan, was in operation in 1923–24. Enthusiasm for the cage game had waned even in such seedbeds as Trenton and Camden, N.J.

On the amateur level, basketball was thriving. The National Amateur Athletic Federation reported that by the mid-1920s 93 percent of the nation's high schools had basketball teams, and in many states there were tournaments to decide state champions. More than thirty state titlists competed in the National Interscholastic Tournament conducted by the University of Chicago. Scores of colleges were building new gymnasiums to handle growing crowds for basketball. The Amateur Athletic Union's basketball program was booming, too; for the finals of the national AAU tourney 9000 fans would pack Kansas City's Convention Center.

Clearly, the game itself was enjoying growing popularity. Why were the professionals not sharing in it?

One of the reasons was the constant jumping of players from team to team to find the top dollar. It was hard for fans to maintain interest in the hometown heroes when they could not be sure who would suit up for a big game. All of the early leagues had failed to stop contract jumping and were unable to stick to agreements among themselves to prevent it. Another factor may have been imbalance in team strength in some leagues. President William J. Scheffer of the Eastern League blamed the dominance of Trenton and Camden for the loss of fans' interest leading to the league's death midway through the 1922–23 season. Trenton had won 19 and lost three, Camden was 18–5, and third-place Coatesville trailed far behind with an 11–13 record when the league disbanded.

Many professionals were loath to admit it, but another reason—perhaps the most important—was the professional style of play, especially in the East. The discontinued (double) dribble with two hands was still in vogue; consequently much of the action at a professional game was the slow movement of a player bulling his way downcourt.

Writing in *Sport Story Magazine* in 1931, Rody Cooney, a veteran of the eastern cage wars, described the dribbling method of a decade earlier:

> A hard dribbler could . . . rush through an entire defensive team, bowling over his opponents by various means—a favorite one being that of butting the opposition in the head.
>
> In this particular case, the dribbler butted—but he didn't look very carefully, and butted his own man, who had stepped in the way. This man toppled backward from the ferocious charge, hit another player on his own team, and the three men fell together, knocked out by the hard impact. All three men of the same team!
>
> Under such conditions, it is no wonder that countless attempts at organized professional leagues ran into failure from lack of patronage. The professional game did not have the appeal of the fast, clean collegiate game.

In most professional games, there was only one official to keep order, and when his back was turned there was a good deal of pulling and hauling in the cage. Free throws were awarded only if the man with the ball was fouled; fouls away from the ball were penalized only by loss of possession. Fights broke out frequently, and often inflamed fans threatened the referee or the opposing team. "In some cities of the New York State League," a sportswriter complained, "gladiatorial combats of the ancient Romans pale into insignificance compared with the rowdyism rampant among some of the fans and some of the players. No effort on the part of the managers to curtail such tactics has apparently been made, with the result that the good old indoor game is getting into disrepute. The games are not fit places on some occasions to take a lady, certainly not the sort of contest they should like to witness."

Rody Cooney agreed. "It wasn't a matter of speed and brains," he wrote. "It was more a case of brute force, hard tactics, and all the dirty tricks you could put into it without arousing the antagonism of the officials or spectators—more likely that of the latter, for the officials were not too strict."

Cooney described one game in which passions were raised to a frightening pitch:

> We were having a pretty hard game of it, with plenty of roughing, tricking, and everything else that passed in the game. It was part of the daily task, and we had to do our work well, or the other fellow would come out ahead.
>
> Well, as was natural, a fight developed, and two of the players staged a word battle that turned into a furious fistfight before we could step between them. Things were going pretty hot, so everyone was carefully warned to cool down before a riot was started. We cooled off—but the fight wasn't over.
>
> A hurried exit by both teams after the game averted a fan scramble, and we

were just beginning to breathe easy down in our locker room, when a man with a drawn gun rushed through the door.

He went directly to the player who had fought with the man on the other side, stuck the gun in his stomach, and demanded an apology for the language he used in the scrap.

As we stood, dumbfounded, players from the other team rushed in and forced the man out of the room. That man was the brother of the other man in the fight, and he was there to avenge the quarrel with a gun.

Yes, we had that kind of fan in those days!

Doubtless the cage contributed to the roughness. When ten men, most of them strong and bulky if not very tall, were moving within the confines of a cage, there were bound to be collisions, both inadvertent and intentional. Bouncing an opponent off the cage was considered fair play, particularly if he had the ball.

Joe Schwarzer, a Syracuse University All-American in football and basketball, recalled that in 1919 when he came home after his first game in the New York State League, he took off his shirt and exposed rope burns all over his back. "Oh, my God," his wife exclaimed, "you've been in a fight!"

Courtside spectators were close enough that they could reach out and touch the cage. From their vantage point, the players must have looked like a zooful of hyperactive gorillas. The memories of some old pros are replete with tales of being stabbed with hatpins and knitting needles and being burned with lighted cigarettes thrust through the cage. In towns in the Pennsylvania coal region, the fans were noted for heating nails with miner's lamps and tossing them high over the net at opposing foul shooters.

A small player had to learn to defend himself if he hoped to survive as a professional. Chick Passon, for instance, a Philadelphia Sphas star who also played for Kingston in the New York State League, remembered, "There were men that thought they could beat the hell out of you, so you had to know how to protect yourself. I had educated elbows. They found places, sometimes in the eyes, sometimes in the nose. I was no chicken."

Some promoters capitalized on the professional game's well-earned reputation for roughness. When the Trenton Tigers were scheduled to play at Madison Square Garden, promoter Tex Rickard would display a seven-foot cut-out photograph of the Tigers' Tom Barlow with the legend, "Caveman Barlow Here Tonight!" Barlow, a tough guard who had played with teams all over the East, recalled that the Celtics' Johnny Beckman urged him to complain to Rickard. Barlow did and wangled $75 out of the promoter.

Rody Cooney was not the only old pro who decried the shortcomings of the professional game. Maurice Tome, a Trenton native who had appeared with many teams during the teens and twenties, told the *Trenton Evening Times*:

> The professional style of play is through in Trenton as in other sections of the country. The intercollegiate game is here and from all indications it is here to

> stay. It has pushed the professional pastime into the background and if basketball is to be restored to its former level, Trenton must adopt the game as played by the schoolboys.
>
> The conclusion is inevitable that the schoolboy game is preferred to the old style of basketball. I have myself played professional basketball for many years and much prefer the school game to the rough, slam-bang cage combats. The sideline game offers more possibilities, is more energetic and appeals to the fans. I predict it is the game of the future.

Tome's judgment may have been colored by the fact that he was then coach of Trenton's Cathedral High School team. Still, even staunch conservatives were beginning to doubt the efficacy of the discontinued dribble. William J. Scheffer, editor of the *Reach Guide* and former league president, wrote in 1925 that college coaches were right in pointing out that restricting the dribble made for more passing. "Being a close student of the game, and one that always favored the unrestricted dribble," he said, "I naturally held out against the restricted dribble, but when the majority of the teams of the country play the college rules and when the majority of that class of teams can outdraw the professional rules, then I, for one, am in favor of making a change."

In the Midwest, where professional teams mostly played by college rules, the pro game was blooming during the 1920s. Attendance at college and professional games was five times as great as in the East, Scheffer said. By 1924, when eastern promoters were delighted with a crowd of 1000, the Cleveland Rosenblums were attracting crowds as great as 10,000. In Detroit the Pulaski American Legion Post team averaged 2500 for Sunday afternoon games. In Chicago, the Bruins were drawing upwards of 2000, and in Fort Wayne the Knights of Columbus team played before packed houses in the 1800-seat Concordia College gym.

There were sharp contrasts between eastern and midwestern teams, not only in the differences in the rules they used but in their styles of play. Nat Holman of the Original Celtics, who was coaching at the City College of New York, discussed them in the *Converse Basketball Year Book* of 1923 after a Celtic tour of the hinterlands. Holman had already published his first book on basketball techniques and was recognized as a canny floor leader, expert passer, and deadly set shooter.

Holman reported that nearly all midwestern players launched set shots underhand, from the field as well as the foul line, and banked most shots off the board. In his scholarly analysis, Holman deplored underhand shooting. He had three objections: "First, since all backboards are not alike and since often, as in the East, in professional leagues, games are played without backboards at all, it is far better for a player to accustom himself to shooting 'clear.' Secondly, the underhand shot when in play is more easily blocked than the overhead shot by an opponent with an arm outstretched in the air. Thirdly, long distance shooting, though poor basketball at any time, is doubly so when players are not in a position to follow-up shots."

Most midwestern teams, Holman said, used a standing guard who remained in the backcourt even when his team had the ball. Because there was then no rule requiring a team with the ball to cross a midcourt line within ten seconds, this meant that if the offensive team laid back, four defenders were guarding five on offense. "Not only is the stationary guard a non-participant on the offense but his particular opponent must be guarded in midcourt by his teammates," Holman noted. "I found that most of the scoring of my team was due to the free opponent of that stationary guard." Holman also criticized the long, looping downcourt pass and the dearth of bounce passing that were common among midwestern teams.

He did not think much of their defenses either. In the Celtics system, switching was the norm, "but the Westerners, not being sufficiently acquainted with that style of play, made no attempt to 'shift,' to take the man going free under the basket," he wrote. "A smart player seeing a teammate eluded by his opponent will leave his own man and run to cover the free one."

Holman said that some midwestern teams used the professional rule-book while others followed the college code. Sometimes games were played half by pro rules and half by college. Like Maurice Tome, Nat Holman was partial to the college rules.

Holman and Tome foretold the future. It arrived in 1925 with formation of the American Basketball League. The ABL was the first truly national league in that it had franchises in cities stretching from New York, Boston, and Washington in the East to Chicago and Fort Wayne in the Midwest. The term "national" is, of course, relative to the times. In the 1920s baseball's National League and American League were also bounded by the eastern cities and Chicago and St. Louis in the Midwest. The days of easy transcontinental travel were still to come; besides, such cities as Los Angeles and San Francisco were just beginning to emerge as metropolitan centers.

The advent of the American Basketball League spelled doom for the old professional game because the new league adopted AAU rules almost in toto. Cages and the double dribble were outlawed in the ABL. Henceforth the professional game would gradually become faster and depend less on bulk and strength and more on speed, agility, and cleverness.

A major national league had been in the offing for several years before the American Basketball League was organized. As early as 1921 there were reports in the *Reach Guide* that a big league was being considered. The rumors simmered for four years before the ABL became a reality for the 1925–26 season.

Joseph F. Carr, president of the five-year-old National Football League and a minor league baseball executive in Columbus, Ohio, was named president and secretary of the new league. On the executive committee were three business-men who sponsored successful basketball teams: George Preston Marshall, owner of the Palace Laundry in Washington and later the owner of the Washington Redskins football team; George S. Halas, owner of the Chicago Bears football team and godfather of the NFL; and Max Rosenblum of Cleveland, owner of a department store and its namesake, the Cleveland Rosenblums.

During the summer, Joe Carr announced that in addition to Marshall's Palace five, Halas's Chicago Bruins, and the Rosenblums, the ABL would include the Boston Whirlwinds, Brooklyn Arcadians, Buffalo Bisons, Fort Wayne Caseys, the Detroit Pulaski Post (American Legion), and the East Liverpool (Ohio) Panthers. East Liverpool never made it to the starting blocks, however, and the league opened with nine teams.

Players were signed to exclusive, written contracts. President Carr promised strict, even-handed enforcement of league rules, which, he said, "would be drastic regarding discipline, and fines and other penalties are provided for covering misconduct of any kind either by players, managers or spectators." Gambling was forbidden at league games, with forfeiture of the franchise as the penalty for permitting it. The ABL hoped to attract college players but, in an effort to keep college coaches happy, Carr pledged heavy fines for any club that signed a player before his college eligibility had expired.

Most of the ABL's players in the first year were either veterans of the East's regional leagues or home-grown products of semipro basketball in the Midwest. Few had had college experience; the exceptions, like Fort Wayne's Homer Stonebraker, a Wabash College star, and Frank Shimek of the University of Iowa, had already played as professionals.

Although the Metropolitan League was still operating when the American League began, it declined somewhat in prestige because the ABL's promise of big-time operation drew the cream of the professional crop except for the touring Original Celtics. The Cleveland Rosenblums, led by Marty Friedman, had a nucleus of established eastern players in John (Honey) Russell, Carl Husta, Dave Kerr, and Richie Deighan, and rookie Nat Hickey. The Washington Palace Laundry boasted Ray Kennedy, its player-coach who led the league in scoring with an 8.0 per game average, and Rusty Saunders and George Glasco, both survivors of countless basketball battles in Trenton. The Brooklyn Arcadians were managed by Garry Schmeelk, who had toured with the New York Nationals during the teens, and featured Red Conaty, Rody Cooney, and defensive stalwart Elmer Ripley, all former Met League stars, and Tillie Voss of Detroit. Rounding out the top four clubs in the league were the Rochester Centrals, whose star was Marty Barry, a high-scoring veteran who had started in the New York State League as a nineteen-year-old after World War I.

The original plan for the league's schedule was to have a split season of 36 games, with the winners of the halves meeting in a "world series." In the event,

The Cleveland Rosenblums, first champions of the American Basketball League.

each team played only thirty games. The Brooklyn Arcadians won the first half by one game over Washington and two over Cleveland. In the second half, the Rosenblums won thirteen and lost only one, finishing two games ahead of Washington and four over Rochester. In the playoffs the Rosenblums beat the Arcadians three straight. The two playoff games in Cleveland drew a total of 20,000 spectators. The final game, played in a Manhattan armory, attracted only 2000.

Original Celtics' manager James Furey promptly fired off a telegram challenging the Cleveland Rosenblums to a best-three-out-of-five series. Max Rosenblum just as promptly declined. *Cleveland News* sportswriter Ed Bang commented, "It seems strange that Furey should become so unduly excited now that the American Basketball League honors have been decided when one stops to consider he wouldn't give the league a 'tumble' when invited to join forces at the time the organization was formed. But there is not a chance for a post-season series because Max Rosenblum is well satisfied that his team is justly entitled to the laurels it won and will give no consideration to the Celtics' defy."

League President Joe Carr called the American Basketball League's first season a "tremendous success," and indeed it was, at least in the sense that all advertised games were played and no players jumped contracts, but not all of the franchises enjoyed prosperity. Boston had dropped out at the end of the first half. The Buffalo Bisons, managed by old Buffalo German Allie Heerdt, finished out the ABL's first season but did not return for the second.

For the 1926–27 season, the ABL replaced Boston and Buffalo with teams in Philadelphia—long a bastion of professional basketball—and Baltimore. The Philadelphia entry, named the Warriors, was owned by Jules E. Aaronson and managed by Eddie Gottlieb, long the player-coach of the Philadelphia Sphas. The Warriors promised a strong lineup with Sphas stars Chick Passon and Lou Schneiderman and former Eastern League standout Jim (Soup) Campbell. The Baltimore Orioles had a young, untried roster.

Meanwhile, the Metropolitan League, which had retained the cage and the double dribble, had visions of joining the American Basketball League in the spotlight. It was renamed the National Basketball League for the 1926–27 season, although it was still centered in the New York metropolitan area. Its guiding light was John J. O'Brien, who had earlier led the Interstate League.

Although the American League had tapped the eastern reservoir for many top players, the new National League still boasted such stars as Benny Borgmann of the Paterson Legionnaires, a 5-foot 8-inch forward who was the top offensive player of the era, Tom Barlow and Teddy Kearns, and Francis P. (Stretch) Meehan, the tallest man in basketball at 6 feet 7 inches. More important, the NBL had the Original Celtics, who joined their third league after three straight seasons of barnstorming.

Five of the NBL's teams represented two cities. The Celtics played in New York and Arcola Park, N.J. The other hybrid teams were the Paterson, N.J., Legionnaires–Kingston, N.Y., Raiders; Ridgewood of Queens, N.Y.–Orange, N.J.; the Trenton–Greenpoint (Brooklyn) Knights; and Jersey City Skeeters–Newburgh, N.Y., club. Only the Brooklyn Visitations had no sister city. For games on the road all but one of the teams got 20 cents of each ticket sold, with a guarantee of $200. The exception was the Celtics, who got 30 cents a ticket with a guarantee of $300. James Furey, the Celtics owner, evidently drove a hard bargain for his champions.

The National League had hardly begun its season before its players started jumping to the more affluent ABL. Stretch Meehan left Ridgewood-Orange to play with the Philadelphia Warriors, and Tom Barlow and Teddy Kearns, Trenton-Greenpoint stars, followed him into the ABL. In early December, while the Celtics were wrapping up the first-half championship, the National League disintegrated.

The American Basketball League was having its troubles, too. The ABL planned a 42-game schedule for its second season. Before the New Year arrived, the Brooklyn Arcadians and Detroit Pulaski Post had dropped out without having won a single game. Detroit was not replaced, but the Original Celtics took over the Brooklyn franchise. Some historians have it that the Celtics were persuaded to join the ABL because the league had forbidden its teams to play them, thus cutting into their opportunities for profit. This seems unlikely because the Celtics had no trouble scheduling 100-plus games a year outside of league play.

The reason the Celtics sought shelter in the league probably was due more to management problems. James Furey, the owner, was also the head cashier of the Arnold, Constable department store in New York. In June 1926 he had been accused of embezzling $187,000 from the store, and soon after his Celtics started play in the National League, he went off to Sing Sing prison for a three-year stay. Johnny Whitty, one of the original New York Celtics who had spent the first ABL season as player-coach of Fort Wayne, rejoined the Celtics and took over the management reins.

Whatever their management problems, the Celtics had lost nothing on the court. Nat Holman, Joe Lapchick, Dutch Dehnert, Chris Leonard, Pete Barry, and Johnny Beckman had played together for five years and were the class of the league. Even when Beckman went to Baltimore to become player-coach of the weak Orioles, the Celtics marched on. They added young Davey Banks, a speedy forward who had learned the game with the Philadelphia Sphas.

Taking over the Brooklyn Arcadians' 0–5 record, the Celtics finished the ABL's first half in fourth place. They won the second half going away—four games ahead of the second-place Fort Wayne club, now called the Hoosiers. The Celtics then defeated first-half winner Cleveland in three straight games to win the league championship.

The Celtics waltzed off with the ABL championship in the following season, too. The league dropped the split-season system and set up two divisions, Eastern and Western, for the 1927–28 campaign. The Celtics ran up a record of 40–9 in the Eastern Division, leading second-place Philadelphia by 10½ games. In the Western Division, the Fort Wayne Hoosiers, led by scoring ace Benny Borgmann, beat out the Cleveland Rosenblums by five games. In the playoff for the championship, the Celtics beat Fort Wayne, three games to one.

Attendance had dropped in most league cities. The Detroit Cardinals dropped out midway through the year, leaving the Western Division with only three teams. In the East, George Preston Marshall gave up on his Washington team and sold the franchise to the Brooklyn Visitations of the Metropolitan League.

One-sided races were only one factor in the box-office decline. Another was complaints of rough play, even with the more open style of the intercollegiate rules. League officials had tried to give the referee, who worked alone, some help during the previous season by adding a second official called the ball tosser. His sole duty was to throw the ball up for the center jump that followed every score, thus giving the referee a better view of that important play. But the roughness was unabated, and so for 1927–28 the ABL adopted the one college rule it had previously scorned—disqualification via personal fouls. The colleges banished a player after four fouls; the ABL made it five. (Free throws, however, were given only if the player who was fouled had possession of the ball. If he did not, the only penalty was giving the ball to the opponents on the sideline.) In a bow to oldtimers who opposed the disqualification rule, the league decreed that a team must have at least seven players in uniform; if three of them were put out of a game for five personals, the one who had first been sent to the bench could re-enter the game. Fines were instituted for fighting and profanity. The standard penalty was $10, with a scale going up to $25 for aggravated offenses.

The Celtics' 1927–28 American League title was their last hurrah as the dominant team of the 1920s. Jim Furey was still in prison, and the team's deficiencies in management led the league to take over the Original Celtics Exhibition Corp. The players were parceled out to other league teams. Joe Lapchick, Dutch Dehnert, and Pete Barry were sent to the Cleveland Rosenblums. Nat Holman and Davey Banks joined the New York Hakoahs, the Big Apple's new representative in the American League.

Before the 1928–29 season began, there was talk of retrenchment to the Midwest, with another National League being formed for eastern teams. But Metropolitan League president John J. O'Brien, who had led the ill-fated National League in 1926, assumed the presidency of the American League. In the process he ended the Metropolitan League and brought into the ABL fold two of its strongest teams, the Trenton Royal Bengals and the Paterson Whirlwinds. The divisional system was scrapped and the split season reinstituted.

Cleveland won the first half and Fort Wayne the second. In the championship series the Rosenblums whipped Fort Wayne in four straight games. The two playoff games in Cleveland attracted only 7500 fans to the 14,000-seat Public Auditorium. In Fort Wayne, which used a high school gym with 3800 seats, paid attendance was 2700 for the first game and 3800 for the finale. Even with the small crowds, the teams and league made money. The winning Rosenblums each collected $500 and the Hoosiers $380 for the four-game series—a significant amount at a time when only stars like Nat Holman and Johnny Beckman were near the $10,000 level for a full season.

By this time, though, the American Basketball League was fraying around the edges. No longer did all players have written contracts; Harry (Jammy) Moskowitz remembered that he had only a verbal contract for $300 a month with the New York Hakoahs. The Trenton Bengals flouted the league rule against cages, using theirs for home games until the season was almost over.

The 1929–30 season was barely under way when the stock market crashed on October 29. Although the American League's owners could not know it at the time, the resulting Great Depression would mean the end of the first attempt at a real national basketball circuit.

The league faced other problems besides economic uncertainties in 1929–30. In the East there was competition from a revived Eastern League. Some players

John J. O'Brien, leader of three early pro basketball leagues. He was president of the Interstate League from 1915 to 1917, the Metropolitan League from 1922 to 1928, and the American Basketball League from 1928 until its demise in 1953. *Basketball Hall of Fame Photo.*

deserted the ABL to play in the Eastern so that they could hold on to their regular jobs back home. The ABL's western flank was also under attack by a new National Basketball League made up of teams in Ohio and Michigan. The new NBL did not directly challenge the American League in its western cities but it did entice some ABL players. Cookie Cunningham of the champion Rosenblums, for example, spent most of the season with the Toledo Red Men of the NBL, although he was on the floor for the Rosenblums for the ABL's championship series. (The NBL's champion was the Toledo Red Men, who beat Dayton, four games to two, in a playoff following a 21-game split schedule. Other NBL teams were the Canton, Ohio, Generals, Jackson, Mich., Elks, Columbus Robert Lees, and a team that started in Pontiac, Mich., and shifted to Detroit.)

In the face of this competition and worries about the economic outlook, the American Basketball League planned its most ambitious schedule yet for 1929-30, with each of its eight teams booked for 54 games. The New York Hakoahs and Trenton Royal Bengals had given up their franchises, but their places were taken by the Syracuse All-Americans and a revised version of the Original Celtics. James Furey had been released from prison and set about reconstructing the Celtics. Three of his stars—Dutch Dehnert, Joe Lapchick, and Pete Barry—had contracts with the Cleveland Rosenblums, but Furey got Davey Banks and Nat Holman back from the Hakoahs. Johnny Beckman also rejoined his old mates after spending the previous season with Rochester and Cleveland. Furey rounded out his roster with Stretch Meehan as center and veteran Harry Riconda and Bill McElwain.

These Celtics were only a pale imitation of the original Originals. They were not successful, either in victories or finances, and by December 10, New York was again without an ABL team. Apparently James Furey turned over his franchise to the league because the ABL financial statement for 1930 shows receipts of $3100 for Davey Banks, who was sent to Fort Wayne, and $500 each for Nat Holman and Johnny Beckman; Holman went to Syracuse and Beckman to Cleveland.

Syracuse dropped out in early January, so the American League, which had started the season with high hopes and eight teams, ended it with six. The Cleveland Rosenblums, with ex-Celtics Lapchick, Dehnert, and Barry, won the first half and the Rochester Centrals, the second. In the playoffs the Rosenblums swept the Centrals in four straight games for their second consecutive league title. The biggest crowd was 3,345 at Cleveland's Public Auditorium for the clincher.

The American League's prospects were not good for the 1930–31 season as the Depression began making itself felt, but president John J. O'Brien was game for another try. In hopes of attracting new fans with new faces, the ABL adopted a rule that each team must have at least two rookies, drawn principally from the college ranks. By mid-season it was ruled that at least one rookie had to be on the floor at all times. In an effort to cut down on roughness by opening passing lanes in the middle, the league also passed a rule that a pivot man could not hold the ball in the foul lane for more than three seconds.

Play began with seven teams: the Brooklyn Visitations, Fort Wayne Hoosiers, Rochester Centrals, Paterson Crescents, Cleveland Rosenblums, Toledo Red Men (NBL champions of the previous year), and the Chicago Bruins. The league began crumbling before the first half ended. The Rosenblums, three-time ABL champions, dropped out on December 8, "Fans have shown by their lack of attendance that they are disinterested in professional basketball," owner Max Rosenblum told the *Cleveland News*. Sportswriter Ed McAuley commented, "It was evident, after the novelty of superlative performance had passed, that professional basketball did not possess the inherent crowd appeal to make it anything but a losing proposition, financially." The Paterson Crescents followed the Rosenblums out of the league three weeks later. Chicago was in bad financial straits, too; at a league meeting in late December, it was noted that the Bruins had not paid their $1000 entry fee and had failed to pay Toledo its full guarantee of $250 for a league game in Chicago.

The schedule called for 48 games over the split season, but by the end of the first half it was clear that it could not be completed. As it turned out, the five teams that finished the season played from 34 to 38 games. The Brooklyn Visitations, first-half winners, beat Fort Wayne, four games to two, in the championship series. (The final game, played in Brooklyn, was broadcast back to Fort Wayne—probably the first radio play-by-play account of a professional basketball game.)

None of the three playoff games in Brooklyn attracted as many as a thousand spectators. Attendance in Fort Wayne was better, with one crowd of 3200, but the champion Visitations earned only $80 per man for the six-game series; each Hoosier got $53.

With such numbers, it did not take a financial genius to see where the league was heading. John J. O'Brien, who had labored valiantly to keep the American Basketball League afloat, was a realist but he did not give up easily. It was not until November 12, 1931, that he threw in the sponge for the first professional league with national ambitions.

Clearly the onset of the Depression was a major factor. By 1932 a quarter of the nation's work force was on the streets, and basketball fans had to watch their quarters if not their pennies. But there was more to the league's demise than that. The ABL had fostered more open play than had been common in the days of the cage and the double dribble, but professional basketball was still a rough game. A New York sportswriter summed it up as the ABL was sinking into oblivion:

> Professional basketball is slowly but quite surely passing out of the picture, and the players have nobody to blame but themselves. Unless some action is taken quickly nothing will be left but the inconsequential semipro outfits.
>
> The "pros" have in recent years persisted in putting on wrestling matches that resemble basketball no more than they do figure skating. It is impossible for a player to be awarded a foul shot under "pro" rules unless he has possession of the ball, and for this reason everything but mayhem and murder goes on in the scramble under the basket. The only penalty the referee is allowed to inflict for

a straightarm violation or a half-nelson is an outside ball, and the pros laugh at that.

The colleges have come along fast in recent years with a speedy, open, clean game that has shamed the old clientele, few of whom stay around now and watch a game that has degenerated into a shambles.

All of this is not as it should be, because the "pro" ranks boast players who really stand head and shoulders over a lot of the collegians in ability. Willie Scrill, the (Brooklyn) Visitations' famous "bad man," would be brilliant and better to watch if he didn't start to spar from the opening whistle. Pat Herlihy could get along without the same sort of thing. The Visitations–ex St. John's stars game last year was more interesting than the average pro game because it was played under rules approximating in some small measure those in force in the colleges.

As it is now the American League is on the rocks from lack of patronage, the old Celtics, gentlemen all from the old school of pro basketball, are about at the end of their string, and the rowdy-dowdy Visitations are taking whatever games they can get, whether they be old men's homes or orphan asylum teams.

John J. O'Brien predicted that if business conditions improved, the American League would resume for the 1932–33 campaign. It was a futile hope. Fifteen years would pass before another league would be started with the scope of the American Basketball League of 1925–31.

The ABL was ahead of its time in trying to put professional basketball on a major-league level, but its acceptance of the faster collegiate style of play—though with the added roughness of the old pros—was a harbinger of the future for the professional game. Even crusty old conservatives like William J. Scheffer were partially converted. In the American League's first season, the *Reach Guide* editor had seen several ABL teams play the Philadelphia Sphas. The games were played half by pro rules, half by the AAU code, and Scheffer admitted that the amateur style was better. He wrote:

> There is no question that the AAU style of play produces more passing and more team play. The fans of Philadelphia have become so accustomed to looking at the dribble that, at times, the AAU style looked dead, but when the ball began to be snapped around the floor the play was just as lively as the professional style. The team to display the best passing combination was Cleveland [the Rosenblums, who won the first ABL title], and when the latter was compelled to play the professional style in the final period, they showed they were head and shoulders ahead of the professional game because the dribble was used only when there was a clear field. That has been the real drawback to the professional game for years, as some teams would dribble entirely too much and cause too much individual work. Basketball was never intended to be an individual game, and passing makes a much prettier contest than too much dribbling.

William Scheffer did not budge in his preference for the cage. "A wire cage or tightly drawn net is the correct way of playing the game," he maintained. It was a claim that would have nonplussed James Naismith.

Some eastern teams continued to use the double dribble into the late 1930s, but it was increasingly viewed as a relic of the pioneer days. The cage was still seen occasionally in small eastern cities as late as the mid-1930s, but not in the major centers after 1929.

William Scheffer was not the only diehard who mourned the cage's passing; some players liked the cage, too. Albert Cooper, Jr., son of one of the first professional stars and a pro himself during the 1920s, said, "I played in cages up to 1929 when they stopped using them in Trenton. When they eliminated the cages, I never cared for basketball after that. All of the basketball players in those days enjoyed playing in a cage because there was less chance of injury than there is today. You learned to protect yourself. If you got jammed against the cage, it didn't bother you."

The passing of the cage and double dribbling helped to modernize the game, but it remained far from modern basketball. Play in the ABL was excruciatingly slow by today's standards. The center jump was still used after every score, and there was still no rule requiring a team to bring the ball across midcourt within 10 seconds. Consequently a team with a slim lead could while away several minutes by playing keepaway all over the court.

Basketball remained a ball possession game.

7

On the Road Again

As the 1920s may be called the age of the Original Celtics, so the thirties may fairly be dubbed the age of the Renaissance Big Five. This all-black traveling club was the most consistently successful team and the biggest attraction of the Depression decade.

The death of the American Basketball League had ended expectations that professional basketball would enjoy a steady march toward prominence on the national sports scene. Few professional games drew more than 2000 fans during the Depression years. There was considerably more interest in college basketball than in the pros.

The demise of the ABL did not mean the end of all professional leagues during the 1930s. In fact, the ABL itself was reorganized by John J. O'Brien as an eastern regional league for the 1933–34 season. It was the major professional circuit for the next half-dozen years and lived on until 1953. Regional leagues were also in business on a small scale in the Midwest, and one of them—the fifth bearing the National Basketball League name—would become one of the parents of the National Basketball Association.

None of the pro leagues of the 1930s, however, excited even the modest attention the old ABL had received. The resurrected American League and the midwestern circuits enjoyed local support, but, like their predecessors, they were little known outside their boundaries. So far as fans in other parts of the country were concerned, professional basketball meant the barnstormers, especially the Renaissance and the Original Celtics, who regrouped in 1931 and hit the road again.

The Renaissance Big Five were barnstormers not by choice but by necessity. As blacks they were not welcomed into the organized white leagues (but league teams were glad to play host to the Rens because their appearance assured a good gate), and there were no organized black leagues for basketball as there were for baseball. Except for the up-and-coming Harlem Globetrotters, who were barnstorming the Midwest and West during the most storied years of the Renaissance, no black team could play with the Rens.

As was true of the Original Celtics, the Rens were eager to play the best, but to meet the payroll they had to play every day and often twice on Saturdays and Sundays, and so the majority of their games were against semipros in small towns and cities, primarily in the East and Midwest, with an occasional foray into the Deep South. In their greatest season—1932–33—the Rens' itinerary included Georgia, Alabama, and North Carolina—states in which by law they could play only black teams because of local ordinances banning interracial competition. In none of those states could the Renaissance players have attended school with whites, used a "white" drinking fountain, had a meal in racially mixed company, or offended the sensibilities of any white man without the possibility of violent retribution. In the northern states, the restrictions were not quite so draconian, but blacks were not expected to appear at the front door of most restaurants catering to whites (they were welcomed in the kitchen) or otherwise avail themselves of public accommodations.

William J. (Bill) Yancey, a Renaissance star who also played on topflight black baseball teams during the 1920s and '30s, recalled how it was for black barnstormers, particularly in small cities where there were no black settlements:

> When I was playing with the Renaissance in basketball, sometimes we used to get treated something awful. We'd go in town and couldn't get any food, and then they'd expect us to make 'em look good! In baseball we didn't get bothered too much except in the South. In the North, we never had problams, not that you'd notice. Because the white ballplayers thought it was an honor to play us. Oh, we used to have problems getting food in the North. The restaurants didn't want to serve us. That was general in the North, but we never had too far to ride. If we were going from New York to Philadelphia, how long is that going to take? And if you were going to Pittsburgh, you could stop at Harrisburg. There's always ways.
>
> Our biggest problem was when we were on the road all the time, like when I was playing basketball. I'll never forget the time we went into West Virginia for the first time and there was no hotel at all where we could go. It took us maybe a couple of hours to find lodging for eight or nine fellas—one stay here, two stay here, like that.

Hosting the Renaissance or Original Celtics was a pleasure for a basketball promoter because it assured a busy box office, but the Rens could present special problems to a promoter who was sensitive to their situation. Gerry Archibald, who owned and managed strong professional teams in Warren, Pa., during the 1930s, remembered one visit of the Rens to Warren, a town of 15,000 people, all white:

> Normally the Rens never tried to stay here. They always stayed in Jamestown, N.Y., when they came in to play us. But for this one game they had come

in from Indiana, and they said they hadn't had time to make reservations so they asked me if I could find a place for them. I said, "I think I can," and I called the Sitler House and asked if they could handle a basketball team. I didn't say they were black. The hotel said yes, so I returned to the Rens' manager and said, "I got a place for you."

So we drove to the Sitler House and the Rens' manager and a couple of the players went in with me. I'll never forget the look on the poor girl's face at the desk when we opened the door. She turned white as a sheet and she said, "Mr. Archibald, I just can't do it," and she burst out crying.

Just like that, the Rens turned around and said, "Okay, Gerry, we'll find some place." And boy, did they ever put on a show that night! I beat 'em a couple of times, but not that night!"

White players were generally mindful of the Renaissance players' problems, and most held them in high regard, both personally and professionally. Frank Baird, a star for the Indianapolis Kautskys, one of the strongest teams in the Midwest, remembered:

> I was very sympathetic. When the Renaissance came in, they had to stay at the colored YMCA at Sennett and Michigan. We'd go out with them and play around the state. There was no place they could get anything to eat, so they brown-bagged it. We'd get to the gym at 6 or 6:30 for an 8 o'clock game, and they'd be down in the locker room already dressed and having a sandwich or something. Maybe they'd save part of it to eat on the way back to Indianapolis. I thought that was one of the most unfair things. They were nice guys and they were tough. I'm pretty sure over the years they beat us more than we beat them.

The Renaissance Big Five was the creation of Robert J. Douglas, a black native of St. Kitts in the British West Indies who had played amateur basketball in and around Harlem in New York City for a dozen years in the early part of the century. In 1923 he decided to form a professional team and challenge the many pro and semipro clubs around New York. He planned to name the club the Spartans after one of his amateur teams but, faced with the need to find a home court, he approached the owners of the new Renaissance Casino in Harlem and offered to take its name if he could use the large, high-ceilinged ballroom on the second floor.

Thus was born the Renaissance Big Five. It was an immediate success, winning thirty-eight and losing ten in its first season.

During the Rens' heyday in the 1930s, the team was on the road almost constantly from November to mid-April, coming home for games at the Casino only over the Thanksgiving and Christmas holidays. When they were at home, the Rens attracted full houses of people in evening clothes who were eager for the game and the dancing that followed. The court was small—perhaps 60 by 35 feet—with the musicians' bandstand on one side and a wooden barrier surrounding the dance floor.

"It was a very slippery floor," Rens' star William (Pop) Gates remembered. "They had baskets that they put up before every ball game and markers they put down for the foul lines and so forth. The spectators were seated at tables in loges on the second tier and in boxes in the third tier. That was supposed to be an elite area," Gates explained.

"The ballroom had a high ceiling, so you didn't have to worry about your shots," he continued. "All you had to worry about was running into that hard wooden barrier around the floor because it had sharp edges. Sometimes when the game got rough, the guys would be flying over that barrier into people's laps."

White teams enjoyed visiting the Renaissance Casino. John J. O'Brien, Jr., who played there several times with the Brooklyn Visitations, recalled, "The fans were the wealthiest black people in Harlem, dressed, believe it or not, in tuxedos. A good-looking crowd—handsome women, good-looking guys—and they loved the basketball game, but they loved to get the game over for dancing afterward."

In their formative years, the Renaissance played mostly in the New York area. By 1927 they could match baskets with the best. Over the three previous seasons, they had beaten the Original Celtics in four out of nine games and had defeated every team in the American Basketball League except the Cleveland Rosenblums, whom they had not met. On the seven-man roster were three of the men who would make up the Rens' best team in the early 1930s—Clarence (Fats) Jenkins, James (Pappy) Ricks, and Eyre (Bruiser) Saitch.

By the late 1920s they were traveling widely and playing 130 games a year. Their victory rate was about 80 percent, even though nearly all of their games were on foreign courts.

Bob Douglas continued to add the best black players he could find, but in their early years nearly all came from New York and Philadelphia. On the 1932–33 team, which established the Renaissance as the best in the country, only 6-foot 5-inch center William (Wee Willie) Smith was an outlander. Douglas had spotted him in Cleveland when he played in a preliminary to a Renaissance game.

That team won 120 games and lost only eight and compiled an 88-game winning streak. The string was ended in Philadelphia late in the season by the Original Celtics, the aging former champions, who met the Rens 14 times that year. The Renaissance took 8 of the 14 matches to cement their claim to the mythical world title. Their only other losses that season were to the New York Jewels (the old St. John's University Wonder Five) and Yonkers of the Metropolitan League. The Rens avenged those defeats by beating both teams twice.

The 1932–33 lineup, which represents the Renaissance in the Hall of Fame, comprised Bill Yancey, John (Casey) Holt, Charles T. (Tarzan) Cooper, and Jenkins, Ricks, Saitch, and Smith. Two of the players, Yancey and Jenkins, were also baseball stars, and Eyre Saitch was a nationally ranked tennis player.

Like the Celtics, the Rens relied on speed, short, crisp passes, and relentless

The Renaissance Big Five in the early 1930s. *From left:* Fats Jenkins, Bill Yancey, John Holt, Pappy Ricks, Bruiser Saitch, Tarzan Cooper, and Wee Willie Smith. *Inset:* Robert L. Douglas, owner-manager. *Basketball Hall of Fame Photo.*

defense. Only Wee Willie Smith and Tarzan Cooper, who stood 6 feet 3 inches, were over six feet. Except for the addition of Johnny Isaacs in 1935, that Renaissance team remained intact for four seasons and never won fewer than 120 games a year.

In March 1939 the first real "world series" of basketball was held in Chicago. (The American Basketball League had billed its championship playoffs as world series, but since the Renaissance were excluded the title was suspect.) The World Tournament was sponsored by the Chicago *Herald-American* over ten years from 1939 through 1948. Each year twelve to sixteen of the nation's best teams competed in Chicago Stadium before crowds that occasionally topped 20,000.

The tourney was recognized by professional players as world championship play, and as a rule it attracted the best professional teams in the country, including champions of various leagues and the black independents, the Renaissance and Harlem Globetrotters. Sometimes, though, the field was filled out with pickup teams. In the first World Tournament in 1939, the Rens' first opponent was a group of American Basketball League players led by Honey Russell and christened the New York Yankees for the duration of the tourney. The duration wasn't very long because Russell's Yankees had the misfortune of drawing the Rens for their second game and were eliminated, 30–21.

The Rens won their next two games, and in the final they beat the Oshkosh All-Stars, champions of the National Basketball League, by 34–25. High scorer for the Rens was Pop Gates, then a twenty-one-year-old, 6-foot 3-inch rookie. His teammates on the championship team were Tarzan Cooper, Wee Willie Smith, Eyre Saitch, Zack Clayton, and Johnny Isaacs. Their coach was Fats Jenkins, the Rens' mainstay for the preceding sixteen years.

Winning the first World Tournament put an official stamp on the Renaissance as champions and climaxed a decade of superior play. They won the big tournament again in 1943, though not under the Rens' name or Bob Douglas's aegis. Because of travel restrictions during that war year, he cut back his operations, and several of the Rens' players played weekends in Washington with the name Washington Bears. As the Bears, the old Rens drubbed the Oshkosh All-Stars, 43–31, in the finale of the World Tournament. The Renaissance continued to operate into the late 1940s, but never again were they the power they had been during the Depression.

In their glory years, the Rens found new blood each fall at a tryout camp in New York. Bob Douglas would invite young black players whom he and Eric Illidge, his road manager, had seen or heard about on their travels to come to New York for a trial. That tryout camp was not only a testing period for the youngsters but also the only preseason training for the regulars. Pop Gates said:

> Remember, this was the only well-known, premier black team in the country, so they would have the best ballplayers come in from all over. The fact that the Renaissance had played for so many years meant that Bob Douglas and Eric Illidge had created friendships in small towns and big cities everywhere. So if people thought they had a ballplayer who could play with the Renaissance, they would let Bob Douglas know about it and he would invite them to the training camp the following year.
>
> That was the training we had; they'd put you on the floor and you played against those trying to make the team. Maybe they'd have a hundred, two hundred guys out there and picked the best eight.

Pop Gates's own route to the Rens was different. He had been an all–New York City selection after his Benjamin Franklin High School team won the city championship in 1938. That fall he went to Clark College in Atlanta, intending to play on its strong basketball team. But he played football, too, and soon found the training table inadequate for his needs. "I was hungry most of the time," he said. So when he got an offer from Arthur Josephs, owner of the semipro Harlem Yankees basketball team, he hustled back home. Gates was earning $2 or $3 a game with the Yankees when they scrimmaged the Renaissance. Bob Douglas was impressed and bought him from Josephs for "maybe a hundred dollars," Pop Gates recalled.

Gates signed with the Renaissance for $125 a month; at the time Fats Jenkins was probably the highest paid Ren at $225. Eight players, road manager Eric Illidge, and a bus driver made up the touring team. "We played every day in the week and sometimes twice on Saturday and Sunday," Pop Gates said. Meal money was $3 a day, and of course the club paid hotel bills. It was not a bad living but the players had to work or collect unemployment compensation in the off-season. Pop Gates himself was a New York City Parks Department lifeguard for ten years and later became a city corrections officer.

The Renaissance players took great pride in their status. Would they have wanted to play in the National Basketball League in their world championship year? Pop Gates said:

> We didn't think about it. The NBL was an excellent league at that time—the top league in the country—but we thought we were the premier team in the country. The Renaissance players didn't give a damn about the National Basketball League at the time because we thought we were their equal or better. So we weren't worried about it. We were happy to be where we were.
>
> I think if the National Basketball League would have offered one of our guys more money than Bob Douglas offered, somebody would have gone. But we loved being with the Renaissance because we thought we were the best, and we were happy and proud to represent the Negro people and give them something they could be proud of and adhere to. And we were happy that a lot of white fans loved us also.

In their last season—1948–49—the Renaissance were the Dayton Rens of the National Basketball League at a time when the racial bars in professional sports were falling. When they disbanded, the Rens could boast of a 2,318 to 381 won-lost record over 26 seasons.

Only the Original Celtics rivaled the Renaissance as a traveling attraction during the 1930s. The Celtics went back on the road for the 1931–32 season after the collapse of the American Basketball League. Joe Lapchick, Dutch Dehnert, Pete Barry, and Davey Banks, who had been on the roster of the last-place Toledo Red Men during the big league's final year, were the nucleus for the barnstorming Celtics for the next four seasons.

They were only a shadow of the powerhouse they had been in their prime, but they were still too much for most of the college and town teams they played on tour. The Celtics remained the symbol of basketball prowess even after they relinquished the top spot to the Renaissance.

In his 50 Years of Basketball, Joe Lapchick remembered: "The one thing that always impressed the Celtics was the number of yellow school buses we would see around the building in which we were to play. Coaches would bring their high school teams hundreds of miles to see us move the ball with that rhythmic free-wheeling that is championship ball at its best. When high school and college players were present, it was like a shot of adrenalin to us. We knew why they came, and we said, 'Let's really turn it on tonight.'"

The Celtics traveled in a seven-passenger Pierce-Arrow, one of the luxury cars of the period. In those Depression days, their guarantee demand was $125, with an option of taking 60 percent of the gate. Gone were the days when they had played before 10,000 at Madison Square Garden or Cleveland Public Auditorium; now the crowd was apt to total 800 or a thousand.

By the mid-1930s the Celtics were no longer playing every night. Moe Spahn, an All-American under Nat Holman at City College of New York, remembered that he was invited to join the Original Celtics after his graduation in 1934:

> They wanted a young guy to do some running for them. I was in graduate school [working on a doctorate in school administration] and an assistant coach for Nat Holman, but there was a Christmas vacation coming up and they came to me. They had Dutch Dehnert, Dave Banks, Carl Husta, Nat Hickey. I think the only ones that weren't with them then were Joe Lapchick and Holman. They said, "Come on, give it a try, see how you like it."
>
> I stayed with them two weeks. We went up to Boston for a three- or four-day trip, and then we took another trip toward the southern end of the New York area. I would say they averaged four or five games a week then. I think they paid me about $20 a game.
>
> They were still a very good team. I had to do some running because I couldn't get into the pivot play. They had Dehnert in the pivot and he was so wide you couldn't see around him. But I did very well and they wanted me to sign up with them, but I said, "No, I've got my studies. I've tasted it and maybe a couple of years hence I'd be interested."

Spahn stayed home in New York and became one of the scoring leaders of the American Basketball League as a member of the Jersey Reds, New York Jewels, and Wilmington Blue Bombers.

For the 1935–36 season popular singer Kate Smith lent her name and money to the Celtics team. Ted Collins, Miss Smith's manager, took care of the promotion and management duties for the Kate Smith Celtics.

Dutch Dehnert and Pete Barry were pushing forty years of age. Joe Lapchick was thirty-five and plagued by knee troubles. Davey Banks, the small speedster, was the only player from the Celtics' great years who was still in his prime. To add some youth and vigor, the Celtics signed on Paul (Polly) Birch of Duquesne University, 6-foot 4-inch Pat Herlihy, former Celts Nat Hickey and Carl Husta, and a promising young set-shot artist named Bobby McDermott.

A telling indication of how far the Celtics had fallen came in April 1936 when they were soundly defeated by a team of New York college stars before 2500 at New York's 71st Regiment Armory. The final score was 46–34. Two of the collegians each scored 15 points, which would have been unthinkable in the Celtics' great days. It was time to quit. Joe Lapchick joined Nat Holman in the college coaching ranks, beginning a long, successful career at St. John's University and with the New York Knickerbockers of the NBA. Pete Barry ended his playing days, too.

Still the Celtics name did not die. Ted Collins added some younger players, and with Pete Barry as coach and the only link to the Original Celtics, the Kate Smith version spent parts of the next two seasons in the American Basketball League. They finished out of the running both times.

Ted Collins followed the Celtics tradition of signing his players to contracts forbidding them to play with other teams. Unfortunately, he could not continue the Celtics tradition of winning. He dropped the team after the 1937–38 season. The Celtics name was carried on by barnstormers, including such old hands as Dutch Dehnert, Pat Herlihy, Davey Banks, and Nat Hickey, until World War II. But the Celtics name was not again in the highest echelons of professional basketball until the Boston Celtics were born in 1946 for the first season of the Basketball Association of America.

The players from the Kate Smith Celtics went to Kingston, N.Y., to play as the Kingston Colonials under the management of dimunitive Barney Sedran, the scoring star from the game's infancy. Unburdened of the Celtics tradition, the Colonials topped the standings in the American Basketball League for 1938–39, but the New York Jewels, fourth-place finishers, won the post-season playoffs.

The Original Celtics and the Renaissance Big Five were not alone on the barnstorming trail during the Depression. In the Midwest, the Harlem Globe-trotters were laying the foundation for the worldwide reputation they have today as an entertainment troupe mixing first-rate basketball and comedy in equal measure. Olson's Terrible Swedes were touring widely and playing almost as many games as the Celtics and Renaissance. Each year there would be several other short-lived barnstorming clubs, some of them based on novelty. Often a collection of players would grow beards and take to the road as the House of David, trading on the fame of a bearded barnstorming baseball team sponsored by the Israelite House of David, a religious sect in Benton Harbor, Mich. Another traveling team used the same whiskery gimmick and called themselves the Bearded Beauties. For one season the Hong Wah Q'ues, a team of Chinese players, wandered through the Midwest playing independent teams.

Probably the best-known of the barnstormers after the Rens and Celtics were Olson's Terrible Swedes. The Swedes were organized in 1920 by C. M. (Ole) Olson of Coffeyville, Kan., a player, manager, and promoter who scouted the AAU ranks in the Midwest and Southwest to fill his roster. During their first decade, Olson's Terrible Swedes covered the Midwest, West, and South, playing eighty to ninety games a season. By 1929 the East was included in their annual itinerary. Like Frank Basloe of the earlier Basloe Globe Trotters, Olson did business out of his hat and hotel rooms, booking games as he went.

Sidney Goldberg, a boxing and basketball promoter in Toledo, Ohio, recalled, "Olson might call me one day from Rochester, the next day from Peoria. He was always figuring where to get a game. He filled up gyms pretty well. The Swedes were a fairly good draw."

Ole Olson was player as well as manager on his early teams and was noted for behind-the-back passes and one-hand shots from the corners. He sometimes shot free throws overhead with his back to the basket, but except for such bits of flashiness, the Terrible Swedes played straight basketball. Naturally, Olson advertised them as "world champions."

Olson's Swedes traveled light, usually carrying only five players. Occasionally that meant trouble as it did one night in 1930 in Akron, Ohio, when Ole Olson was ejected from a game. The game with the Akron Goodyear Wingfoots was stopped for 10 minutes until a spectator, James (Soup) Campbell, an Eastern League veteran who was then with a team in Pontiac, Mich., could don Olson's uniform and join the fray.

In 1935 Olson took the Swedes off the road. The following year he began touring with the All-American Red Heads, a women's team which for the next forty years was surpassed only by the Harlem Globetrotters as a barnstorming attraction. Playing exclusively men's teams, mostly amateurs in small towns, the Red Heads typically covered thirty states and played 185 games during their six-month seasons. In some years their travels took them to Mexico, the Philippines, and Hawaii.

Olson recruited Red Head players from AAU teams and high schools. In their ranks were several well-known players, including Hazel Walker, a seven-time AAU All-American for teams in Tulsa and Little Rock and one of the best women players of the 1930s and '40s. She held the women's free-throw shooting championship and regularly defeated male contenders during half-time contests at Red Heads' games.

During their first decade on the road, the Red Heads claimed a victory rate of 50 percent against men's teams. In later years they did better than that, according to Orwell Moore, who began coaching the Red Heads in 1948 and bought them from Olson seven years later. "I would say that from 1950 to 1975 we probably won 85 or 90 percent of the time," Moore said. Beginning about 1950 the organization was so successful that two or three Red Head teams were on the road at the same time.

The appeal of the Red Heads was based on equal parts of skillful basketball, the novelty in those pre-women's liberation years of watching accomplished women athletes working up a sweat, and the battle of the sexes. The word "glamour" popped up often in magazine stories about the Red Heads, but given their travel schedule, their life could not have been all that glamorous. Over the years the Red Heads built up a repertoire of trick plays and gags to amuse the fans—dribbling with the knees, a variety of trick shots, and the piggyback play in which a petite guard climbed on the back of 6-foot 4-inch Gene (Careless) Love and dropped the ball through the hoop.

The Harlem Globetrotters have been by all odds the most successful and long-lived of basketball's barnstormers. Since their formation in 1927, the 'Trotters have played on six continents (missing Antarctica only because of the paucity of basketball fans in that bleak land), most of the world's capitals, and virtually every country with the remotest interest in basketball. Undoubtedly they have been seen by more people than any other sports team in the world.

For many years the key to the popularity of the Harlem Globetrotters has been comedy, but that wasn't so in the beginning. For more than a decade, they played straight basketball and gradually developed into a superior team. Almost from the start the Globetrotters were performing the "circle" before each game, though not to the accompaniment of "Sweet Georgia Brown," their theme song in later years. The circle was an exhibition of fancy ball-handling, behind-the-back and between-the-legs passes, bouncing the ball off knees, elbows, and heads, and other sleights of hand and foot. "When I booked them into Toledo for the first time in 1931—and gave them $43—the circle wasn't that good," promoter Sidney Goldberg recalled. But as the Globetrotters' fame grew the circle improved and became an integral part of every show.

The Globetrotters had their genesis in Chicago's Savoy Ballroom, one of the best-known dance halls in the dance-band era. It was one of many ballrooms which booked basketball games when no dance was scheduled and had its own team, the all-black Savoy Big Five. In 1926 an enterprising twenty-three-year-old native of London, England, who had grown up on Chicago's North Side, began booking the Savoy team around Chicago for their nights off from the dance hall. He was A. M. (Abe) Saperstein, a short, stocky man who had played on the Lake View High "bantamweight" team and from 1920 to 1925 with the semipro Chicago Reds. Saperstein's basketball background was modest but his promotional instincts were unexcelled.

In early 1927 he decided to expand his horizons. With the Big Five's best players as a nucleus for a new team, Saperstein booked his first barnstorming game in the village of Hinckley, Ill., about twenty miles west of Chicago. So on January 7, 1927, the Globetrotter legend was born with a victory over the village team for a purse of $75. The five-man squad led by the diminutive white man was called Saperstein's New York, implying a well-traveled, sophisticated organization. Over the next few years Saperstein's New York became just plain New York, then Saperstein's Harlem New York, and finally, in the mid-1930s, Saperstein's Harlem Globetrotters. Despite the name changes, the 'Trotters were still confined to Illinois, Michigan, and Ohio, and they were playing most of their games in towns that were mere dots on the map. When they did hit a big city, fans did not turn out in droves. In one of their first appearances in Chicago,

The Harlem Globetrotters of 1930, when they were simply called "New York." Despite the name, the Trotters were still barnstorming in the Midwest. *Standing, from left:* Abe Saperstein, Toots Wright, Fat Long, Inman Jackson, and Kid Oliver. Runt Pullins is seated. *Harlem Globetrotters Photo.*

for example, the 'Trotters attracted 27 spectators and earned $5 for the night's work.

Abe Saperstein persisted, and gradually the Globetrotters' territory included much of the Midwest and Pacific Northwest. Like the other barnstormers, the 'Trotters played on a wide variety of courts—high school gymnasiums, armories, second-floor social halls, and even a drained swimming pool. Like the Renaissance, they suffered the consequences of de facto segregation, finding it hard to locate food and lodging because they were blacks in a white world. Their lot may have been even harder than the Rens' was because there were few black oases along the highways and byways of the rural Midwest and West.

Bernie Price, who joined the Globetrotters in 1936, remembered, "In some small towns the kids had never seen blacks before and they would rub our skins to see if the black would rub off." Price continued:

> We were treated poorly practically everywhere. I remember one occasion in Omaha, Neb. After the game a boy came on by and said, "I got a place for you."

So we go by this big fine hotel. The kid on the desk must have been young or new on the job because he gave us rooms, but about 4 o'clock in the morning we had to get up and get out. So we got in the bus and drove on down toward the town where we were playing next. We drove all night, just kept on going.

Saperstein would intercede for us, but hell, there wasn't anything he could do about it. But we were mostly young and we didn't pay much attention to it.

Given the level of competition to be found in the small towns, the Globetrotters won almost to the point of boredom. During the Depression, they were playing from 150 to 175 games a year and winning more than 90 percent. Their show routines during games began to evolve to relieve the tedium of one-sided games. The first showman was Inman Jackson, who joined the team about 1930. He was a 6-foot 3-inch strong man who learned to palm the ball and roll it up one arm, across his shoulders and down the other arm. He was also an accomplished faker and could so bewitch an opponent that the man would be looking for a ball that was perched on his head. Babe Pressley, who came to the 'Trotters a few years later, became expert at putting such strong backspin on a bounce pass that it would come back to him yo-yo fashion. All of the 'Trotters were soon learning such crowd-pleasing tricks as spinning the ball on a fingertip. The fancy dribbling, trick shooting, and comedy routines that are now staples of a Globetrotter performance did not appear until the 1940s.

By 1939 the Globetrotters had never ventured further east than western Pennsylvania and were virtually unknown in most of the citadels of professional basketball. On the strength of their 148–13 won-lost record, however, they were invited to the first World Tournament in Chicago. They acquitted themselves very well, losing to the champion Renaissance, 27–23, in the second round and placing third in the tourney.

The following year they won the World Tournament, ousting the Renaissance in the second round and defeating the Chicago Bruins of the National Basketball League in the final by 31–29. On that team, which established the Globetrotters as bona fide champions, were veterans Inman Jackson and Babe Pressley, Sonny Boswell, Hillery Brown, Ted Strong, and Bernie Price.

The 1940 world championship was the apex of the Globetrotters' years in "straight" basketball. In subsequent years they never made it to the finals of the World Tournament, although twice they extended the eventual champions in early-round games. Following World War II, they beat the world champion Minneapolis Lakers twice in exhibitions before sell-out crowds in Chicago Stadium.

By the time the National Basketball Association began its first season in 1949, the Harlem Globetrotters were at the height of their game as skilled players and entertainers and were basketball's biggest attraction.

8

Metamorphosis

During the heyday of the barnstormers, professional basketball as a whole remained a backwater on the national sports scene. The college game was in the ascendancy. Basketball had long since supplanted baseball and track as the number two attraction on campus after football.

The collegians could fill seats off campus, too. In January 1931, as the Great Depression was deepening, New York Mayor Jimmy Walker's Committee for the Relief of the Unemployed and Needy staged a tripleheader with six metropolitan college teams. Some 14,500 spectators were drawn to the old Madison Square Garden on Eighth Avenue and contributed $24,000 to the unemployed. Tripleheaders later that year and again in the next two years also yielded gratifying results, not only for the needy but as portents of basketball's future.

Intercollegiate basketball was flourishing in the Midwest. The Big Ten averaged 7800 fans per game in the 1933–34 season, and one game—Purdue at Minnesota—attracted 13,600. Crowds were smaller in the East, but a Penn-Princeton game in Philadelphia's Palestra drew 10,000.

Some college coaches were challenging the conventional belief that ball possession, conservative shot selection, and tight defense were the keys to good basketball. Frank Keaney's University of Rhode Island team played run-and-shoot that year and averaged an unheard-of 46.9 points per game. Purdue's Big Ten champions, coached by Ward (Piggy) Lambert, weren't far behind with a 41.6 average.

The growing popularity of college basketball was not lost on a New York sportswriter named Edward S. (Ned) Irish. He had been assigned to cover a game at Manhattan College's tiny gym in 1933 and found the place so jammed that the only way he could get in was by crawling through a window in the athletic department's office. In the process he ripped his best pants.

That unhappy experience (and probably also the tripleheaders for the needy) convinced Irish that basketball—at least the college variety—deserved a bigger showcase. He quit his job on the *New York World-Telegram* and signed a rental contract with Gen. John Reed Kilpatrick, president of Madison Square Garden, to promote college doubleheaders there. Kilpatrick was glad to have the business, even at the bargain rental of $4000 a night, because the Garden was often dark in the Depression years.

Irish's first college basketball promotion was so successful that even he was astounded. It was held on December 29, 1934, and 16,180 fans turned out to see New York University defeat Notre Dame, 25–18, and Westminster (Pa.) trim St. John's, 37–33. Irish staged seven more doubleheaders that year, and soon a bid to Madison Square Garden was the ticket to national prominence for college teams. Irish's promotions were not the first intersectional college games (Yale had toured the Midwest before the turn of the century), but national interest in intercollegiate play began with the Garden doubleheaders.

The seeds of the scoring surge to come in basketball were sown at one of the Garden doubleheaders in 1936. Ned Irish's booking for December 30 called for the Indians of California's Stanford University to meet Clair Bee's Long Island University Blackbirds. LIU was a heavy favorite, having won 43 straight games against the best in the East. They were led by 6-foot 8-inch Art Hillhouse and All-American Jules Bender. New York sportswriters knew that Stanford had a sound team, since they had whipped Temple, 45–36, on their way to New York, but they were not thought to be a match for the Blackbirds.

That illusion was shattered before the first half ended with Stanford leading, 22–14. The real revelation, though, was the shooting of Stanford's 6-foot 2-inch Angelo (Hank) Luisetti. He was firing one-hand shots—and making them! Heresy! Everyone knew that the proper way to shoot from farther than 10 feet was to plant your feet together, hold the ball with both hands—seams parallel to the floor—and push the ball up from the fingertips. Luisetti's feet left the floor slightly as he launched his one-handers, but it was not a true jump shot in which the player springs high and releases the ball at the apex of his jump. That would come later.

Hank Luisetti was an excellent ball handler, dribbler, and floor general, but it was his one-hand shots that captivated the 17,623 spectators as Stanford defeated LIU, 45–31. Luisetti scored 15 points—a high but not terribly unusual total for the time—but it was the way he scored them that presaged a basketball revolution. The New York Times reported, "It seemed that Luisetti could do nothing wrong. Some of his shots would have been foolhardy if attempted by another player, but with Luisetti doing the heaving, these were accepted by the crowd as a matter of course."

Two old original Celtics were not converted. Nat Holman, "Mr. Basketball" and the coach at City College of New York, groused, "That's not basketball. If my boys ever shot one-handed, I'd quit coaching." Even five years later, when one-hand shooters were fairly commonplace in the colleges and were beginning to appear in the pros, St. John's coach Joe Lapchick deplored the one-hand shot.

Luisetti's demonstration that in fact one hand is as good or better than two in shooting did not immediately set kids in school gyms, playgrounds, and barnyards to shooting one-handers because in those pre-television days relatively few people had seen him. But his example opened up new possibilities for coaches and players whose mind-set had long been conditioned by the received wisdom about shooting methods.

Hank Luisetti, twice an All-American selection, never appeared in professional basketball. After his graduation from Stanford in 1938, he played for AAU teams and in the Navy during World War II. While he was in the Navy he was struck by spinal meningitis and was told by physicians that his days in competitive basketball were over.

While intercollegiate basketball was booming, the professional brand languished. The pros were not welcome in Madison Square Garden or most of the nation's big arenas. A few professional teams had big-league digs (the Indianapolis Kautskys, for example, sometimes rented the 15,000-seat Butler Fieldhouse), but most teams were confined to armories, high school and college gyms, and dance halls. Some played in even stranger places. Moe Spahn, who played with semipro teams immediately after graduating from CCNY, remembered that one of the courts was a fire station, where the firemen rolled out their engines and the game was played on an improvised court.

Professional basketball had a brief vogue on theater stages during the 1930s. The Kate Smith Celtics played some home games in the Hippodrome, a huge theater in Manhattan, and the Brooklyn Jewels were an attraction on the 80- by 40-foot stage of the Brooklyn Paramount Theater. Jewels' manager Eddie Wilde reported enthusiastically in the 1936 *Converse Basketball Year Book* that the introduction of basketball had boosted theater attendance from 1500 to 5000 on some movie nights. Sammy Kaplan, a star for the Kate Smith Celtics and American League teams, remembered playing on stage in Albany, N.Y., where the game complemented a movie and a vaudeville bill headlined by Red Skelton. There was some talk of a theater basketball circuit for deluxe theaters with big stages, but nothing came of it.

The success of basketball in theaters was not a sign that prosperity was just around the corner for the professionals. Nevertheless, while the pro game was stagnant at the box office, in retrospect the period can be seen as the harbinger of a new age. The game itself was speeded up as the professionals adopted rules designed for faster action and more scoring. By the end of the Depression decade, game scores tended to be in the '30s and '40s rather than the teens and '20s.

The intercollegiate rules-makers made two important changes in 1932, and both were accepted for most professional games. One change divided the court in half with a midcourt line and required the team with the ball to cross that line within 10 seconds of getting the ball, whether from a center jump, out-of-bounds play, interception, or defensive rebound. It had the effect of curbing stalling to some extent by forcing the offensive team to play a half-court game. The second change prohibited a pivot man from camping permanently with the ball within the six-foot wide foul lane and thus clogging the area around the basket. The rule said that when a player got the ball in the foul lane, he had three seconds to pass, shoot, or dribble out of the lane. Three years later the pivot man was further restricted when it was ruled that a player could not stay in the lane, either with or without the ball, for more than three seconds. (The three-second rule is one of the few instances in the early days of basketball when the pros preceded the colleges in rule-making; the American Basketball League had passed it in 1930.)

Not all professional teams adopted the new rules immediately. The touring Original Celtics, for one, were reluctant. Presumably in deference to their aging stars, the Celtics insisted on playing under the old professional rules which did not require so much movement.

The most striking rule change of the decade was elimination of the center jump after every score. It had been proposed as early as 1928 by Justin M. (Sam) Barry, coach at the University of Iowa. Nat Holman was an early advocate of the idea, and in 1933 he staged a demonstration game without the center jump, except to start each quarter, before a skeptical audience of eastern intercollegiate officials. Holman's plan was to have the teams alternate in taking possession of the ball at the midcourt sideline after each score, rather than giving it to the defending team at its endline as Barry had proposed.

Several college conferences also experimented with ending the center jump before the change was finally adopted by the National Basketball Committee in 1937. The rule followed Barry's version, giving the ball to the team that had been scored upon at its endline.

Elimination of the center jump was the most radical change in basketball's early evolution. It speeded up play considerably because the ball did not have to be brought to center court for a tip-off after each score. It also contributed to the development of the skills of tall players because teams could no longer afford to carry a big center whose only value was to get the tip-off. The consensus of coaches was that ending the center jump would help small players most, but in fact the day of the dominating big man was still in the future.

Not all basketball men, either amateur or professional, welcomed the change. Notre Dame coach George E. Keogan said eliminating the tip-off penalized good teams because they had no chance to get the ball back immediately after a score via a center jump. James Naismith, basketball's inventor, wasn't too pleased either. "I'm not wedded to the jump, mind you," he said, "but I think that it has slowed the sport up. . . . In the old days it took the referee four seconds to throw the ball up after a score," Naismith continued. "Now the team scored against can take 15 seconds (including five to put the ball in play) to bring it beyond the center line. I also think the new style is monotonous."

Naismith reserved his harshest criticism for the zone defense, which was reaching the height of its popularity among college and high school teams, though not among the professionals. "I have no sympathy with it," the founder told the New York Metropolitan Basketball Writers Association. "The defensive team is stalling which lays back and waits for the offense to come to it . . . Officials should penalize a defensive team for stalling. The rules committee, unfortunately, puts the responsibility on the wrong team. Roughness is the result. A zone defense has no part in basketball. It is a violation of the fundamental principles of the game."

Responding to Naismith's complaints in a letter to the sports editor of the *New York Times*, Hy Fliegel, who had been captain of Nat Holman's first CCNY team in 1919, pointed out that zone defenses were rooted in basketball history. Many college coaches taught the zone even before 1919, Fliegel said, and advised, "Don't be alarmed, Dr. Naismith. Basketball is still in the ascendancy and the zone defense will be broken through by good players and good coaches just as it has been broken through in the past."

Professional teams could ignore the flap over the zone defense since none of them used it, chiefly because pro teams had set shooters who could destroy a zone with long-range shots, but they were ambivalent about ending the center jump. Teams with a tall center tended to favor the tip-off after scores; those without one liked the new rule. The National Basketball League, which was in its first season in 1937–38, gave the home team the option of deciding whether to use the center jump. A typical hassle occurred when the Pittsburgh Pirates visited the Warren Penns in February and learned that the Penns did not plan to use the tip-off. "Elimination of the center jump caused a lengthy argument before the game was started, the Pittsburghers claiming that National League rules made the center jump mandatory," the *Warren Times-Mirror* reported. "They finally agreed to play the first half without the tip, and during intermission manager Archibald removed all doubts by exhibiting the league rules to the visiting manager, proving that the center jump is optional with the home team."

Gradually the nay-sayers were won over as it became clear that ending the center jump added to basketball's appeal by fostering more scoring and faster action.

Even more important than the rule changes in the metamorphosis of professional basketball during the 1930s was the influx of former college players. College-trained players were rare in the pro game's infancy; Barney Sedran, who graduated from CCNY in 1911, and Syracuse University All-American Joe

Schwarzer, who started in the New York State League in 1919, were exceptions that proved the rule.

During the 1920s, a handful of college men turned professional after graduation, notably Homer Stonebraker of Wabash College and Frank Shimek of the University of Iowa. Late in the decade, the American Basketball League recruited several college stars, including Vic Hanson of Syracuse University, Lou Spindell of CCNY, Cookie Cunningham of Ohio State, Tiny Hearn of Georgia Tech, Branch McCracken of Indiana University, and Charley Murphy of Loyola of Chicago. But most professional rosters were still filled by alumni of the school of hard knocks in regional leagues, YMCAs, high schools, and settlement house teams.

That began to change in the 1930s. Two factors were at work. First, with the onset of the Depression, it was hard for even a college graduate to find a job—any job—and professional basketball offered a good living in season and sometimes a job for the off-season. And for a lucky player who *did* have another job, pro basketball was a pleasant way to supplement his income. The second factor was the game itself. Players who had benefited from good coaching in college and had played the game with a high level of skill welcomed the chance to continue playing. It was pure love of the game that sent them into the professional ranks.

Frank Baird, a Helms All-American in 1934 at Butler University, was typical of the collegians who turned to the pros after graduation. He had been trained as an accountant and was offered a job by Firestone Tire & Rubber in Akron, where he would have played on the company basketball team and, incidentally, worked in accounting. But, he said, he did not want to leave Indianapolis, and he was one of the lucky ones—he got a teaching and coaching post there at Broad Ripple High School. Baird played for a year with the Hilgemeier Packers, a semipro team, before joining the Indianapolis Kautskys, one of the strongest professional teams in Indiana—then, as now, a basketball-mad state. Frank Baird remembered:

> I would say that when I started with the Kautskys in 1935, eight out of the ten players were coaching some place. I was one starting guard and Johnny Wooden was the other. He was coaching at Central High of South Bend, and he would drive 130 miles down to Indianapolis and back again for every game. Bill Perigo, who was a great ballplayer at what is now Western Michigan, was coaching at Markleville. Cy Proffitt, a forward, was coaching at Spencer. Our starting center, George Chestnut, was different—he was working at Delco Remy in Anderson, Ind. But most of the players who joined our club were coaching someplace. Basketball was a pretty profitable sideline, and of course a lot of fun.
>
> Our schedule was irregular. Sometimes we would play just one game a week, sometimes two or three. If the Celtics, Renaissance or Globetrotters came

through, we'd play them Tuesday, Wednesday and Thursday around the state, skip Friday and Saturday because those were high school basketball nights, and then play someplace else Sunday.

We never really barnstormed. We'd go, play the game, and turn around and try to get back in time to get to work the next morning. Maybe we'd go to Akron and play the Goodyears Saturday night and the Firestones Sunday afternoon, and then drive like wild to get back home. Or we'd go up to Wisconsin, play Oshkosh Saturday night and Sheboygan Sunday afternoon and then drive like wild to get back. It was mighty tough. Lots of times we would get back to Indianapolis at 5 o'clock in the morning—if it was real icy, maybe 6 or 6:30— and there were a few times I was late getting on the job Monday morning.

The Indianapolis Kautskys were owned and managed by Frank Kautsky, owner of two grocery stores on the city's south side. He had started the club in 1930, apparently as a labor of love, although of course the team advertised his stores. "I don't think Frank Kautsky was ever an athlete himself," Frank Baird said, "but he was a very fine fellow, very outgoing, he liked people and he liked athletics."

Like nearly all owners in the Depression years, Frank Kautsky paid his players by the game. Frank Baird recalled:

When I started with the Kautskys, I got $25 usually, which seemed like a good bit of money. It was 1935, and I was teaching school and coaching two sports for $100 a month for ten months, so I was making more money playing basketball than I was teaching school. But it wasn't so much the money— although I enjoyed the money—but I just loved to play.

All the time I was with the Kautskys, I didn't get much more than $25 a game. Whether the other fellows were getting more, I have no idea. Probably Johnny Wooden got more because he was a great drawing card; he had been All-America at Purdue for three years.

Maybe I didn't have the name or reputation to draw people, or maybe I didn't dicker. To tell you the truth, I enjoyed playing and if he wanted to pay me I was just tickled to death to take the money.

Frank didn't put your money in an envelope. He carried a roll of bills with a rubber band around it. While you're getting dressed after the ball game, he'd take some money off the roll and hand it to you. Everyone would just stick it in their pockets. If he was particularly pleased, or if you had had a good ball game, sometimes he would give you a little bit extra.

Indianapolis had three play-for-pay teams during Frank Baird's young manhood, so he was aware of the professional game when he graduated from Butler. Not every collegian was. Buddy Jeannette, for example, had only a dim awareness that pro basketball existed when he was graduated from Washington and Jefferson College in Washington, Pa., in 1938. He had starred for the W&J team for three years and was looking forward to a coaching job. Jeannette recalled:

I thought I had a coaching and teaching job lined up in a little town called Claysville, Pa. Well, school started and another guy got the job. I was staying in our fraternity house and the college year was starting so I had to get out. Some guy I went to school with said, "Why don't you two"—me and another player named Bill Laughlin—"go up to Warren, Pa., and play basketball."

So we got in touch with Gerry Archibald, who had the Warren Penns, and we bummed up there one day and met Arch and worked out. He said come back on Thanksgiving; they started the season then. And that's how I got started in professional basketball.

I made a hundred dollars a month. During the season I did nothing but play basketball and drive that 1928 Pierce-Arrow we rode around in. After the season, Arch got me a job with the National Transit Co. in Warren for $15 a week. It was the hardest job I've ever done in my life. Warren is an oil area, and we used to go out to the farms that had oil wells and drain them into a pipe that emptied into the refinery. I really had to work for that $15. Playing basketball was nothing compared with that.

Buddy Jeannette went on to a long career as player, coach, and front office man in the years when professional basketball was becoming a major sport, all due to his failure to get the coaching spot in Claysville, Pa. "Now," he said, "every time I go through Claysville I stop and say a little prayer."

One of Jeannette's teammates on the Warren Penns, Emmett W. Morrison, didn't wait for graduation before turning professional in 1937. Morrison was in his junior year at the University of Pittsburgh and playing under Dr. H. C. Carlson, one of the era's most famous coaches, when he got an offer from Gerry Archibald, Morrison said:

I had a basketball scholarship at Pitt that paid my tuition, but I had to buy my books and pay board. I parked cars at football games, waited tables at the Syria Mosque, and carted coal in bushel baskets to deliver it to people. Ever walk three flights up with a bushel basket of coal?

At Pitt I was just hanging on, working at anything to make ends meet. So when Archie offered me, I think it was $15 a game, and guaranteed two games a week, and also said he'd get me a job in a local plant, I jumped right at it. I enjoyed Pitt, I enjoyed Doc Carlson, and it was great being a Pitt basketball player. But I told him, "I have to leave, I can't go on like this. I don't know whether I'll have enough to eat tomorrow."

Another player who turned professional for lack of better opportunities was John J. O'Brien, Jr. A six-footer and the son of the American Basketball League's president, O'Brien had captained the Columbia College team and graduated in 1938. "When I graduated, it was still the Depression period," he said. "You couldn't buy a job, so I decided to play basketball. I went with the Brooklyn Visitations ball club. John Donlon was the manager. He was a Jimmy Cagney type of Irishman; he wore a derby hat. He couldn't tell us anything about basketball, but he knew how to handle seven young men."

O'Brien went along when the franchise moved to Baltimore. "All the time I'm working at different jobs outside of basketball," he said, "but I'm not too happy with the progress I'm making, basically because I'm starving. So I wanted to make a change in my employment." He visited Columbia's placement service and was told to get in touch with Goodyear Tire & Rubber in Akron. O'Brien remembered:

> So I wrote to them and they sent me a telegram saying, "Come out to Akron at our expense." I couldn't believe this! This sort of thing didn't happen. So I hop on a train and go out to Akron, and I'm saying to myself, "I've got to give Goodyear credit. Even though I'm 500 miles away, they recognize that I'm brilliant, I'm a great engineer."
>
> I go into Goodyear's personnel department and they say, "Jack, we'd like you to meet the basketball coach at Goodyear." They don't want me for my brains, they want me to play basketball! I say, "Okay, what job is open? I want industrial engineering." And they say, "You got it, no problem."

Firestone Tire & Rubber and Goodyear were the principal industries in Akron and arch-rivals in basketball. Their players had jobs in the plants and were not paid extra for playing on the company team. (This practice was common for Amateur Athletic Union teams; consequently Goodyear and Firestone teams played in both professional and AAU competition at various times.) Jack O'Brien said he was paid about $3000 a year for his work in the plant, but of course nothing more for playing. He later became a well-known official in the ABL and the young National Basketball Association.

Professional rosters were studded with Jewish names during the 1930s, especially along the eastern seaboard. Probably half of the players in the reincarnated American Basketball League were Jewish.

A few Jews, notably Nat Holman, Barney Sedran, Marty Friedman, and Doc Sugarman, had been professional stars during the Roaring Twenties and before, but it was the Depression decade that brought a wave of Jewish players into the professional ranks. Most were first-generation Americans, the sons of European Jews who had flocked into eastern cities in the late nineteenth and early twentieth century.

Jewish athletes were prominent in other sports, too. Baseball's pre-eminent slugger, Hank Greenberg, was Jewish. Benny Leonard, Max Baer, Barney Ross, and Sammy Mandell were among boxing's luminaries, and football had coach Benny Friedman of Michigan, Marshall Goldberg, an All-American fullback at Pitt, and Columbia's passing ace, Sid Luckman.

But basketball was even then the city game and the one sport that was easily accessible to Jewish boys growing up in the teeming cities of the Northeast. Baseball diamonds and football fields were scarce because of their space require- ments, but nearly every schoolyard and playground had a basketball hoop. If there was none near by, the boys made their own courts in alleys behind their tenements. Joel S. (Shikey) Gotthoffer got his start on an alley court in the Bronx. The son of Austrian immigrants, Gotthoffer, who was born in 1911, began playing very early:

> I guess I started playing basketball before I could read. I can't recall *not* playing. We had a unique situation when I moved to the Bronx from Manhat- tan. I was getting old enough to handle a basketball. We had a group that was very much entrenched in basketball, and we consequently built a court behind the tenements we lived in on Union Avenue between 165th and 163rd Streets. We had the Bronx Owl Seniors, Bronx Owl Juniors, and Bronx Owl Midgets— all basketball teams.
>
> The regular courts that were primarily used by people like myself were at public schools. I can't recall when I didn't go to school with my basketball clothes underneath my school clothes so that at 3 o'clock I could stay on the playground and play basketball. The school had a gym but when we played after school it was on the outdoor court.

Shikey Gotthoffer was luckier than some youngsters because he had access to real basketballs. Not everyone did. In Harry (Jammy) Moskowitz's neighborhood in the Brownsville section of Brooklyn the kids improvised. Moskowitz, born in Brooklyn in 1904, remembered:

> When I was a little kid—10 or 11 years old—we played in the street. We used ashcans for baskets but we didn't have a basketball. No kids did in that neighborhood then. Kids wore knickers and black stockings, so you took a stocking or a skating hat and you filled it with rags. That was the basketball. Now you couldn't dribble it and you couldn't run with it, so you dribbled it by hitting it in the air—an air dribble.
>
> My beginning in organized basketball was in fourth grade at P.S. 84. Then I went to Commercial High School. We had a good basketball team there. We lost the city championship to Commerce High, Lou Gehrig's team. Later when Gehrig made a name for himself in baseball, he had a basketball team in the winter; he would play about five minutes a game. I played with his team a number of times.

Another Brownsville boy, Sammy Kaplan, born in 1912 to Russian immi- grants, learned the game in schoolyards and summer recreation programs. He recalled:

> Basketball was the big sport there then. We played a little baseball, but there was no football or tennis or golf, of course. They were out of our reach; we were too poor for that. But the schoolyard was always there. My biggest problem

coming home from school was whether I should do my homework now and have the rest of the day off, or go out in the schoolyard and play immediately and then, when it got dark, come home and do the homework.

Sammy Kaplan's first formal team was the Dux Athletic Club, a group of eight Jewish teenagers who formed a summer playground team. The Dux (pronounced "Dukes") were named by a young Latin scholar who told the boys that *dux* means leader. The name not only had a nice ring to their ears but it had the additional virtue of having only three letters, which meant small expense to add it to their uniform shirts.

At this time, there was much concern in the cities about "Americanizing" the children of immigrants, and so settlement houses and municipal recreation programs required children to learn as well as play. Sammy Kaplan remembered:

> The Dux Club's members joined the evening recreation center program, which was in the schools at night. They let us use the gymnasium. Also, they insisted that we hold meetings. They wanted us to learn how to run a meeting and keep minutes and so on. They wouldn't let us use the gym unless we had the meeting. As young kids, we weren't interested in having meetings but we did all right. We even had a minute book. All the business had to do with the basketball team. New business might be that we had found out that the 92nd Street YMHA was booking games, and we wanted our booking manager to write to them.

The Dux A.C. even published a newspaper for Evening Recreation Center 184. The paper covered social activities at the center as well as sports, and the editors took care to get as many names into the paper as possible to ensure a large circulation at five cents a copy.

In 1928, when the Dux A.C. won the metropolitan recreation center basketball championship, the story was, of course, bannered on Page One. Until about 1935 the Dux A.C. was the best amateur team in Brooklyn, playing metropolitan colleges, YMHA teams, and occasionally full professionals. Sammy Kaplan went on to become a well-known professional player with the New York Whirlwinds, an independent team made up largely of former college team captains, the Kate Smith Celtics, and teams in the American Basketball League. (Incidentally, when he was with the Wilmington Blue Bombers in 1941, he was advertised as having played under Nat Holman at CCNY. Kaplan had been a student there but never played college basketball. But by that time, collegiate experience added cachet to a player's résumé and so the Blue Bombers appropriated the Holman-CCNY imprimatur.)

Why such a disproportionate number of Jewish players in professional basketball during the 1930s? Most old pros say it was because Jewish kids played basketball all the time. But the sons of Irish and Italian immigrants used the schoolyards, too, and did not become professionals at the same rate as Jews. Shikey Gotthoffer suggested another possibility:

> Jews by the very nature of the fact that they were constantly under some kind of pressure had to do a lot of thinking and developing of the mind in order to be able to live and act in society. Since there was so much hatred attached to them, they had to be able to outwit a person. Knowing that these kinds of conditions existed . . . you learned cunning, you learned finesse, you learned how to avoid a situation as opposed to fighting. Jews thought things out instead of throwing their bodies at each other. That's a very amateurish view, I know.

Sports journalist Stanley Frank took much the same tack in *The Jew in Sport,* published in 1936. "The Jewish boy," Frank wrote, "having made all diplomatic arrangements at home, starts to play basketball and makes rapid progress since the elements of the game are admirably suited to those qualities commonly attributed to him. This is a sport in which instincts largely figure . . . Intellectually and emotionally, the Jew comes to basketball well equipped. As a type, the Jew is commonly regarded as being squeamish about absorbing bruising punishment, yet he dominates the fastest and most taxing team game men play on their feet."

That seems a clear case of the racial stereotyping that was more prevalent then than it is today. It reflected the belief that Jews were a distinct race with attributes of cunning and guile. As a consequence, bias against Jews was widespread in society. Anti-Semitism was occasionally manifested on the basketball court, but it was not very intense, according to the Jewish players who were interviewed for this book. Outbursts rarely went beyond shouts of "Jew bastard," although Moe Goldman recalled that when the all-Jewish Philadelphia Sphas played at Brooklyn's Prospect Hall, which was in an Irish neighborhood, the Sphas would sometimes be the targets of burning cigarettes as they ran along the sidelines. "We had a lot of fights with the ballplayers there, too," he said.

Anti-Semitic incidents may have been more flagrant in basketball's earlier period. In his biography of his father, John (Honey) Russell, author John Russell wrote that Barney Sedran and Marty Friedman were the frequent prey of bigots. "Coffins and hangmen's nooses would sometimes be painted on a hometown floor to mark their spots," he wrote, "and in one hall the team was greeted with signs around the balconies saying, 'Kill the Christ-Killers.' In those provinces the rough going of pro basketball was 'twice as tough,' in my father's words. 'The Jew-baiters got there early—they'd have stones inside the snowballs and it was hell getting inside the hall, much less playing the game.'"

A predominantly Jewish team, the Philadelphia Sphas, was the only legitimate rival to the Renaissance for dominance during the 1930s and may have been the

The Philadelphia Sphas in the mid-1930s when they dominated the American Basketball League. Eddie Gottlieb, manager and coach, is at left. *Clockwise from him:* Red Rosen, Inky Lautman, Gil Fitch, Red Wolfe, Moe Goldman, Cy Kaselman, and Shikey Gotthoffer. *Basketball Hall of Fame Photo.*

only team that beat the Rens at the Renaissance Casino. The Sphas were also the dominant team in the American Basketball League from its rebirth in 1933 until World War II. Their leader was Edward (Eddie) Gottlieb, the most knowledgeable professional coach of the time and later one of the moving spirits in the National Basketball Association.

The Sphas had their origin in 1910 as a team of Jewish grade school boys who called themselves the Combine Club. The team, led by Harry Passon and Abe Radel, won several titles in settlement house and Jewish junior leagues. As teenagers, most of the players played for South Philadelphia High School. In 1917 the team won the backing of the South Philadelphia Hebrew Association, whence the name Sphas. Their jerseys were adorned with the Hebrew letters *samech, pey, hey, aleph.* Because they had no home court, they were sometimes called the "Wandering Jews," even though they rarely wandered out of Philadelphia in their early years. Finally, in 1921, the Sphas leased the New Auditorium Hall in Philadelphia for home games.

By 1926, the Sphas were among the best in the nation. They had won three championships in the minor Philadelphia League and also took the title in the briefly rejuvenated Eastern League. Augmented by two non-Jews—Stretch Meehan and Tom Barlow—the Sphas, playing as the Philadelphia Hebrews, beat the Original Celtics two out of three, won both of their games with the Renaissance, and defeated three teams in the new American Basketball League, then in its first season. They lost, however, to the Cleveland Rosenblums, the ABL's first champion.

Gottlieb took his mixed team of Jews and gentiles into the American League for the next two seasons. Playing as the Philadelphia Warriors, they finished in the middle of the standings for 1926–27 and in second place behind the Celtics the following year. Gottlieb withdrew from the league in 1928 and spent four years in the smaller Eastern League. When the ABL was reborn in 1933, Gottlieb joined it with an all-Jewish team, and it remained entirely Jewish from then on. The Sphas early stars—Harry and Chick Passon, Edwin (Hughie) Black, Lou Schneiderman, and Doc Newman—were gone. In their places came a new generation of accomplished players—CCNY All-American center Moe Goldman, sweet-shooting Cy Kaselman, Shikey Gotthoffer, Red Wolfe, and Petey Rosenberg.

Over the next dozen years, the Sphas (often under the name Hebrews) won six American League championships and were the wintertime toast of Philadelphia's sports fans. "We became the darlings of Philadelphia," Gotthoffer said. "We couldn't go anywhere in Philadelphia without being recognized. It was a very nice feeling. We were very well-loved. Even William Penn's statue on top of City Hall used to bow to us when we came by," he laughed.

The Sphas' fame, however, was not universal. Moe Goldman remembered that when Eddie Gottlieb approached him with an offer, he didn't know who Gottlieb was. Agreeing to join the Sphas for $35 a game after the college season ended, Goldman got a quick introduction to professional basketball. He played his final college game one Saturday night in 1934 and was told to be at Arcadia Hall in Brooklyn the next night for his pro debut. Goldman recalled:

So I went to Arcadia Hall and the man at the gate wouldn't let me in. I said, "I'm playing for Philadelphia," and he said, "I don't know you from Adam." That's how big the game was then. And incidentally, I would have been a number one draft choice if they had the system they have today.

Finally Eddie Gottlieb comes and gets me in. I go down to meet the ballplayers and he gives me a uniform. I thought, well, I'll probably go out and watch them play. We get into the gym and get ready to start the ball game, and Eddie says, "Goldman, you're at center." I had never played with these fellows, I just met them that night.

Sphas players were paid by the game—generally $35 for rookies up to $100 or more for veterans in the Sphas' latter years. As a rule, they played two games a

Honey Russell, player-coach of the Brooklyn Jewels when their home court was the stage of the Paramount Theater. Russell's pro career lasted 28 years. *Basketball Hall of Fame Photo.*

week in the ABL and two games outside the league. Gottlieb permitted his men to play with other teams, too, and so Goldman, Gotthoffer, and others played as "imports" in the minor Penn State League and with independents on their nights off from Sphas games.

The Sphas' home court was the ballroom of the Broadwood Hotel. Their games were highlights on the social calendar of Jewish singles, in part because they liked basketball and in part because of the dancing that followed the game. When ex-Temple star Gil Fitch was on the Sphas' roster, he would change quickly into a tuxedo after the game and lead his band for the dance.

The Sphas stuck quite close to home along the eastern seaboard, except for a western trip each year around Christmas. Then they would take off in a nine-passenger car and head for Oshkosh, Wis., stopping off for games in Pittsburgh, Akron, Detroit, Chicago, Sheboygan, and other waystops on the professional basketball circuit. Occasionally they went west again in March for the World Tournament in Chicago. They never won it; by the time the tournament began in 1939 the Sphas were past their prime.

The Sphas were successful because Gottlieb recruited excellent players and kept them together until they could anticipate each other's every move. "Eddie didn't have to coach us," Shikey Gotthoffer said. "He had a principle that you were professional ballplayers, you were schooled in your trade, you knew what you had to do. You had to be cohesive, you had to be a team. And we jelled and became a team with him sitting there," Gotthoffer continued:

> We moved as a team, not as individuals. The man who had the ball would pass it as we moved up the court, not dribble it as they do today. Today the man with the ball is in the backcourt and the rest of the ballplayers are down in the area where the basket is. We played on the supposition that if all the men were advancing, they had to guard us that way. When we came sweeping down, we came down with full force. They didn't know where the ball was going to go or who was going to handle it.
>
> The ball always moved—it was always off the floor. Of course we dribbled, but in most of the action the ball was being moved. That brought about opportunities because of the changes that were taking place.

When the Basketball Association of America began play in 1946, Eddie Gottlieb entered the Philadelphia Warriors as charter members. The Warriors' roster included only Petey Rosenberg from the great years of the Sphas. The Sphas' name was continued into the late 1940s by a team that barnstormed with the Harlem Globetrotters.

Seeds of the NBA

If ever a major professional sports league had modest parentage, it is the National Basketball Association. The genesis of one of the NBA's parents can be traced to 1935 and a loose coalition of professional and quasi-amateur teams called the Midwest Basketball Conference. Two years later, the name was changed to the National Basketball League, and it was under that title that it joined with the newer Basketball Association of America in 1949 to become the NBA. By that time none of the original entries was still in the league.

The Midwest Basketball Conference had four types of teams. First, there were the company teams—Akron Goodyear Regulars, Akron Firestone Non-skids, Fort Wayne General Electrics, and Indianapolis U.S. Tire and Rubber. The players were company employees with year-round jobs who were not paid for basketball but owed their jobs to their basketball skills. The second type was operated by a basketball man but supported by a business and took its name. An example was the Warren, Pa., Hyvis Oils, operated by Gerry Archibald with financial support from an oil refinery. Third, there were teams like the Indianapolis Kautskys and Whiting (Ind.) Ciesars which were both named for, and operated by, businessmen. Finally, there were independents like the Buffalo Bisons and the Pittsburgh YMHA.

Paul Sheeks, recreation director of Firestone Tire & Rubber and coach of the Nonskids, and Indianapolis businessman Frank Kautsky are often credited with having organized the Midwest Conference. One of them may have had the original idea but many other team operators were thinking along the same lines about the value of formalized competition, according to Gerry Archibald, who became conference vice-chairman. The conference schedule was informal at best. Each team booked its games, although they were expected to play a minimum of ten league games, at least four of which had to be on the road. No team could play another more than four times to count in the conference, which sprawled from Chicago and Fort Wayne in the Midwest to Buffalo and western

Pennsylvania. The conference used intercollegiate rules with two exceptions: five personal fouls disqualified a player instead of four, and home teams had the option of choosing to play four 10-minute quarters or three 15-minute periods. (The American Basketball League was using three periods at the time.)

In the league's two years of life as the Midwest Basketball Conference, the Chicago Duffy Florals won the first championship and the Akron Goodyears the second. Before the start of its third season, the league's owners changed its name to the National Basketball League, ostensibly because on sports pages "Midwest Conference" often referred to the Big Ten conference of major midwestern universities. In fact, though, said Gerry Archibald, "we were trying to give it more of a national effect by changing the name." M. B. (Buck) Ghefsky of Pittsburgh was elected president, and Hubert Johnson of Detroit was named commissioner.

Despite its grander ambitions, the NBL in its first season was just as casual as the Midwest Conference had been about scheduling. Again the eighteen teams made their own bookings, with the result that the league champion Akron Goodyear Wing-foots played eighteen league games and the Buffalo Bisons only nine in the Eastern Division race. In the Western Division, the Fort Wayne General Electrics led the league for its number of games, with twenty, but finished third behind the Oshkosh All-Stars and Whiting Ciesar All-Americans for the divisional title.

The looseness of the league's structure in its first year is made plain by Gene Scholz, who played for the Columbus Athletic Supply club, last-place finishers in the Eastern Division. "I didn't even know we were in a league," Scholz said. "I didn't know what was going on. I was just picking up a few bucks on the side playing basketball."

With their backing by major corporations, teams like Akron's Goodyears and Firestones were on solid financial footing, but several operators of independent teams struggled to stay alive. One of them was Gerry Archibald, the young owner, coach, and occasional player for Warren. In a change of management at Hyvis Oil he had lost the refinery's support, but he renamed his team the Warren Penns and entered the NBL.

Archibald was the son of Lyman W. Archibald, one of the eighteen men in James Naismith's class of "incorrigibles" who played the first basketball game at Springfield in 1891. Father and son were prospering as fox breeders in Warren, giving the younger Archibald the wherewithal to indulge his love of sports. Gerry, who was in his late twenties, was operating strong football and baseball teams as well as the Warren Penns. Three of the Penns' players were semipro stars, from Erie, Pa., and Archibald recruited college men from Westminster, Duquesne, Pitt, Edinboro State Teachers College, and other colleges in western Pennsylvania. "In the beginning," he said, "I was paying them $5 or $10 a game. Later, when we got into the National Basketball League, I was paying $100 or

The Akron Goodyear Wingfoots, champions of the National Basketball League in 1937–
38, the league's first season. *From left:* Russ Ochsenhirt, Wes Bennett, Bob Cope, Charlie
Shipp, Wilson Fitts, LeRoy Lins, Chelso Tamagno, Chuck Bloedorn, Mal Rush, and Ray
Morstadt. *Courtesy of Wayne O. Rumlow.*

$125 a month. But these kids had been driving from Erie—about 60 miles—for a
$5 bill, and paid a driver, too. What I'm getting at is in that era, the boys wanted
to play, plus the fact that a few bucks was a lot of money in those days."

The Penns played home games in the Beaty Junior High School gym, which
seated about 900. They rarely filled it. Even when they hosted the Hammond
(Ind.) Ciesars with All-American Johnny Wooden or Lou Boudreau, the University of Illinois star who would later become a famous baseball player with the
Cleveland Indians, fewer than half of the seats would be occupied. "In a small
town like Warren," Gerry Archibald said, "you may get three or four good
crowds, like when the Celtics or Renaissance come in, and everybody thinks
you're making a lot of money, but they don't count the times when you lose
money."

Midway through the NBL's second season—1938–39—Gerry Archibald decided he had to move to survive. When he secured the backing of White Horse
Motors in Cleveland and made arrangements to play in the Cleveland Arena, the
Warren Penns became the Cleveland White Horses of the NBL. Cleveland
sportswriters were underwhelmed. Al Sutphin, president of the Arena, had
called a press conference to announce a "stupendous" story, and the sportswriters believed it would be a revelation that Sutphin's Barons hockey team

would enter the National Hockey League. It was a letdown when they learned that the old Penns were coming to town.

Still, when the White Horses played their first game at the Arena, they drew a crowd of 7500 fans who "displayed a surprising amount of enthusiasm," the *Cleveland News* reported. They also saw a pretty good game, with the White Horses losing to the Akron Firestones, 32–29. The fans were entertained by a pre-game parade led by an American Legion post and two White Horses players riding—what else?—white horses.

Reduced to eight teams in 1938–39, the National Basketball League played only a 28-game schedule, and so each team had to book outside games to meet the payroll. Gerry Archibald's booking problems were solved when he was invited to represent Elmira, N.Y., in the New York–Pennsylvania League, as well as Cleveland in the NBL. For the remainder of that season, the Cleveland White Horses–Elmira Colonels shuttled between Elmira, Binghamton, and Wilkes-Barre in the East and Cleveland, Oshkosh, and Indianapolis in the Midwest, with an occasional game back home in Warren. They tied for second place in the NBL's Eastern Division and won the New York–Penn League title.

The White Horses–Colonels played in one of the last cages that season. Buddy Jeannette, a rookie who became an all-star during World War II, remembered:

> One day we were supposed to play a New York–Penn League game in Hazleton, Pa. In those days, to find the gym you drive into town and you look for the biggest building. We drove up to this bar and I got out of the car and ran inside and said to the bartender, "Hey, we're supposed to play a basketball game in this town today. Can you tell me where it is?" He said, "This is the place." I look around and there are tables all over the room.
>
> So we went in and got dressed, and when we came out to play they had shoved all the tables back. They had a basket on one wall, and on the other side they let down a basket that had been drawn up to the ceiling. The floor was maybe 70 or 80 feet long. The referee went out to the middle of the court and drew a big round circle, and at each end he marked off 15 feet for the foul lines. Then they let a net down on the side where the people sat at the tables. And when the game began, the damndest fight you ever saw started. That was a real education.

Undaunted by such hardships, Gerry Archibald persisted. He moved his franchise to Detroit for 1939–40 and signed several All-Americans—Urgel (Slim) Wintermute, a 6-foot 8-inch center, and Lauren (Laddie) Gale from the University of Oregon, Irv Torgoff of Long Island University, and Bernie Opper of the University of Kentucky—plus old pro Nat Frankel from the American Basketball League. With holdovers Buddy Jeannette and Bill Holland, Archibald's Detroit Eagles did very well. They were beaten in a three-game playoff for the NBL's Eastern Division title by the Akron Firestone Nonskids. (The final playoff game brought air travel to professional basketball. After losing the second game, Firestones coach Paul Sheeks flew his team home to Akron from Detroit to rest them for the finale the next night. As always, the Eagles drove.)

Gerry Archibald, who had been losing from $1000 to $1500 a year on basketball, sold his franchise to a cigar manufacturer in Detroit for $1500 and went home to Warren. "I wouldn't trade the experience," he said. "I'd have been happy if I had just broken even, but it was the love of the game that kept me in it. I really had no hope of making a dollar."

By this time salaries were rising in the National Basketball League. Buddy Jeannette said that when the team moved to Detroit, his monthly wage jumped to $300. "I said to my girl, 'Jesus, let's get married. Nobody makes that kind of money!'" he recalled. "So what happens is, in Detroit I'm doing all the playing and the guys with big names are getting 1500 a month."

Gerry Archibald's tribulations in search of a solid base of fan support were not unusual. In Toledo, Sidney Goldberg, who had been promoting boxing and basketball for years, strove mightily to establish a professional team in his city.

For the 1940–41 season, Goldberg had the backing of White Huts, a hamburger chain, and organized a team to play barnstormers and semipros. Although the White Huts were not in the National Basketball League, they were invited to the World Tournament in Chicago. Goldberg recalled:

> White Huts gave me $125 to go to the tournament. That was a lot of money in those days. We didn't even have uniforms. I bought University of Toledo jerseys for $20, and I think I had some pants left over from my amateur teams.
>
> The Rochester Seagrams got knocked out in the first round, so I asked Les Harrison, their owner and coach, if I could borrow their pants.

Thus uniformed in patchwork fashion, the Toledo White Huts did much better than anyone expected. They knocked off the Sheboygan Redskins and Chicago Bruins of the NBL before losing to the Oshkosh All-Stars in the semifinals and then to the New York Renaissance in the consolation game. Toledo's Charles (Chuck) Chuckovits led all scorers in the tourney with 82 points in four games.

Chuckovits was the key to Sidney Goldberg's hopes for an NBL franchise in Toledo. One of the first of the one-hand shooters, the 6-foot 1-inch Chuckovits had singlehandedly put the University of Toledo on the college basketball map with his scoring feats. In three years of varsity play he eclipsed Hank Luisetti's record per-game average. He was well behind Luisetti's four-year point total because he played 43 fewer games, but he finished with a 17.4 per game average to Luisetti's 16.2.

By the time he graduated with All-American honors in 1939, Chuck Chuckovits was a Toledo folk hero. When it was revealed in his senior year that Chuckovits had married, it was a Page One story in the *Blade*. His one-handers were the talk of the Midwest. "But some of the high school coaches around here wouldn't let their kids come out to watch us play because I was throwing one-handers," he laughed.

Chuckovits was approached by Dutch Dehnert of the Original Celtics but elected to sign with the Hammond Ciesar All-Americans of the National Basketball League for the 1939–40 season. It was an unhappy experience. "It was a fly-by-night outfit to start with," he said. "Our contract read that we'd get $50 a game, but Eddie Ciesar would withhold $5 from every check in case we skipped the club. Lou Boudreau was our coach, but Ciesar let him go after a few games, and I thought it really wasn't fun anymore." After 14 games, Chuckovits quit and stayed home in Toledo.

His professional debut had been a considerable come-down from his collegiate career. "At the University of Toledo," Chuckovits said, "we'd have 5000 spectators—maybe 7000 for Michigan with standing room only. At Hammond, we'd have maybe 750 or a thousand, even when we played good ball clubs."

On the strength of Chuckovits's showing in the 1941 World Tournament, Sidney Goldberg was welcomed by the National Basketball League when he applied for a franchise for the 1941–42 season. "They were after me," he remembered. "They wanted Toledo and they needed teams. I paid $350 for a franchise. They also insisted on a $1500 deposit in case of forfeits, which I couldn't raise, but I got the backing of Jim White Chevrolet. Jim White also bought us uniforms and gave us two station wagons to use."

The Toledo Jim White Chevrolets, composed of Chuck Chuckovits and a supporting cast of players who came and went, had a disastrous season, winning only three games and losing twenty-one in the NBL. But Chuckovits set new league scoring marks, averaging 18.5 points per game, 5.3 more than runnerup Bobby McDermott.

Despite the opportunity to pad their scoring averages against the hapless Jim Whites, the other league teams hated to come to Toledo. "They didn't like it because we had a miserable floor in the Civic Auditorium," Chuckovits said. "It was terrazzo and slipperier than hell. They would get shinsplints from running on that floor."

After his record-breaking year with the Toledo Jim Whites, Chuck Chuckovits never again played in a professional league. For the following season, while Sidney Goldberg was struggling to hang on in the NBL, Chuckovits was coaching high school basketball in a Toledo suburb and playing an occasional game with pickup teams who furnished opposition for the Harlem Globetrotters. After Army service during World War II, he became an executive for Owen-Illinois Corp. and a well-known basketball referee.

On December 7, 1941, the Toledo Jim Whites and Indianapolis Kautskys were sliding around the terrazzo floor at Toledo's Civic Auditorium when the announcement came that the Japenese had bombed Pearl Harbor, plunging the United States into the second World War. Soon NBL players were being called to military service. By the time the 1942–43 basketball season rolled around, Sid Goldberg, who had already lost Chuck Chuckovits, was desperate for players. So was the new franchise in Chicago, which was backed by the United Automobile Workers union local at Studebaker, an auto manufacturer. Both Goldberg and the Chicago Studebakers solved the player shortage by tapping the pool of black players and bringing racial integration to the National Basketball League.

Integration came without fanfare or fuss, either because of the NBL's obscurity or because the nation was at war and had more pressing concerns—perhaps both. Sid Goldberg recalled, "I went to the league and I told them, 'I don't know what you fellows are going to do, but if you want me to stay in'—and they wanted my team—'I'm going to use blacks.' Some of them didn't relish it, I suppose, because they thought it would bring problems, but I don't think any of them objected."

Goldberg signed four good black players from Toledo—Al Price, Casey Jones, Shannie Barnett, and Zano Wast—plus six whites. But continuing calls to military service bled the team, and the Toledo Jim White Chevrolets disbanded in early December, having lost all four of their league games.

In their short season, Sid Goldberg was introduced to the realities of black life. Curiously, his education began in Oshkosh, Wis., the league's northernmost city. Goldberg remembered:

> I never thought I'd encounter the problems I did there. I went into a hotel to register the team, and they said, "We don't accept blacks." So I had no place for them to sleep. The blacks couldn't even go in a hamburger place. I had to go in and get the hamburgers.
>
> The blacks had to sleep in the car. It was cold, and I remember taking the uniforms out and putting them in the car to use for blankets. I had a room, but I felt guilty so I went out and slept in the car with them.
>
> We were there for a two-game series, and the second night I finally found a place in Oshkosh. This guy had one room, and the blacks and I slept there.
>
> So now we go to Sheboygan for a game. A great guy, Carl Roth, ran the team there—a wonderful fellow. I called Carl and said, "I don't want what happened in Oshkosh to happen again." A minor league first baseman named Joe Hauser owned a hotel on the waterfront, and Carl called him. He told me, "Joe says you can stay in the hotel." I said, "Should I bring them in the back door?" and Joe said, "You bring them in the front door and they stay right here." So that helped the situation.
>
> The crowds were good and the players cooperated. I can't recall any of the black players coming to me and saying they heard the remarks that Jackie Robinson got later as the first black major leaguer. They were accepted because they were good ballplayers.

In some accounts of the NBL's 1942–43 season, the integrated Chicago Studebakers are said to have been fractured by racial strife. Not so, in the memories of the coach and players. The Studebakers were half Harlem Globetrotters and half white college stars; all were working in the Studebaker plant, which had converted to war production, exempting them from the draft.

Coach Johnny Jordan, who later coached for many years at Notre Dame, and Paul Sokody, a former star with the Sheboygan Redskins, said there was no racial tension on the team. "There was no strife at all," Jordan said, "and the blacks were treated well by players and fans because, you know, people knew the Globetrotters as great ballplayers. They were well received."

Bernie Price, a five-year veteran of the 'Trotters when he joined the Studebakers, agreed with Jordan. "We played all year together and didn't have any problems," Price said. "The only time we had a break-up was for the World Tournament at the end of the year. I think it was a matter of egos. I don't believe it was racial."

Another Globetrotter veteran, Roosevelt (Roosie) Hudson, said the friction was between Mike Novak, a former Loyola of Chicago star, and Globetrotter Sonny Boswell, but, he said, "It had nothing to do with race. It was just about Sonny taking too many shots and not giving the ball up. That's all that was."

On the whole, the Studebakers got along well on the road. Unlike Sid Goldberg's Jim Whites, they were served in Oshkosh restaurants but, Bernie Price said, they did not try to lodge there. Instead they headed back to Chicago after games in Oshkosh. "They didn't like us up there, though," Price added. "I imagine it was because we were black, but it could be because they were crazy about the team they had up there—and they had a good team. The fans used to shoot staples and everything else at us."

The season was a milestone for professional basketball: for the first time black players had joined a league in appreciable numbers. Their arrival did not portend a rush to sign up other black players. It would be four more years before blacks would again be in the National Basketball League.

(The blacks on the Studebakers and Toledo Jim Whites were not the first ever in white leagues. A black player named Bucky Lew was with Newbury and Haverhill in the New England League as early as 1904. Three years later Frank (Dido) Wilson integrated the minor Mohawk Valley League, playing with Fort Plain, N.Y. Historian William F. Himmelman believes the Eastern League may have had a black player in 1911 and again in 1917. And in 1935, the first season of the Midwest Basketball Conference, the Buffalo Bisons center was Hank Williams, a 6-foot 4-inch black man.)

Not all of the National Basketball League's teams were quite so unstable as the Toledo Jim Whites or Gerry Archibald's Warren Penns-Cleveland White

Horses-Elmira Colonels-Detroit Eagles. It would not do to leave the impression that all NBL franchises were here today, gone tomorrow.

Three NBL teams were solid rocks—the Oshkosh All-Stars, Sheboygan Redskins, and Fort Wayne Zollner Pistons. All three made it through the tough years of World War II (when gas was rationed, automobile tires impossible to find, and players not much more plentiful) and emerged as postwar powers. One team, the Fort Wayne Zollner Pistons, lives on today as the Detroit Pistons of the National Basketball Association.

They had quite different origins. The Oshkosh All-Stars were basically a one-man operation, started and run by Lon Darling, a local businessman. The Sheboygan Redskins, a civic corporation with 120 stockholders drawn from the business and professional elite of the city, were operated by a volunteer board of directors. The Fort Wayne Zollner Pistons were the wholly owned team of the Zollner Pistons Co. (now Zollner Corp.).

The Oshkosh All-Stars were conceived by Arthur Heywood, sports editor of the *Daily Northwestern,* who suggested to Lon Darling that a professional basketball team would relieve the tedium of the long Wisconsin winters for Oshkosh's 40,000 citizens. Darling agreed and organized the All-Stars as a semipro team for the 1929–30 season. From then until 1948, Darling, who had never played a game of basketball, coached or managed the All-Stars.

The All-Stars did not join the Midwestern Basketball Conference but they were charter members of the National Basketball League in 1937. Over the next twelve years, the All-Stars won six divisional titles and were league champions in 1940–41 and 1941–42. In 1942 Oshkosh also won the World Tournament.

For the NBL's first three years the All-Stars had the league's top scorer. He was Leroy (Cowboy) Edwards, a 6-foot 4-inch center who had dropped out of the University of Kentucky in 1935 after an All-American year to turn professional. Edwards, a strong pivot man with a devastating hook shot, was what was then called a "gunner" because he hated to give up the ball if a shot was possible. He led the NBL in its first season with 16.2 points a game. His average dropped a bit in the next two years but was high enough to take the honors both times.

Many other college stars were lured to Oshkosh. One was Scott Armstrong, a 6-foot 3-inch corner man who had played under Tony Hinkle at Butler and with the Fort Wayne General Electrics. Armstrong remembered his one season with Oshkosh—1938–39—as the highlight of his years in basketball:

> I was offered a contract for $250 a month—$1500 for the season. Playing in Oshkosh was a horse of a different color. I'll tell you, you were king of the hill up there. The people held you in high esteem. You'd get invitations to this and that and meals here and there. People would speak to you on the street and ask for your autograph.
>
> The fans in Oshkosh were really rabid. Sheboygan was the big rival, of course. We were playing the Redskins at home one night and a Sheboygan

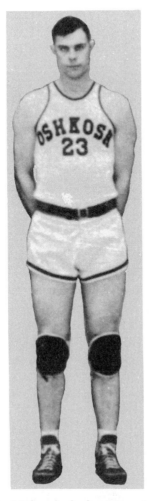

Leroy (Cowboy) Edwards, leading scorer in the National Basketball League during its first three seasons. *Basketball Hall of Fame Photo.*

player named Paul Sokody and I got our hands on a rebound near the sideline. I knew the whistle was coming so I let go of it and Sokody fell backwards. He came up with his hands up as if he was going to hit me, and I pushed him and he went back into the first row of seats.

Well, you'd think I had just made the greatest stunt in the world! Of course, the crowd didn't like him in the first place because he played for Sheboygan. Some fellow in Oshkosh even offered to buy me a hat.

The National League schedule called for only 28 games that season, so the All-Stars played another 50 games as exhibitions. "We went out on what we called the kerosene circuit," Scott Armstrong said. "We'd go up north in Wisconsin and play colleges and little town teams maybe a couple of times a week. The gyms had electric lights, but a lot of the homes were still lit by kerosene. Things were still *rural* in those areas."

The Sheboygan Redskins were organized specifically to enter the NBL, presumably to challenge Oshkosh's supremacy in Wisconsin basketball. A group of civic leaders formed the club and promptly it was granted an NBL franchise for the league's second season in 1938. The stockholders named Dr. E. H. Schutte, a local dentist, as manager and coach, and rounded up young college players, mainly from Marquette University and Wisconsin State at Oshkosh. The rookies included Kenny Suesens, a University of Iowa star who became a fixture in Sheboygan and coached the Redskins in their one year in the NBA in 1949–50.

The Redskins played in the 1500-seat Eagle Auditorium for their first four years until a new auditorium and armory was built on the shores of Lake Michigan to handle twice that number. Sheboygan compiled a less scintillating record in the National Basketball League than Oshkosh but was never less than respectable. Over eleven straight years in the NBL, the Redskins won two Western Division titles and in 1943 they took the league championship by beating the Fort Wayne Zollner Pistons in the playoffs after finishing second in the Western Division race.

Sheboygan would go to some lengths to improve its team. Buddy Jeannette recalled that in early 1943, when he was working in a defense plant in Rochester, N.Y., and playing for the non-league Rochester Eber-Seagrams, he got a call from the Sheboygan management:

> They wanted me to come out there and finish the season with them. They wanted me bad. I hemmed and hawed and finally said, "Well, I'll take $500 a game." They said, "Be here Saturday."
>
> The New York Central ran through Rochester, so on Friday night I'd catch the train at 10 o'clock and sleep into Chicago. I'd get up then and run over to the Milwaukee Line and grab a train that got me into Sheboygan at noon. I'd play Saturday night and Sunday afternoon. Then I'd catch a train out of Sheboygan at 2 o'clock in the morning, change to the New York Central in Chicago, and sleep the whole way back to Rochester. Then I'd work the rest of the week.

Jeannette not only earned $500 a game, a fabulous payday, but he got a bonus—a five-pound box of cheese for each trip. "I remember that they paid me in cash," he said, "and when I got on the train at 2 o'clock in the morning, I'd keep my hand over my money in my inside pocket. The cheese came from Magnus Brinkman, a cheese manufacturer who was a Redskins' officer. I'd ask the train porter to put it between cars so it would stay cold, but by the time I got home, the cheese was pretty ripe. Everybody on my block who liked limburger got some."

Fred Zollner, owner of the Fort Wayne Zollner Pistons. His players were employees of the Zollner Pistons Company and split net receipts from games at the end of the season, making them the best-paid players in the early 1940s. *Basketball Hall of Fame Photo.*

In his short season with Sheboygan, Jeannette helped the Redskins to the league championship in the playoffs. He also attracted admiration—and a contract offer—from the Fort Wayne Zollner Pistons, who were emerging as the dominant team in the National Basketball League. The Pistons were the pride of the Zollner Pistons Co., which was headed by Fred Zollner, a passionate fan. His company sponsored national champion fast-pitch softball teams as well as basketball.

In the opinion of some players, Fred Zollner was the first owner to make professional basketball financially worthwhile. Like Goodyear and Firestone in Akron, Zollner gave his players jobs in his piston plant but he put all basketball receipts beyond expenses into a kitty. At the end of the season, the kitty was divided up and usually each player received several thousand dollars. "At a time when guys were playing for $5 a game or $50 a game," Jeannette said, "the Zollner Pistons were getting eight or nine thousand at the end of the year. That was a pretty good piece of change. Zollner took us out of the nickel and dime league."

The Pistons were organized in 1939 and played at first in a Fort Wayne industrial league, using local players. In 1941, Fred Zollner suggested to his sports manager, Carl B. Bennett, that maybe he should book exhibition games with National Basketball League teams. "So I went to Chicago to talk to the NBL commissioner, Leo Fischer of the *Herald-American*," Bennett recalled, "and he said, 'Why don't you guys join the league?'" Bennett promptly began scouring the country for players. With the attractive job-cum-kitty deal offered by Zollner, Bennett soon lined up Bobby McDermott and Paul Birch of the Original Celtics, Indiana University stars Paul (Curly) Armstrong and Herm Schaefer, Carlisle (Blackie) Towery of Western Kentucky, and Elmer Gainer of DePaul.

Led by high-scoring Bobby McDermott, the Pistons finished second to the Oshkosh All-Stars in the NBL. For the remainder of the war years, they were supreme. In 1942–43 they topped the league standings but lost to Oshkosh in the playoffs. With the addition of Buddy Jeannette and 6-foot 6-inch John Pelkington, the Pistons then won two straight outright league titles and the World Tournament twice. They won the first postwar World Tournament, too, making it three in a row.

Following the lead of other great teams, the Zollner Pistons got the best players they could sign and kept them together. During the war, Zollner's company was making pistons for military aircraft and heavy equipment, and so the players, as employees of a defense plant, were not drafted into service. While other NBL rosters were decimated by the draft, the Pistons lost very few players.

World War II ended in atomic holocausts over two Japanese cities in August 1945. Soon scores of old pros and college stars were trooping home from the military. The National Basketball League rejoiced at the prospect of a banner season in 1945–46, with all travel restrictions lifted and plenty of good players ready to go. Ward (Piggy) Lambert, famed coach of Purdue, was named commissioner. The league welcomed back the Indianapolis Kautskys after an absence of four years and two new franchises, the Chicago American Gears and the Rochester Royals. The American Gears are not much more than a footnote in basketball's history, notable only because in 1946 they brought the first dominating big man, George Mikan, into professional basketball, but the Rochester

The Fort Wayne Zollner Pistons, the dominant professional team during World War II, after winning their third straight World Tournament title in 1946. *In front, from left:* Buddy Jeannette, Bob McDermott, and Paul Armstrong. *Center:* Jerry Bush, Chick Reiser, Bob Tough, and Charlie Shipp. *Standing:* Manager Carl Bennett, John Pelkington, Bob Kinney, Ed Sadowski, and owner Fred Zollner. *Courtesy of Wayne O. Rumlow.*

Royals quickly became one of the powers in the NBL and later in the National Basketball Association.

The Royals were the creation of Lester Harrison, a Rochester fruit and vegetable purveyor who had been operating amateur and semipro teams since his graduation from East High School in 1923. By the time of America's entry into the war, he had assembled perhaps the strongest team in the country with five All-Americans—Johnny Moir and Paul Nowak of Notre Dame, both of whom had played for the Akron Firestones, Jerry Bush of St. John's, Gus Broberg of

Dartmouth, and Jack Ozburn of Monmouth (Ill.) College—plus scrappy Al Cervi, who commuted to Rochester from his Buffalo home. The team played independent ball with the backing of the Seagram liquor company and Eber Bros., a fruit, vegetable, and liquor wholesaler. For a time they were called the Rochester Seagrams. "In those days," Les Harrison said, "the Rochester newspapers were dry and would not take liquor advertising. They said we're only going to let you use the name one year and then you have to be Ebers. So we used Seagram-Ebers for one year and then we dropped Seagram and became Ebers."

When the war ended in 1945, Les Harrison and his younger brother Jack, who was a lawyer and handled the team's business affairs, were determined to step up in class. "Eber Bros. and Seagram didn't want to go big-time," Les Harrison said, "and my brother and I mortgaged everything we had or could lay our hands on and we got a franchise in the National Basketball League, the only big league at the time. I think it cost us $25,000."

To stock the Royals' roster, Harrison looked to eastern universities. One of his first acquisitions was Andrew (Fuzzy) Levane, a star of the St. John's team which won the National Invitation Tournament in 1943. At the time it was considered good for the box office to appeal to various ethnic groups, and Harrison hired Levane under the impression that he was Jewish. Actually Fuzzy Levane was the son of an Italian immigrant who played violin in the Metropolitan Opera orchestra. He was in the Coast Guard when Harrison spotted him playing service basketball. "I got a call from Les offering me $50 for a practice and $110 to play against Sheboygan," Levane said. "Now I was from Brooklyn, and I had never heard of Sheboygan," he laughed. "I played seven or eight games at the end of the 1944–45 season and did very well."

When Les Harrison learned that Levane was not Jewish, he asked him to recommend a good Jewish player for the Royals. That request brought to the Royals, William (Red) Holzman—who had played under Nat Holman at CCNY—and Jack (Dutch) Garfinkle of St. John's. Holzman became an outstanding guard in a backcourt that included Al Cervi and Bobby Davies, a Seton Hall All-American who pioneered the behind-the-back dribble. (Holzman later coached the New York Knicks to their first NBA championship in 1970.) The big men on the first Royals team were 6-foot 6-inch George Glamack of North Carolina and 6-8 John Mahnken of Georgetown University. The roster also included Otto Graham of Northwestern, later the all-pro quarterback of the Cleveland Browns, Del Rice, a catcher for the St. Louis Cardinals, and Chuck Connors, a fair-to-middling center and briefly a major league first baseman who found his real niche as television's "Rifleman."

The Royals wasted no time in making their presence felt in the National Basketball League. They finished in second place in the Eastern Division, two games behind the Fort Wayne Zollner Pistons. In the playoffs, they beat the

Pistons, three games to one, and then swept the Sheboygan Redskins, Western Division winners, in three straight for the league championship.

The addition of the Rochester Royals extended the National League's geographical boundaries beyond the Midwest and brought a fourth solid franchise into the fold to complement Fort Wayne, Sheboygan, and Oshkosh. The NBL seemed to be on the path to national attention as it continued to attract most of the college stars, especially in the Midwest and West. As the NBL rose, the American Basketball League declined in relative prestige, although it still had such stars as Meyer (Mike) Bloom of Temple, Art Hillhouse of Long Island University, and Sonny Hertzberg of CCNY.

Recognition of the National League as *the* major circuit seemed assured, even though most of its franchises were in small and medium-sized cities. Still, time and expansion could be expected to lift the league out of its regional base.

So the NBL looked to 1946–47 with well-founded confidence. It expanded from eight to twelve teams, including a franchise in Detroit, and increased its schedule from 34 to 44 games per team. Even the birth of the Basketball Association of America, with franchises in large cities of the East and Midwest, caused little anxiety in NBL circles. Anxiety would come later.

But before telling the story of the war between the leagues, it would be well to take a look at the game on the floor. It had evolved considerably since the halcyon years of the Original Celtics, Renaissance, and Philadelphia Sphas. Game scores were in the 40s and 50s—10 to 15 points higher than they had been when the Depression began. The two-hand set shot, the hook, and the layup were still the weapons of choice; only a handful of players were emulating Hank Luisetti's one-handers.

The fast break was increasingly common, but most teams played a controlled offense patterned on the "scientific" basketball taught by such masters as Nat Holman and Joe Lapchick. The pivot play was universal, and all teams had set plays for out-of-bounds balls and the center jump that started each quarter. Picks and screens were used to free a teammate for an unobstructed shot, just as they are today.

Double-teaming and trapping defenses were unknown but switching when a defender was picked off was routine with all teams. The zone defense was popular in colleges and high schools but not among professionals because every pro team had one or two set shooters who could stay on the zone's perimeter and hit shots from 25 feet or farther. The king of the set-shooters was Bobby McDermott, the greatest long-distance shooter in history, according to many old professionals.

McDermott, a speedy, 5-foot 11-inch guard who came off the New York City sandlots in the early 1930s, led all American League scorers twice and the NBL's

Bob McDermott, who is generally regarded as the premier two-handed set shooter, in the uniform of the Fort Wayne Zollner Pistons during the 1940s. *Basketball Hall of Fame Photo.*

once. Like all two-hand set shooters, he needed a second to set up by bringing his feet together. Then he would lean slightly backward and fire a high arching shot. Statistics were not kept on shooting percentages in those days so we must rely on the memories of old players. They are unanimous in marveling at McDermott's accuracy.

Al Cervi, one of the era's best guards, believes that with today's three-point shot, McDermott would be among the scoring leaders in the National Basketball Association. "We're talking 30 points a game," he said. Cervi continued:

> I played against him three years, and I made my credits playing him. He was my best rooter. He could run like hell but he couldn't jump; I could outjump him.
>
> The first time I saw him I had just got out of service and joined Rochester. I had read about McDermott. We were in Fort Wayne, and in the dressing room Les Harrison told me, "Cervi, you've got McDermott." The other players looked at me and said, "Better you than me."
>
> Before the game started he was putting on an exhibition. He made 10 for 10 out here, 15 for 15 here. The crowd is clapping. I'm clapping too and asking myself, "Doesn't the sonuvabitch ever miss?"
>
> You couldn't let him get the ball. I remember a game in the Chicago Amphitheater, which had the longest court in the United States—112 feet. He scored three baskets from the midcourt line—that's 56 feet—on me that night and two flicked my fingers. Oh, he could shoot! If he shot 10 times from 30 feet, I'd guarantee he'd make eight in game conditions.

McDermott's prime came at a propitious time for a shooter because basketball's most basic piece of equipment—the ball itself—had become easier to handle and shoot than it had been in the time of Al Cooper, Harry Hough, and Ed Wachter. During the 1930s, manufacturing improvements had given the ball a much more reliable bounce. More important, the ball was slightly smaller, making it more easily controlled with one hand. The change came in the mid-'30s when rules-makers decreed that the ball's circumference must be between $29\frac{1}{2}$ and 30 inches—about an inch-and-a-half smaller than the original official basketball.

Gone were the droopy-drawers shorts and the warm-up sweaters of the pioneers. Now the players were nattily dressed in colorful jerseys, abbreviated shorts and sweatsuits much like today's uniforms except that they were of wool and other natural fabrics. Great advances had been made in footwear. Basketball shoes had canvas uppers, sponge insoles with cushioned arches, and soles designed for good traction.

There was another significant development as the game evolved during the Depression and war years. It deserves a chapter to itself.

10

The Big Man Cometh

It is self-evident that in basketball a tall man has a considerable advantage over a short man simply because he is closer to the goal. Yet in the game's early years, most professional players were not much taller than the average American male—at that time, 5 feet 8 inches.

There are no reliable statistics on average heights of the early pros, but we do know that until about 1930 a six-footer was considered a big man. Some indication of the sizes of the pioneers can be gleaned by examining "all-time" teams chosen by knowledgeable basketball men in 1931 and again in 1940 because we do know the heights of these stars.

In 1931, Frank Morgenweck, who had been connected with professional basketball since his brother Bill managed Camden in 1898, chose an all-time lineup whose heights averaged 5-foot-9½. The center was William Keenan, a six-footer. Morgenweck's second-team choices were slightly bigger— 5-foot-11—with 6-foot-2 Maurice Tome at center.

Nine years later, Ed Wachter, the Troy Trojan and later coach at Harvard and other colleges, tried his hand at selecting all-timers. Wachter named thirty players—first, second, and third teams with ten players each. His first-team choices averaged 5 feet 10 inches and included 5-foot 4-inch Barney Sedran and three six-footers—his teammate Chief Muller, John Wendelken of the New York Wanderers, and Chris Leonard of the Original Celtics. The tallest man on Wachter's three squads was 6-5 Joe Lapchick of the Original Celtics, his selection for second-team center. Wachter himself is often mentioned by oldtimers as the best center of the early days, and he was 6-feet 1-inch tall.

(Wachter, incidentally, seems to have suffered the common oldtimer malady of believing that his contemporaries were the best; most of his choices were at their peak before 1920 and none were still playing regularly in 1941. Six of the thirty were old Troy Trojans.)

Speed and agility were more highly prized than height in basketball's early

Barney Sedran, at 5 feet 4 inches the shortest player in Basketball's Hall of Fame. When he became a professional in 1911, speed and quickness were valued more than height. *Basketball Hall of Fame Photo.*

days, as was shown in 1904 when George T. Hepbron, secretary of the AAU's basketball committee, edited the first book on the game. The book, titled *How to Play Basket Ball,* included contributions by several YMCA and AAU experts on the game. One of them, T. J. Browne, had this to say about the qualifications for center:

> Height is a more important consideration in choosing a centre than in choosing a forward. Without height many good plays between centre and forward, when the ball is put in play, cannot be carried out. But along with height the centre must be able to correctly determine the exact time at which to jump in order to get the ball at just the right height, not too low nor too high. The ability to thus judge the jump correctly, of course, improves with practice.

However, let a quick man be the first choice, height being of secondary importance.

The value of big men as rebounders was not recognized at the time, perhaps because so few shots were taken and thus there were few rebounds. The center's chief task was to control the tip-off after each score; if he could do that, it gave his team many more chances to score. Many professional teams carried a center who was expected to get the tip and then get out of the way while the other four men played the ball.

The first tall man (by the standards of the day) to achieve fame was 6-foot 7-inch Francis P. (Stretch) Meehan, who began playing in the Eastern League in 1919 after starring at Seton Hall. Meehan was said to have earned as much as $100 a game, a fabulous salary during the 1920s. He was not much of a scoring threat, although he was a good foul shooter. Albert Cooper, Jr., who was himself a big man at 6-feet 4-inches when he played for the Trenton Tigers during the 1920s, said, "Stretch got the tap, but once he did that you might as well have taken him off the floor because he was of no value to the team. He was slow. If he scored three points a game, that would be average. All he did was get the tap, but the tap meant everything in those days."

Stretch Meehan's slightly younger comtemporary, Joe Lapchick, was generally regarded as the premier center of the time, although his reputation may have benefited from the fact that he played for the Original Celtics. But Lapchick contributed in other ways besides his ability to control the tip-off because he learned to pass, dribble and play a role in the Celtics' give-and-go offense.

It is puzzling that there were so few men over 6 feet 4 inches tall in professional basketball during its first thirty years. Today NBA centers hover around 7 feet, small forwards are 6 feet 8, and even most point guards are 6-3 or taller. Did such giants not exist in basketball's pioneer days?

They did indeed, though probably not in today's abundance. In 1912, a study made for insurance companies found that among male policy holders from 1885 through 1908, only one in 221,800 was 6 feet 11 inches tall. Just four per thousand were 6-5 or taller. The average man's height was 5-8½ with shoes on.

Average heights for men grew steadily, though not spectacularly, over the next fifty years. Research for the Society of Actuaries published in 1959 found that 20- to 29-year-old men averaged 5-9½ with shoes. Only three-tenths of one percent were 6-foot-5 or taller. In 1965 the National Center for Health Statistics reported that 25- to 34-year-old men averaged a hair over 5-foot-9, but only one percent topped 6-4.

Since in some studies height was measured with shoes on and in others with shoes off, comparisons are imprecise, but it appears that men's heights increased by an inch to an inch-and-a-half between the time the first professional basketball players took the court and the early years of the National Basketball Association. But there is no reason to believe that the bell curve of height distribution has changed, and so there should have been plenty of tall prospects for basketball in the 1920s and before. Perhaps not many as big as 6-foot-8, but surely a few 6-foot-6ers. Why weren't they playing basketball?

The answer is twofold. First, really large men were considered slightly freakish. Looking back to his playing days when he was coaching the New York Knicks in the 1950s, Joe Lapchick remembered, "I was a freak. It was real embarrassing. Wherever we went people stared at me and pointed to me like something in a sideshow." As a consequence, many big men tended to shrink from the limelight.

Second, and perhaps more important, the conventional wisdom was that large men were too clumsy and uncoordinated to play basketball. Better a six-footer who was fairly fast, quick and graceful than a really large man who stumbled over his own feet. No doubt many big men accepted that judgment and never seriously tried to learn the game, or, if they did try, faced ridicule for their initial efforts and dropped out.

A few big men did persevere and reached the professional ranks in the late 1920s and early '30s. Six-foot 9-inch Tiny Hearn joined the Rochester Centrals after graduating from Georgia Tech in 1929 to become the first American Basketball League player taller than Stretch Meehan. Howie Bollerman at 6-8, a Colgate All-American, played for the Brooklyn Visitations in the revived ABL during the '30s. "Neither Hearn nor Bollerman could run," said Moe Goldman, the Philadelphia Sphas' 6-foot 3-inch center at the time. "In our day, when they were 6-foot-6 or taller, they never ran. And I could get rebounds from the big fellows, I could outjump them. I could jump and run, and I was one of the few center men who could shoot two-hand set shots from a distance fairly accurately."

When the National Basketball League began its first season in 1937, the players on its thirteen teams averaged about 6-feet 1-inch, but there were only six men over 6-foot-5 and none of them was among the league's top scorers. The tallest was Milas (Slim) Shoun, a slender 6-11, 200-pounder who was a seven-year veteran of the Akron Firestone Nonskids.

By 1940 the trend toward taller, stronger centers was becoming apparent. With only half as many teams as in 1937–38, the NBL had nine players who topped 6-foot-5, and two of them began demonstrating the value of a large, strong center. Ed Sadowski, a 6-5, 220-pounder from Seton Hall, led the Detroit Eagles scorers with a 10.7 average. The Eagles finished fourth in the NBL but won the 1941 invitational World Tournament, with Sadowski leading the scoring with 11 points as Detroit beat the Oshkosh All Stars, 39–37, in the tourney final. Elsewhere in the NBL, young John Pelkington of the Akron Goodyear Wingfoots was clogging the lanes with his 6-6, 220-pound bulk, and 6-6 Paul Nowak of the Firestones, 6-7 Ed Dancker of the Sheboygan Redskins, and 6-9 Mike Novak of the Chicago Bruins played key roles in their teams' successes.

Mike Novak, by the way, was the first well-known goaltender as an All-American at Loyola of Chicago. At the time there was no rule against deflecting an opponent's shot on its downward arc, and in the semifinal game of the 1939 National Invitation Tournament, the high-flying Novak batted away nine sure baskets as Loyola beat St. John's 51–46. There is no record that he had similar success in the NBL before goaltending was outlawed in 1945.

By this time, basketball's traditionalists were beginnning to deplore domination of the game by big men. "There has been such a profound change in the theory, technique, and tactics of the game that a bloc of conservative coaches and free-lance critics, concentrated in the East, no longer call it basketball," Stanley Frank reported in the *Saturday Evening Post*. Frank continued:

> They refer to it, rather contemptuously and caustically, as "scarom," an ingenious trade name which is derived by combining the word "carom" and the second element of harum-scarum.
>
> "Scarom" describes perfectly the general scheme under which too many teams operate these days. The big idea is to barge down the court in harum-scarum fashion, let someone unload a wild shot and, if it fails, have one of those 6-foot 6-inch human skyscrapers—standard equipment for every top-notch team—slap the carom off the backboard into the basket or grab the rebound and dunk the ball through the hoop.

Various remedies were proposed for reining in the big men, who were often derided as goons. Forrest C. (Phog) Allen, a pioneer coach who was still at the University of Kansas, proposed raising the baskets to 12 feet to annul some of the advantage of height. Coach Paul Mooney of Columbia University suggested removing the backboards so that all shots would be made "clear" as they had been in the old New York State League. Ed Wachter offered another solution: Raise the baskets five inches and set them out 20 inches from the backboard. Putting the basket a little higher and much farther from the board, Wachter said, would put a greater premium on skillful shooting:

> Aside from the tap-ins, hooks and layups, most of the basket shooting right now is being done without dependence on the backboards. And the tap-ins we can do without because even when they are not lucky, they are usually the reward for size, not skill.
>
> But how about layups, the heart of good scoring? Well, there is no question that even the skillful player will miss the bankboards at first in some shots. But it won't be long until you'll find even the school kids using the "lift" shot which was such a sight to behold in the early days of professional basketball when open baskets without any backboards were the rule. For grace and skill, there were

Big George Mikan shooting a left-handed hook over Howie Schultz of the Anderson Packers during the last World Tournament in 1948. Ready for the rebound is the Packers' Price Brookfield (No. 3). *Wide World Photos.*

few sights in American sports to compare with a Nat Holman or a Jack Inglis driving toward the basket, leaping into the air and lifting the ball in a controlled arc to find its way into the bare, unadorned hoop unerringly. That kind of scoring shouldn't be counted in the same column with tap-ins and blind shots.

Nothing came of these ideas, and nothing stopped the march of the big men into basketball. In the 1946–47 season there were 25 players standing 6-6 or taller on the twelve teams of the National Basketball League—four times as many as had been in the circuit when it began with thirteen teams nine years earlier. One of them was the league's first seven-footer, Don Otten of Bowling Green University, who played for the Tri-Cities Blackhawks. But the next tallest player, at 6-foot 10-inches, was a rookie who would demonstrate conclusively that a giant could be a complete basketball player.

His name was George Mikan. Before he had played more than a half-dozen games as a professional, the bespectacled Mikan was being acclaimed as the most valuable player in the National League, if not the universe. He quickly became the game's biggest drawing card, and in 1950 he was selected as the greatest player of basketball's first half-century.

It did not come easy. Like many tall youngsters before him, George Mikan was clumsy and uncoordinated. In his freshman year at Joliet, Ill., Catholic High School, he was cut from the basketball squad. Transferring to Quigley Prep Seminary in Chicago, he made the team but did not set the world on fire and drew no college scholarship offers when he graduated in 1942.

Enrolling at Chicago's DePaul University, he had just begun his studies when Notre Dame invited him to try out with the Irish. (Mikan was, after all, already about 6 feet 8 inches tall, an attractive attribute for any prospect.) The big youngster was unimpressive in his trial at Notre Dame, and coach George Keogan advised him to go back to DePaul and concentrate on the books. Fortunately for George Mikan, DePaul had a brand-new coach named Ray Meyer who saw potential in the ungainly youngster. He also found that Mikan was a determined young man who was perfectly willing to work hard.

By his senior year, George Mikan was a three-time All-American and clearly the choice plum of the graduating basketball players. His only rival as the dominant big man among the collegians was Bob Kurland of Oklahoma A&M, a seven-footer who was, like Mikan, strong in the pivot and an adept shot blocker and defender, though not as high a scorer. (Kurland never played professionally, choosing instead to join Phillips Petroleum and play with its AAU team.)

George Mikan became a professional immediately after his final college game. He signed a five-year contract worth $60,000, including bonus provisions, with the Chicago American Gears of the National Basketball League. He played seven games with them at the end of the 1945–46 season. Five of the games were in the 1946 World Tournament in Chicago. If there was any doubt that a new "Mr. Basketball" had arrived, it was dispelled when Mikan scored 100 points in the five games and was named the tourney's MVP. (His American Gears, however, were knocked out of the running by the Oshkosh All-Stars after Mikan fouled out in the third period.)

It is sometimes said that George Mikan revolutionized basketball. It would be more accurate to say that he took the game as he found it and lifted it to a new level.

Mikan was slow afoot and not a great leaper. But he had an unsurpassed will to win and was strong as a bull. He was the immovable object in the pivot, had an accurate hook shot with either hand, and could take and give punishment to the other strong men in the league. In the course of his nine-year professional career, Mikan suffered several fractured bones and required 166 stitches for various wounds.

Bob Calihan, Mikan's teammate in his first year as a professional, summed it up this way:

> He was really the first good big man. There were other big men, but he was the first outstanding big man. He made the defenses double up on him. I think it was the first time I had seen double-teaming on a big man.
>
> I don't know that Mikan changed the game, but he was outstanding on rebounding and short hook shots. He was slow, and he'd have a time playing today. Of course, we'd *all* have a time playing today.

Mikan's arrival came at the right time for professional basketball. He was the game's first true superstar, and when he appeared on the scene, the pro game was poised to begin its bid for recognition as a major part of the national sports scene.

11

The BAA and
War Between the Leagues

In the summer of 1946, while the National Basketball League was looking forward to its next season with George Mikan as its stellar attraction, another major league was taking shape. It would be the most ambitious effort at establishing a truly national circuit since 1925 and the birth of the American Basketball League.

The new league would be called the Basketball Association of America, with franchises in major cities of the Northeast and Midwest. Unlike the NBL, which had grown out of the desire of basketball managers and promoters to formalize competition, the BAA was born because arena managers wanted to fill seats. None of the franchise owners was a professional basketball man.

Several of them, notably Ned Irish of Madison Square Garden, were profiting handsomely from staging college games, and some, not necessarily including Irish, believed the time was ripe for a big professional league. The leaders in the organizational effort were Walter A. Brown of Boston Garden and Al Sutphin of the Cleveland Arena. They and all but one of the other founders of the BAA had hockey teams as their principal sports properties and tenants for their arenas. There is a certain irony in the fact that basketball, the uniquely American sport, would play second fiddle to the Canadian import and be used to provide an attraction for arenas when the hockey teams were out of town.

The idea for a new professional basketball league had been discussed by members of the Arena Managers Association of America for several years. It was given impetus by sports editor Max Kase of the *New York Journal-American,* who went so far as to draw up a charter for a proposed league. Kase hoped to rent Madison Square Garden and operate a New York franchise himself. But Ned Irish squelched that notion on the grounds that, if New York had a team, Irish and the Garden would be the owners. Kase was shut out of the planning but got a cash settlement for his trouble.

The BAA's organizational meeting was held in New York, June 6, 1946, with

Maurice A. Podoloff, president of the Basketball Association of America, and first president of the National Basketball Association. *Basketball Hall of Fame Photo.*

Maurice Podoloff, operator of the New Haven, Conn., Arena, in the chair. Podoloff was a small (just over 5 feet tall), rotund man who had been born in Russia and raised in New Haven. His family had built the Arena in the Connecticut city. Podoloff was a Yale graduate, a lawyer, and president of the American Hockey League. He knew little about hockey and less about basketball, but he was an experienced executive.

The intent of the league's founders was articulated by Podoloff in his remarks. "The Chairman called to the attention of the members the fact that the newly organized Association was a major league in every possible meaning of the term," the minutes of the meeting reported. At the urging of Walter Brown, Podoloff was promptly elected president.

In line with the BAA's big league aspirations, the founders decided that its teams should be named for their cities rather than for industrial companies, as was common in the National Basketball League. The fee for a franchise was set at $1000, and a team salary limit of $40,000 was established for the ten-man rosters, not including coach and trainer. (Before the BAA actually began play, the player limit was raised to twelve and the salary cap to $55,000.)

Thirteen franchises were granted over the summer, but two of them—for Buffalo and Indianapolis—were withdrawn. The eleven teams in the first year of the BAA were:

· Boston Celtics, owned by Boston Garden, operator of the Boston Bruins of the National Hockey League.
· Chicago Stags, owned by Chicago Stadium interests, operators of the Chicago Blackhawks of the NHL.
· Cleveland Rebels, owned by the Cleveland Arena, operator of the Barons of the American Hockey League.
· Detroit Falcons, owned by the Detroit Olympia, operator of the NHL's Detroit Red Wings.
· New York Knickerbockers, owned by Madison Square Garden, operator of the New York Rangers of the NHL.
· Philadelphia Warriors, owned by the Philadelphia Arena, operator of the AHL's Philadelphia Rockets. (The Warriors' coach was Eddie Gottlieb of the old Philadelphia Sphas, the only professional basketball man at the organizational meeting.)
· Pittsburgh Ironmen, owned by Duquesne Gardens, operator of the AHL's Pittsburgh Hornets.
· Providence Steamrollers, owned by that city's arena, operator of the Providence Reds of the AHL.
· St. Louis Bombers, owned by the St. Louis Arena, also an AHL operator.
· Toronto Huskies, owned by Maple Leaf Gardens, operator of its namesake NHL team.
· Washington Capitols, owned by the Uline Arena in Washington, the only building without a hockey team.

On October 3, the organizers met again in New York to complete preparations for the first season. Among items of business was a decision to play four 12-minute quarters, making a 48-minute game—eight minutes longer than the game the National Basketball League and the colleges were playing.

Jackie Robinson had just completed his first season as the first black man in organized baseball in modern times, and the color question was evidently on the minds of the BAA's founders because, the minutes stated: "An inquiry was made as to whether or not there was any rule which might be regarded as discriminatory with reference to the engagement of players, and the ruling from the chair was that there was no such rule in the Association." None of the organizers leaped at the chance to sign black players, though, and none appeared in the BAA's three years of existence.

The operators of the National Basketball League took a tolerant view of the new league. *Basketball Magazine* quoted Carl Bennett, manager of the Fort Wayne Zollner Pistons, as saying, "We are not interested in a so-called war with the newly formed Basketball Association of America and we are certain there are enough players to go around. We plan to operate together and in harmony, and perhaps even have a world basketball series between the two league champions like they do in baseball."

One of the officers of the BAA's Chicago Stags, who would have to compete for fan support with the NBL's Chicago American Gears, was equally conciliatory. "Our team will become the second professional club in Chicago," Judge John Sbarbaro told the magazine. "I think the town is big enough for two teams. There's no reason we can't work in harmony with the other league."

The BAA's player rosters were a mix of old pros, college stars, and men who had played in the military services during the war. The BAA took the cream of the American Basketball League and netted a handful of the top graduating college stars. Ernie Calverley, Rhode Island's scoring ace, joined the Providence Steamrollers, Tony Jaros of Minnesota was signed by the Chicago Stags, and Kenny Sailors of Wyoming went to the Cleveland Rebels. But other college standouts, such as Max Morris of Northwestern and Bill Hassett of Notre Dame, opted for the National Basketball League. Most important, the NBL had George Mikan and Don Otten, the two big men from the Class of '46.

A handful of National Leaguers switched to the new league. Big Ed Sadowski, the Fort Wayne Zollner Pistons' center, became player-coach of the BAA's Toronto Huskies, but left them after twelve games to join the Cleveland Rebels of the new circuit as a player. Before leaving Toronto, Sadowski brought Roy Hurley of the NBL's Indianapolis Kautskys to the Canadian city. Chuck Connors (the "Rifleman") and Jack (Dutch) Garfinkle left the NBL's Rochester Royals for the Boston Celtics of the BAA, and Bob Feerick of the Oshkosh All-Stars went to the BAA's Washington Capitols. But there were no wholesale defections from the NBL because players could do at least as well financially in the established circuit as in the unproven Basketball Association of America.

Most of the coaches in the BAA were former high school and college mentors. Among them was Arnold (Red) Auerbach, a feisty twenty-nine-year-old former high school coach who convinced Mike Uline that he could make Uline's Washington Capitols a winner right away. He did. The coaching ranks also included old pros Honey Russell (Boston), Eddie Gottlieb (Philadelphia), Dutch Dehnert (Cleveland), and Paul Birch (Pittsburgh).

The BAA's eleven teams were divided into Eastern and Western Divisions. A 60-game schedule was set up for the inaugural season, sixteen games more than the NBL was playing. Exhibition games were forbidden in the first year. This was in contrast to the NBL, where games outside the league were icing on the financial cake.

The new league began play on November 1, 1946, when the New York Knickerbockers defeated Toronto, 68–66, on the Huskies' floor. The game's high scorer was Toronto's player-coach Ed Sadowski, the old National Leaguer, with 18 points.

The Knicks, who clearly would be a key to the BAA's success because their home city was basketball's prime venue, had a nucleus of home-grown stars who had played in the American Basketball League—Sidney (Sonny) Hertzberg, Leo Gottlieb, Oscar (Ossie) Schechtman, and Ralph Kaplowitz. Another local player was rookie Nat Militzok. Adding a touch of glamour from precincts outside New York were John (Bud) Palmer of Princeton, who brought an effective two-hand jump shot to the Knicks, and Stan Stutz, who learned the run-and-gun style at Rhode Island. The coach was Neil Cohalan, formerly of Manhattan College, one of the metropolitan area's strongest college teams.

The Knicks' debut in Madison Square Garden augured well for the new league. A near-capacity crowd of 17,205 was on hand at the old Garden on Eighth Avenue as the Knicks lost in overtime to the Chicago Stags, 78–68. It was, the *New York Times* noted, the first major league professional basketball game at the Garden since 1929. As a between-halves treat, the fans saw a fur fashion show and a brief game, ending in a 1–1 tie, between a team of New York Giant football players and the old Original Celtics—Nat Holman, Johnny Beckman, Dutch Dehnert, Joe Lapchick, Chris Leonard, and Pete Barry.

Possibly because the Garden had to book events far in advance of the BAA's schedule making, or possibly because Ned Irish had lingering doubts about the viability of the new league, the Knicks played only five more games at the Garden in 1946–47. Their other 24 home games were at the 7000-seat 69th Regiment Armory.

The Knickerbockers had a successful season artistically, winning 33 and losing 27—good enough for third place in the Eastern Division of the BAA. Taking first place easily, with a 49–11 record, were the Washington Capitols led by Red Auerbach. The young coach (later to become famous as builder of the Boston Celtics dynasty) had Bob Feerick and Fred Scolari, a former AAU player, in the backcourt, 6-foot 8-inch John Mahnken, formerly of the Rochester

Jumping Joe Fulks, who popularized the jump shot, launching one of his patented two-handers against the New York Knicks in 1951. Trying vainly to block it are, from left, Ray Lumpp, Ernie Vanderweghe, and Nat Clifton. *The Bettmann Archive.*

Royals, at center, and Bones McKinney of North Carolina, John Norlander from Hamline, and Irv Torgoff, the LIU All-American who had played with the prewar Detroit Eagles, on the front line.

Although they won the divisional title in a cakewalk, the Capitols were not the

First champions of the Basketball Association of America, the Philadelphia Warriors of 1946–47. *Seated, from left:* Jerry Rullo, Angelo Musi, Peter A. Tyrrell (general manager), Petey Rosenberg, Jerry Fleishman. *Standing:* Cy Kaselman (assistant coach), George Senesky, Ralph Kaplowitz, Howard Dallmar, Art Hillhouse, Joe Fulks, Matt Guokas, Eddie Gottlieb (coach). *Basketball Hall of Fame Photo.*

hottest team in the BAA. The big news was the coming of the first well-known jump shooter, Joe Fulks of the second-place Philadelphia Warriors. There may have been other jumpers before him, but Joe Fulks was the first to exploit the shot to the fullest. Within a decade it would be the primary offensive weapon in the National Basketball Association.

Jumping Joe Fulks, a 6-foot 5-inch self-described hillbilly, had played at Murray State Teachers College in western Kentucky and with Marine Corps teams during the war. On the recommendation of old Philadelphia Sphas player Petey Rosenberg, who had seen Fulks in the service, Warriors Coach Eddie Gottlieb tracked him down after the war and signed him, beating out the Chicago Stags for his signature.

Joe Fulks proved to be well worth the chase. In sixty games, he scored 1,389 points, more than 400 over the next best individual total. His per-game average was 23.2. In second place in the scoring race, but nearly seven points behind, was Ed Sakowski, with 16.5 points per game.

Fulks could shoot hook shots with either hand, but it was his turnaround jumpers from the pivot (released from over his head) that captivated crowds. His high-arching shots seemed to float toward the basket. Knowing a good thing when he saw it, Eddie Gottlieb had his Warriors feed Fulks, who soon became the darling of the young league. He had some accomplished teammates in 6-foot 7-inch Art Hillhouse, a refugee from the American League, Howie Dallmar, Angelo Musi, and George Senesky, but more than anyone else, it was Joe Fulks who brought attention to the Warriors and the BAA as a whole.

In the BAA's Western Division, the Chicago Stags, with Max Zaslofsky, one of the era's great two-hand set shooters, and 6-9 center Chick Halbert, edged out the St. Louis Bombers for the divisional title.

As men who had cut their promotional teeth on hockey, the BAA's founding fathers planned an intricate playoff system similar to that used in professional hockey for the championship of the league. Curiously, they decided to have the divisional champions play each other in the opening round, thus ensuring that one of the best teams would be eliminated right away. The first casualty was the Washington Capitols, the club with far and away the best regular season record. They lost four of six playoff games to the Chicago Stags. The Philadelphia Warriors won the first BAA championship, beating Chicago, four games to one, in the finals. Joe Fulks poured in 34 points in the last game, but the winning score was made by Howie Dallmer as the Warriors won, 83–80.

It was a satisfying year for the players in the new league. The BAA had promised to be big league all the way, and it was, at least for some teams. Nathan (Nat) Militzok of the Knickerbockers remembered, "Everything the New York team did was in style." Militzok had played at Hofstra College before the war and at Cornell while he was in the Navy. In his last year in service, he was on a Navy team at the Brooklyn Armed Guard Center coached by Neil Cohalan. When Cohalan was named to coach the new Knicks, Militzok, a 6-foot 3-inch forward who was an excellent defender, was among the first players signed. Militzok recalled:

> It was a very exciting year. I remember that when I went to the Garden to negotiate a contract, Ned Irish offered me $4,000. He was sitting there with Neil Cohalan, and Cohalan said, "Let's give him $5,000 because he'll be the best defensive ballplayer in the league." So through Neil Cohalan, who had been my coach in the service, I was able to get $5,000. I was very, very pleased. I'd just gotten out of service and I'd never seen that kind of money. I thought it was the epitome of all salaries and that I'd never earn more than that the rest of my life.
>
> Everything on the Knicks was done in a first-class manner. When we travelled, we would have our own railroad car. Each player would have both an upper and lower bunk, and you would throw your luggage in the upper bunk and sleep in the lower. I think we were the only team that was able to travel that way.

Travel was almost entirely by railroad in the BAA's first year, and although passenger rail service was much more extensive than it is today, there could be problems with connections. Roy Hurley, who was with the Toronto Huskies, remembered:

> Sometimes we would have to take three or four cabs and drive to Buffalo— about 90 miles—to make our connections. I remember once we had bad weather and we missed our train connection in Buffalo, and we were playing the next night in Providence, R.I. So we just stayed in the four cabs and drove all the way to Providence. That was a tough trip, but there was a forfeit fee if we didn't show up so we had to do it.

Hurley, who had starred at Butler University under Tony Hinkle and with the Indianapolis Kautskys of the National Basketball League, had a contract for $4400 with Toronto. The Huskies finished in a tie for last place in the Eastern Division with the Boston Celtics. They did not generate much enthusiasm among Toronto's sports fans, as Hurley recalled:

> Toronto wasn't really a basketball city. Their game was hockey. Another big sport—and this was amazing to me, coming from the Midwest—was wrestling. They would fill Maple Leaf Gardens for wrestling. It was unbelievable. We were really ahead of our time.

The fact that basketball shared ten of the eleven BAA arenas with hockey had an unanticipated effect on the game. Ice-making methods were relatively primitive, and if a hockey game was scheduled for the night after basketball, the ice was frozen and the basketball court was laid over it. "I remember at Chicago Stadium, they had the floor over the ice," Nat Militzok said. "When the people started coming in and the temperature got a little higher, the ice melted and there were puddles all over the basketball court. When the referee threw the first ball up, eight guys fell down," he laughed.

Buddy Jeannette, who came to the BAA in its second year with the Baltimore Bullets, said there was another consequence of the hockey-basketball marriage:

> In those days nobody knew anything about putting down insulation before they laid the floor over the ice. Fog would come up in the arena—you couldn't see. It was terrible.
>
> And it was so damned cold. I remember going to Providence with my gang when I was coaching Baltimore. They gave us blankets to sit on the bench with, and there were heaters behind the bench. You still froze! I told my gang every time we went into Providence, "I don't know about you guys, but I'm playing 48 minutes. I'm not going to sit on that bench."

All eleven teams that started the BAA's first season finished their 60-schedule, and the league had an authentic headliner in Jumping Joe Fulks. But any owner who had visions of immediate financial success was soon disabused of that notion. Financially the BAA's first season was a disaster. The Basketball Association of America would not displace college doubleheaders as an attraction any time soon.

Average attendance was just over 3000, and even that figure was padded with freebies. Only the Philadelphia Warriors averaged more than 4000 paying customers for thirty home games. Complimentary tickets were handed out by the bucketful in some cities. The Chicago Stags, who were competing with George Mikan and the American Gears for fan support, papered the house so briskly that more fans got in free than paid for the privilege of watching the Western Division champions.

In early December, with the season barely a month old, the BAA's founders— now called the Board of Governors—bemoaned the meager gate receipts. Some owners suggested having doubleheaders to make a full evening's entertainment and attract more fans. President Podoloff noted approvingly that the Philadelphia Warriors had booked a Sphas-Renaissance game as a preliminary one night and netted $10,000. No doubleheaders were held that year but they did come later. Another suggestion was to lengthen games to sixty minutes of play to give the spectators extra value. The idea was tried by Chicago and the Detroit Falcons without noticeable effect at the box office.

For the full season, with BAA tickets priced from 70 cents to $2.50, the eleven teams had net receipts of $1,089,949—about what an NBA star expects today for a year's work. The attendance figures and receipts are worth inspecting in full for the picture they paint of the owners' financial bath in 1946–47.

| | | Attendance | | |
	Paid	Complimentary	Total	Net Receipts
Boston	50,454	44,541	94,995	$ 57,875
New York	103,703	25,626	129,329	204,043
Philadelphia	128,950	5,882	134,832	191,117
Providence	77,883	3,828	81,711	117,740
Toronto	64,056	10,816	74,872	43,590
Washington	65,693	7,734	73,427	98,901
Chicago	70,474	83,952	154,426	93,951
Cleveland	67,778	—	67,778	64,638
Detroit	37,195	25,690	62,885	48,236
Pittsburgh	40,970	9,956	50,926	56,005
St. Louis	93,601	21,286	114,887	113,808
League Totals	800,757	239,311	1,040,068	$1,089,949

With such numbers, it is hardly surprising that Cleveland, Detroit, Pittsburgh, and Toronto dropped out after the first season. The only surprise is that they were able to complete their 1946–47 schedules since three of them did not have even enough income for player salaries.

Meanwhile, the National Basketball League was having trouble of its own in 1946–47. The trouble was spelled M-I-K-A-N. Although only in his rookie season, George Mikan was clearly destined to be the NBL's pièce de résistance, and so when he quit the Chicago American Gears with the season only a month old, it was a severe blow to the league.

His widely heralded $60,000 contract for five years was made up of $7000 per year salary (the NBL's cap), $50 for making an occasional appearance in the legal department of the American Gear & Manufacturing Co. (Mikan was a law student at the time), plus $5 for each field goal and $2 for a free throw. When Maurice A. White, the owner of both the company and team, reneged on some of the payment details, Mikan left the club for six weeks. Fortunately for the American Gears and the National Basketball League, the trouble was smoothed over, and Big George came back in time to help the Gears get into the NBL playoffs.

While George Mikan was temporarily unemployed, Maurice White applied the piecework principle to his other players. One of them was Robert (Bob) Calihan, an All-American at the University of Detroit who had played with the Detroit Eagles in the 1940–41 season and joined the American Gears in 1945 after service in the Navy. Calihan remembered:

> We had a crazy owner. After Mikan quit the team with his contract dispute, the owner came up with a plan to pay us $6 a basket, $3 a free throw, and $3 for an assist, but only if we won. If we didn't win, we didn't get that bonus. We got our salaries, but this was a bonus for winning.
>
> Most of us got together and wanted to pool the bonuses and split it, but White wouldn't do that unless it was unanimous. We had one guy who was against it, so White wouldn't pay the bonuses after that. The player who didn't agree didn't get the ball too many times after that.

During Mikan's absence, the American Gears maintained a .500 won-lost record but were no threat to the Western Division leaders, the Oshkosh All-Stars, the Indianapolis Kautskys, who had a budding star in 6-foot 9-inch Arnold (Arnie) Risen, a rookie from Ohio State, or the veteran Sheboygan Redskins. Things began looking up for the Gears even before Mikan's return when they got Bobby McDermott from the Fort Wayne Zollner Pistons. The firebrand McDermott was thirty-two years old but still the game's best long-distance shooter. "He was a hellion off the court, though," said Carl Bennett, the Pistons' general manager, "and if he drank liquor, he was mean, and I mean mean." Going home to Fort Wayne on a train one night, McDermott and another player beat up a third Piston; McDermott had to go.

Fort Wayne's loss was Chicago's gain. Bobby McDermott was named player-coach of the American Gears and drove them to greater effort by his intensity. When George Mikan rejoined the team, they had a winning combination. Despite their slow start, the Gears finished in a tie for third place with Sheboygan in the Western Division, trailing Oshkosh by only two games and Indianapolis by one.

The 1946 champion Rochester Royals had little trouble in the Eastern Division, leading Fort Wayne by six games at the end of the 44-game schedule. In the final match of the NBL's playoffs, the slick Royals lost to Mikan and Company, three games to one.

Overall the 1946–47 season had been a considerable success for the National Basketball League. The circuit now had twelve teams, up from eight the previous year. One of the additions was Syracuse, N.Y., the easternmost terminus the league had ever had. Still, the NBL's heart was in the Midwest. Because traveling costs and overhead in the league's small cities were less than in the more ambitious Basketball Association of America, the NBL could flourish while the BAA struggled.

The '46–'47 season brought black players into the National Basketball League for the first time since 1943. William (Pop) Gates, of the Renaissance world champions of 1939, and William (Dolly) King, a thirty-year-old former star at Long Island University, were signed by Les Harrison of the Rochester Royals. He sold Gates to Leo Ferris of the Buffalo Bisons, and when the Bisons moved to Moline, Ill., as the Tri-Cities Blackhawks early in the season, Gates went along. Willie King, a former Harlem Globetrotter, played for the Detroit Gems, and another black player, Bill Farrow of Kentucky State, was with the Youngstown Bears.

Relationships between the NBL and the Basketball Association of America were cordial in the BAA's first year. Maurice Podoloff of the BAA and Commissioner Ward Lambert of the NBL agreed in December to respect each other's player contracts barring jumping. After the playing season ended, the leaders of the two circuits held a joint meeting and hammered out a wide-ranging interleague agreement. It called for:

· A uniform player contract for both leagues.
· A joint draft of college players. (Agreement on the draft was reached only after heated debate because NBL teams had already signed 11 players who were on the BAA teams' lists of desirables. It was decided that each BAA team would have one choice before NBL teams began drafting.)
· Provisions for interleague trading of players.
· A possible world series between league champions.

In October, just before the start of the 1947–48 campaign, the two leagues held another amicable conference. They settled a player contract dispute between the Baltimore Bullets of the BAA and the NBL's Tri-Cities Black-hawks. They also considered the idea of an all-star game between the leagues.

The sweetness and light would not last the season.

Stung by the meager financial returns in its first season, the Basketball Association of America retrenched for 1947–48. Eight teams were entered—seven survivors of the first season plus the Baltimore Bullets, who had won the championship of the American Basketball League the year before. The schedule was reduced from 60 to 48 games and the team player limit was decreased from twelve to ten men.

From the standpoint of fans, the BAA's divisional races in '47–'48 could not have been better. The Philadelphia Warriors, with Joe Fulks averaging a league-leading 22.1 points a game, nipped the New York Knickerbockers, now led by Joe Lapchick of Original Celtics fame, by one game in the Eastern Division. In the West, the St. Louis Bombers won the hottest possible race. Its three pursuers—the Baltimore Bullets, Chicago Stags, and Washington Capitols—were all just one game back. In the playoffs, the Baltimore Bullets emerged with the BAA's second championship after defeating Philadelphia in the finals, four games to two.

Attendance at BAA games increased marginally over the '46–'47 season. New York and Philadelphia drew more than 4000 paying spectators per game, but the league's average was just over 3000. (The crowds were again swelled by complimentary tickets.) The shorter schedule meant less income, though, and so even with smaller rosters, the BAA's team balance sheets were again awash in red ink.

The National Basketball League was having its own problems. The first came before the season began when Maurice A. White pulled his champion American Gears—and of course the league's biggest drawing card—out of the NBL. In a costly miscalculation, White set up a sixteen-team league called the Professional Basketball League of America with franchises in thirteen midwestern and southern states stretching from New Orleans and Atlanta to Chicago and St. Paul. The linchpin was the Gears with George Mikan.

The new league was dead within a month. Maurice White lost $600,000 in a hurry and dropped out of basketball, much to the relief of Maurice Podoloff and others who found him an irritant at basketball meetings. The American Gears, a separate company from White's manufacturing concern, declared bankruptcy and the Gears players had to sue for their back salaries. They got fifty cents on the dollar, Bob Calihan remembered.

The National Basketball League took title to the Gears players and parceled them out to its other teams. The big prize, George Mikan, went to Max Winter and Ben Berger, who had bought the weak Detroit Gems' franchise and moved it to Minneapolis as the Minneapolis Lakers. The new Lakers already had Jim

Pollard, a 6-foot 4-inch forward who had starred at Stanford and played on Coast Guard and AAU teams during the war, plus a nucleus of experienced pros.

While the Basketball Association of America was cutting back its schedule, the National League went to a sixty-game season—fourteen more than it had ever played. The Minneapolis Lakers walked off with the Western Division title by thirteen games over Tri-Cities. In the East, the Rochester Royals, augmented by the purchase of Arnie Risen from the Indianapolis Kautskys, led the division by two games over the Anderson Duffey Packers. Minneapolis took the playoffs by beating Rochester, three games to one, and capped their inaugural season by winning the last World Tournament in Chicago.

The 1947–48 season was the highwater mark of the National Basketball League. It had the majority of the name players, six solid franchises in Fort Wayne, Rochester, Minneapolis, Oshkosh, Sheboygan, and the second-year Syracuse Nationals, and a ten-year history behind it—albeit a sometimes turbulent history. What the NBL did not have was the potential for much growth because most of its franchises were in small to medium-size cities.

The Basketball Association of America was weaker in players and less stable financially, but it had franchises in most of the cities that were considered major league in that era. With constant prodding from Madison Square Garden's Ned Irish, the BAA also held to its big-league aspirations even as it retrenched and began promoting doubleheaders, often with the Harlem Globetrotters as the second attraction.

To sum up the picture, the NBL had most of the better teams and players, the BAA had arena seats to fill in major cities. Did that suggest anything? It did: to bring the choice pieces together. At this far remove, it is not known who first offered the suggestion but it probably was Maurice Podoloff. Soon after the New Year in 1948, Podoloff conferred with several NBL leaders, including Fort Wayne's Carl Bennett, Frank Kautsky and Paul Walk of Indianapolis, Max Winter of Minneapolis, and Les Harrison of Rochester, about defecting to the Basketball Association of America.

By early February it was an open secret that Fort Wayne, Minneapolis, and Indianapolis were likely to jump to the BAA. Rochester was also mentioned as a possibility. Speaking to New York's basketball writers on February 10, Podoloff made no effort to squelch the rumors.

Still, eviscerating the National Basketball League was by no means a foregone conclusion. Podoloff and Paul Walk, president of the NBL, had inconclusive discussions of a possible merger of the two circuits in April. On May 10 the governors of both leagues held separate annual meetings at the Morrison Hotel in Chicago. That session was the death knell of the National Basketball League. At the BAA's governors' meeting, Fort Wayne, Indianapolis, Minneapolis, and Rochester were given franchises in the Basketball Association of America. Lon

Darling of the Oshkosh All-Stars and Virgil Gladieux of the NBL's Toledo franchise had also asked to join, but their applications were tabled. In one stroke, the upstart BAA had crippled the older NBL.

The National League's leaders promised to fight. "There will be no respect of player contracts and open war on signing players now," Leo Ferris of Tri-Cities told Podoloff. The National League refused to go through with the planned joint draft of rookies and said it would assign the player contracts of the four jumping teams to its remaining clubs.

The next day, Leo Ferris, who was named NBL president to succeed Paul Walk of the defecting Indianapolis Kautskys, threatened court action. The NBL's suit, he said, would be based on a resolution passed in April by the league's directors, including those from the four jumping teams, that if any club withdrew without permission of the league its players would become property of the National League. In the general turmoil, it was hardly noticed that Ward Lambert had submitted his resignation as NBL commissioner. He was succeeded by Doxie Moore, general manager and coach of the Sheboygan Redskins.

Hard feelings simmered through the summer, although in late July, Maurice Podoloff and Carl Bennett of Fort Wayne, now a member of the BAA's Board of Governors, met with Ike Duffey of the Anderson Duffey Packers, who had taken over the NBL's presidency from Leo Ferris. They got nowhere in attempting to smooth the National League's ruffled feathers. Podoloff reported to the BAA's owners that he and Bennett had come to a tentative agreement with Duffey for interleague cooperation. Then he dropped a bombshell. Podoloff wrote: "After Mr. Duffey had left the room, Mr. Bennett found on one of the tables in the room the following in Mr. Duffey's handwriting: 'Members, Executive Board, National Basketball League: No possible chance agreement with BAA stop Consider yourself free to operate as you see fit in contacting and signing any of their players stop Ike W. Duffey, President NBL.'"

Under the circumstances, Podoloff wrote to the BAA's team owners, feel free to raid the National Basketball League. He pointed out, however, that raiding can be a double-edged sword. Podoloff concluded, "I am hopeful that when tempers have cooled a bit and there is less irritation on the part of the National Basketball League because of the loss of four of its teams, which reduces its condition to a very precarious one, there will be the possibility of a mutually beneficial agreement, and that possibility should not be unnecessarily destroyed."

Podoloff and Duffey had another fruitless meeting in August. Duffey said afterward that they could find no common ground for an interleague truce. Podoloff agreed and added, contrary to what he had told his owners earlier, "I have instructed BAA teams not to raid NBL teams. However, if raiding starts, we will retaliate."

Despite the chilly atmosphere and warm rhetoric, no wholesale jumping occurred from league to league. Only the contract of Al Cervi, who left the Rochester Royals to become player-coach of the National League's Syracuse Nats, was a bone of contention between the leagues.

In September, the BAA's Board of Governors had an extended discussion on a policy for raiding NBL teams. The question was dropped in President Podoloff's lap. The minutes of the meeting stated, "It was decided that any players offered were to be routed through the Association office." At the same meeting the BAA banned NBL teams from its arenas and forbade BAA teams to play them.

The war between the leagues was effectively over, but the National Basketball League was not ready to admit defeat.

12

The Infancy
of the NBA

In the official annals of the National Basketball Association, its birth is given as June 6, 1946, when the Basketball Association of America was founded. It is certainly true that there is a steady progression from that date to August 3, 1949, when the BAA and remnants of the National Basketball League formally merged and took the National Basketball Association name.

But the contributions of the NBL have often been minimized. Without the box office appeal of the NBL players who came into the league with Minneapolis, Rochester, Fort Wayne, and Indianapolis, it is at least doubtful that the BAA could have continued long enough to evolve into the NBA. The BAA got players whose names meant something to professional basketball fans—George Mikan and Jim Pollard of the Lakers, Bob Davies, Arnie Risen, Bobby Wanzer and Red Holzman of the Royals, Bruce Hale and Curly Armstrong of Fort Wayne, Price Brookfield of Indianapolis.

Anyone wishing to test the temper of an old National Leaguer has only to suggest that the NBL didn't matter. As Al Cervi, a man of positive opinions, put it, "The NBL was the strength! The BAA was a high school league. If they don't steal four clubs from the NBL, they're out of business. That's how they perpetuated their league." Cervi may have overstated the case, but not by much.

The former National League teams wasted no time in establishing their quality in their first season in the Basketball Association of America. All four were put into the BAA's Western Division. The Rochester Royals and Minneapolis Lakers ran one-two in the standings over the sixty-game regular schedule. In the Eastern Division, with all old BAA teams, the Washington Capitols won by six games over the New York Knicks.

The league had changed its playoff system so that it was possible for division champions to meet in the finals. Under the new system, the first- and fourth-place and second- and third-place teams in each division met in the first round. The survivors of these series then played in the division finals for the right to meet the winner of the other division's playoffs. Under this more rational system, the Minneapolis Lakers won the BAA's championship, defeating Washington, four games to two, in the league finals. It was the first of seven consecutive championships by former National League teams.

While the revitalized Basketball Association of America was enjoying its new status as *the* major league, the decimated National League was playing out the string. It still had strong franchises in Syracuse, Oshkosh, Sheboygan, and Anderson and such stars as Al Cervi and Dolph Schayes, a promising, 6-foot 7-inch rookie center, in Syracuse, Louisiana State star Frankie Brian in Anderson, Don Otten in Tri-Cities, Harry Boykoff in Waterloo, and Gene Englund in Oshkosh.

To replace the four teams that had defected to the BAA, the National League added the Hammond (Ind.) Calumet Buccaneers, the Waterloo (Iowa) Hawks, the Denver Nuggets, a former AAU team, and the Detroit Vagabond Kings. Detroit dropped out after nineteen games and was replaced by the Dayton Rens. (In their final season, the Renaissance, with Pop Gates as coach, became the only all-black team ever to play in a "white" league.)

The Anderson Duffey Packers won the Eastern Division and swept through the playoffs, taking three straight from the Oshkosh All-Stars in what proved to be the NBL's swan song.

Although the National League was now overshadowed by the Basketball Association of America, it was not totally without appeal to players. The league office announced in May 1949 that the NCAA champion University of Kentucky team would turn pro as a group and join the NBL for the following season. Since several of the Kentucky players had played on the U.S. Olympics team in 1948, the club would be called the Indianapolis Olympians.

By late spring, the NBL's leaders were having second thoughts about continuing. They held fruitless talks with the BAA in June concerning merger or a new interleague agreement. On July 1, Leo Ferris, Ike Duffey, and Magnus Brinkman of the NBL told the BAA's executive committee that eight of their teams wanted a merger. So it was done. On August 3, the National Basketball Association was born, with ten teams from the BAA and seven from the NBL. Maurice Podoloff was elected president and Ike W. Duffey was named chairman of the NBA's Board of Governors.

The word "unwieldy" might have been coined to describe the NBA's situation in its first year. The seventeen teams were divided into Eastern (six teams), Central (five), and Western Divisions (six teams). Bearing in mind that most teams were still traveling by train, it was a schedule-maker's nightmare. Even Eddie Gottlieb, a mathematical wizard who had been making schedules for the Negro baseball leagues as well as the Basketball Association of America, was overwhelmed. As a result, three teams played 62 games, four had 64, and ten played 68. When it was over, the Syracuse Nationals were atop the Eastern

First NBA champions, the Minneapolis Lakers of 1949–50. *From left:* Slater Martin, Billy Hassett, Don Carlson, Herm Schaefer, Bob Harrison, Tony Jaros, Coach John Kundla, Bud Grant, Arnie Ferrin, Jim Pollard, Vern Mikkelsen, George Mikan. *Sporting News Photo.*

Division by 13 games over New York; Minneapolis and Rochester tied for first in the Central Division, with the Lakers winning the tie-breaker; and the glamorous Indianapolis Olympians, with Alex Groza, Ralph Beard, Wah Wah Jones, Joe Holland, and Bruce Hale—its only experienced pro—edged out the Anderson Duffey Packers in the Western Division.

Twelve teams qualified for the playoffs. At the end, the Minneapolis Lakers were again champions, this time with the first NBA title.

The most casual observer could see that a seventeen-team league with franchises in Sheboygan and Waterloo as well as New York, Boston, and Philadelphia was inherently unstable. Even Fort Wayne, the most solid franchise among the league's small cities with the backing of millionaire Fred Zollner, could not keep pace forever with the big boys because, for one thing, the Pistons were still playing in the 3800-seat North Side High School gym. (Later the city built the

The Boston Celtics' Bob Cousy, one of the NBA's brightest stars in the 1950s, gets off a shot in heavy traffic against the New York Knicks. Defending are the leaping Ernie Vanderweghe, Harry Gallatin (No. 11), and Sweetwater Clifton. *The Bettmann Archive.*

10,000-seat Coliseum to house the Pistons; the franchise did not move to Detroit until 1957.)

The smaller cities began dropping out immediately, and for its second season the NBA was down to eleven teams. Three of the NBA rejects—Sheboygan, Anderson, and Waterloo—made a valiant attempt to revive the old National League for 1950–51 as a new midwestern circuit called the National Professional Basketball League, with Doxie Moore, the former NBL commissioner, at its head. The NPBL, which had teams in St. Paul, Louisville, Grand Rapids, Mich., Evansville, Ind., and Kansas City as well as the three ex-NBA entries, never really made it off the ground. By December cracks in the enterprise were already evident when the St. Paul Lights appealed in vain for an NBA franchise. The new league succumbed at the end of the season. The old Sheboygan Redskins compiled the best record, 29 victories and 16 defeats.

Having brushed off the weak challenge of the NPBL, the National Basketball Association continued its shakeout of franchises over the next four years, dropping from eleven teams in 1950–51 to eight in 1954–55. Scores of fine young players had come into the league. Vern Mikkelsen and Slater Martin joined Mikan and Pollard on the Minneapolis Lakers. Easy Ed Macauley went to the St. Louis Bombers, and Paul Arizin and Neil Johnston increased the firepower of the Philadelphia Warriors. Bob Cousy, a clever passer and floor general and the league's biggest attraction after Mikan, and Bill Sharman went to the Boston Celtics as building blocks for the Celtics' dynasty. The Fort Wayne Pistons boasted Larry Foust, Fred Schaus, and George Yardley, who would become the first scorer to reach 2000 points in a season.

The first black players appeared on NBA rosters in 1950. Baseball's major leagues had been integrated three years earlier. In retrospect, it seems curious that the NBA (and the BAA before it) had not followed suit earlier because so many good black players were coming out of the colleges.

There seem to have been two reasons. First, the NBA already had a host of problems with shaky franchises and the owners were reluctant to add yet another, fearing that they might lose white patronage. Second, and probably more important, was their relationship with Abe Saperstein and his Harlem Globetrotters. Whenever the 'Trotters appeared on a double bill with NBA teams, gate receipts soared, and so the owners were loath to challenge Saperstein for the rights to black players.

In 1949, according to Carl Bennett of the Fort Wayne Zollner Pistons, there had been a straw vote against signing black players by the NBA's Board of Governors. Since the league had no rule barring blacks, the straw vote would have had no effect if a black had been signed, but it did indicate the owners' fears. A year later, Bennett said, Ned Irish of the Knickerbockers told the Board of Governors, "I'm not drawing, and I want approval to buy Sweetwater Clifton from the Globetrotters to help me win ball games. If I don't get it, I'm going to walk out of this room and we're going to withdraw from the NBA. We're not going to continue to lose ball games just because you fellows won't approve it."

Irish, an imperious magnate, had often threatened to leave the league if he didn't get his way. Nevertheless, the other owners paid attention because the NBA needed New York more than Irish needed professional basketball in Madison Square Garden. So, in another straw vote, the governors voted 6–5 in favor of signing black players, Bennett said.

"When we walked out of the room, one of the other governors asked how I felt about it," Bennett recalled. "I said, 'Hey, if they're good ballplayers and can help win games, what's wrong with it?' And he said, 'Bennett, you dumb sonuvabitch, do you know what's going to happen? In five years we'll be 75 percent black—if we survive. We won't draw any people, and we've just ruined the game of basketball.'"

Integration finally came during the college draft in the spring of 1950. In the second round, Walter Brown, owner of the Boston Celtics, took Charles (Chuck) Cooper, a 6-foot 5-inch forward from Duquesne University. In a later round, Bones McKinney, coach of the Washington Capitols, tapped 6-6 Earl Lloyd of West Virginia State. A month later, Ned Irish made good his promise by buying Nat (Sweetwater) Clifton from the Harlem Globetrotters; evidently Abe Saperstein realized that his monopoly on the best black talent was ending.

Saperstein could, however, still match or beat NBA salaries and so signing Chuck Cooper took some persuasion. After his graduation from Duquesne, Cooper toured with the Globetrotters in their annual series with the College All-Stars, and Saperstein presumably expected to make him a permanent member of his comedy basketball troupe. Walter Brown's offer was no better than Saperstein's.

It happened that the Globetrotters' eastern representative was Haskell Cohen, a freelance writer and publicity man who had his office in the NBA's small suite on the eighteenth floor of the Empire State Building. Cohen, who later became the NBA's publicity chief and the most knowledgeable basketball man at headquarters, remembered:

> I had grown up in Pittsburgh and I was close to the Duquesne team. One day Maurice Podoloff called me in and said, "I know you're close to the Duquesne picture. You know Cooper, don't you? He's been drafted by the Celtics."
>
> I said, "Yes, I know Chuck pretty well." As a matter of fact, I had gotten him a summer job one year at a resort hotel in the Catskills. At that time basketball was very hot in the mountains.
>
> Podoloff said, "Walter Brown can't sign him. Will you go to Pittsburgh and see if you can?" So I went to Pittsburgh and signed him for $7,500.

Chuck Cooper, the first black player drafted in the NBA. He was chosen by
the Boston Celtics in the first round of the 1950 draft. Earl Lloyd, selected by
the Washington Capitols in a later round, was the first black player to appear in
an NBA game. *Basketball Hall of Fame Photo.*

At the time, Saperstein was reported to be paying stars like Sweetwater
Clifton $10,000 a year, well over the average in the NBA, so $7500 was probably
not the best offer Chuck Cooper had in his pocket.

The first black player to take the floor in an NBA game was Earl Lloyd in
Washington's season opener against the Rochester Royals on October 31, 1950.

The next night Chuck Cooper appeared with the Boston Celtics in their game with Fort Wayne. Nat Clifton made his NBA debut on November 4 at Fort Wayne.

The NBA's black players had no bed of roses. They were routinely shuttled to black hotels in Baltimore and Washington. In Indianapolis they were permitted to stay in the same hotel with their white teammates but could not eat in the hotel's restaurants. When their teams played exhibition games in southern cities they were routinely left at home. But the color line on the court had finally fallen for good. It would be another decade, though, before black players were in the NBA in appreciable numbers.

By the time Lloyd, Cooper, and Clifton entered the league, the NBA was unquestionably offering the best basketball in the world, though not necessarily the best basketball show. The Globetrotters still held that spotlight.

Player salaries were rising slowly. A league report for the previous season showed that marginal players earned about $4000, journeymen were in the range of $5000 to $7000, and eight players were in five figures. The highest salary was $17,500.

Income was not keeping pace. The NBA's attendance report for the 1950–51 season showed that paying spectators at league games averaged 3,267—just slightly better than it had been in the first season of the Basketball Association of America four years earlier. One of the league's small cities, Syracuse, was strongest at the gate despite a fourth-place finish in the Eastern Division race. The Nats averaged 5,185 paid attendance for 33 home games. Minneapolis was second with 4,728, and among the other eight clubs, only New York and Philadelphia topped 4000.

Radio play-by-play accounts of NBA games were common but televised games were rare. Like the NBA, television was still in its infancy. A few American Basketball League and college games were televised to the relative handful of New Yorkers who had sets as early as 1946, but basketball's promoters were not yet impressed with its potential to excite interest in the game. In fact, some owners resisted TV for fear that it would hurt the gate receipts.

It was not until 1953 that the NBA got its first contract for television. Haskell Cohen, then the league's publicity chief, recalled:

> I brought in the first television contract. It was with the old Dumont Network. I met with Tom McMahon of Dumont, and he gave me an offer of 13 games for $39,000, and the league adopted it.
>
> I don't think the owners knew how big it would get ultimately. But they felt that it was good exposure for the game, and that $3,000 a game was nice little revenue in those days, so they were very keen on it. I don't think any of the

174

CAGES TO JUMP SHOTS

owners objected. They were so anxious to get that $3,000 that they said, "Let's try it."

Maurice Podoloff was more sanguine than the average owner. He told the governors that the day might come when "the proceeds may supplement gate receipts to the point where the latter lose their importance."

For the first six years of the post-World War II period professional basketball continued to lag behind the college game in fan interest. The National Invitation Tournament and the NCAA's championship playoffs both attracted more attention than the playoffs in professional leagues. Arenas in New York, Chicago, Cleveland, Philadelphia, Buffalo, and San Francisco were packed for major collegiate games. Only the NBA's all-star game, with the twenty best players in the world on display, could match the big college games for national attention. The first NBA all-star contest was played March 2, 1950, at Boston Garden, with the East winning, 111–94. Maurice Podoloff, reporting approvingly on the spectacle, told the owners that net receipts were $10,941. Each participating player got a $100 U.S. Savings Bond.

The tables began turning in the winter of 1950–51, not because the NBA did anything dramatic to call attention to its superior product but because the college game became suspect. The shift began in January when Junius Kellogg, Manhattan College center, told the Bronx District Attorney's office that two teammates, Henry E. Poppe and John A. Byrnes, had tried to persuade him to help fix a game with DePaul at Madison Square Garden. Poppe, Byrnes, and three professional gamblers were arrested on bribery and conspiracy charges. A month later, players on Nat Holman's City College team and Long Island University were implicated in fixes.

In most cases the players were not asked to lose a game—only to win by less than the point spread. Bookmakers had introduced point spreads about a decade earlier to increase action on games in which one team was heavily favored. A bettor might be reluctant to wager on a weak team, even with 10 to 1 odds, but would cheerfully bet on the margin of victory.

Coaches around the country tended to dismiss the college basketball scandal as a New York aberration peculiar to that sink of iniquity, Madison Square Garden. But Manhattan District Attorney Frank S. Hogan pressed the investigation, and it was soon evident that teams outside of New York were involved. Bradley University in Peoria, Ill., the quintessential All-American city, had been touched by gamblers. So had the University of Kentucky, whose famous coach Adolph Rupp had assured his myriad fans, "They couldn't touch my boys with a ten-foot pole." By the time the last revelations wound down in 1953, the investigators had strong cases of fixed games against six college teams and 33 players. At least 49 games had been fixed between 1947 and 1951 and there were suspicions about as many more.

The college scandal should not have surprised anyone. Only the year before it broke, a Bradley University player reported that he had been offered up to $500 to fix the point spread in National Invitation games in New York. Earlier, in 1945, Brooklyn College players had been charged with fixing games, but the news made no lasting impression.

The college scandal of 1951 could not be brushed off so easily. It involved not only CCNY's "Cinderella team"—which had won both the NIT and NCAA tournaments in 1950—LIU, and Manhattan but also Bradley, the University of Toledo, and Kentucky's two-time NCAA champions and Olympics heroes.

Suddenly, the colleges were the guys in the black hats. Suddenly, the pros were the good guys. While the NBA's owners held their breath in fear for their own game, not a hint of point-shaving or fixing was raised about professional game results. (In professional basketball's pioneering years, occasional innuendoes were heard about some unusual game results, but nothing was ever proven and the pro game was so obscure that few paid any attention.)

The college scandal did have direct effects on the NBA. Two of its all-star players, Alex Groza and Ralph Beard of the Indianapolis Olympians, had fixed games during their years at the University of Kentucky and so they were banned by the NBA. Several potential professional stars who had been implicated in fixes lost their opportunity to play in the league.

The scandal also led to the end of the American Basketball League. The ABL had been in continuous operation since 1933 under the leadership of John J. O'Brien and had enjoyed a good relationship with the NBA. The fallout from the college scandal killed the league in the 1952–53 season when O'Brien refused to approve ABL contracts for Groza, Beard, Sherman White of Long Island University, and Bill Spivey, a 7-foot center who had succeeded Groza in the pivot at the University of Kentucky. Two ABL teams dropped out and the league died. (Bill Spivey denied having been a party to fixes at Kentucky, and his trial on perjury charges in January 1953 ended in a hung jury, but the NBA's Board of Governors barred him from the league anyway.) Several of the players who were tainted by the college scandal wound up in the Eastern League.

Although the National Basketball Association escaped irreparable harm from the college scandal, it had its own problems with gambling soon afterward. Fortunately, the league took prompt action. Referee Sol Levy was barred in 1953 after being charged with taking $3000 in bribes to affect game results three years earlier. And in January 1954, Jack Molinas, a 6-foot 7-inch rookie for the Fort Wayne Zollner Pistons, admitted that he had bet on NBA games, though only in small amounts and only on the Pistons to win. Fred Zollner suspended him and the league banned him for life. The fast, decisive action on Levy and Molinas saved the NBA from losing its credibility.

The college scandal opened the way for the major professional league to take top billing in the basketball world after all the years as second banana. In theory, it was supposed to be easy. In fact, it was not.

The reasons are manifold but they can be boiled down to one: the product on the floor. The players were bigger and better than ever, but too often NBA games degenerated into brawls. Parades to the foul line were more frequent than fast breaks. Stalling for several minutes was the accepted—and perfectly logical— tactic when a team held a slim lead in the waning minutes. The referees were constantly reviled, not only by fans but by players, coaches, and even owners, who were sometimes permitted to sit on their team's bench in the guise of assistant coaches.

Ah, the referees. Before further considering the NBA's product in the early 1950s, let us digress for a brief historical review of basketball officiating.

The first thing to be said is that a basketball referee has the hardest job in sports. His problems are built into the game and have been there since the beginning. James Naismith's hope was for a non-contact game in which skill and finesse were rewarded over size and strength. Basketball was hardly a month old before it became clear that non-contact was wishful thinking.

The original rules forbade shouldering, holding, pushing, tripping, or striking an opponent. It is usually easy enough to spot a culprit who trips or takes a punch at an opponent. It is not so easy to decide who is at fault when there is shouldering, holding, and pushing during a scramble for a rebound. Chances are that all hands are shouldering and pushing, and the official's angle of vision on the play is bound to influence his determination of blame.

So it is no surprise that there were complaints about officiating even before the embryo professional teams moved out of the YMCAs. Too many officials did not know the rules. Too many were "homers," favoring the home team (which paid their wages).

The official's lot was no better in the early professional game. He worked in proximity to hundreds of partisan fans who were not sparing in verbal abuse. More than one pioneer referee climbed out of a dressing room window rather than run a gauntlet of enraged fans after a game. More than one needed a police escort to the train station on his way out of town.

Basketball was a relatively simple game then. There was no midcourt line, no three-second violation, no ban on zone defenses, no rule against goal-tending, and, of course, no 24-second shot clock. As the rules changed, the official's task became infinitely more complex during the 1930s and '40s. Now he was expected to watch simultaneously for contact outside the normal bumping and decide who had wronged whom, determine whether a shooter had been hacked before or after the shot, decide whether an offensive player had stayed too long in the foul lane, and watch the man with the ball for traveling violations. In short, he was given an impossible task.

By the late 1920s when the American Basketball League was striving to maintain a big-league image, it was paying referees a respectable $25 a game. Among its noted officials were John J. Murray, who had managed Tex Rickard's New York Whirlwinds back in 1921, Louis (Doc) Sugarman, a veteran player and referee, and two youngsters, William C. (Chuck) Solodare and Matthew P. (Pat) Kennedy, who would set the officiating style for a generation. Solodare, a baseball umpire as well as basketball official, was not learned in the rules but he was the best at controlling a game according to the unwritten professional code of "no harm, no foul," and he could not be intimidated. Pat Kennedy was the prime exemplar of the arm-waving, foot-stamping, gesticulating showman who calls, "No-ooo! I caught you that time" when he spots a foul. The crowd—or at least that portion of it rooting for the offended team—loved Kennedy's act. (In his later years, Pat Kennedy found a compatible showcase for his act with the Harlem Globetrotters.)

Chuck Solodare's courage was celebrated. John J. O'Brien, Jr., who became a referee after his playing days, remembered that he was inspired by Solodare:

> It was about 1932 and he was refereeing a game between the Brooklyn Jewels and the Sphas in Broadway Arena in Brooklyn. The place is jammed with 1,200 fans, and they're getting on Solodare. So he picks up a chair from the front row and brandishes it over his head and challenges 1,200 people, "Come on, you bastards, I'll kill you!"
>
> Well, you know, the fans don't attack *that* guy. I love a guy who has intestinal fortitude. Chuck had it. I said to myself—I'm just a kid—I'm going to become an official.

Solodare and Kennedy worked in the National Basketball League as well as the ABL and Basketball Association of America. Both also joined the staff of the young National Basketball Association, and for a time Kennedy was chief of officials. In all three leagues officials were paid by the game, with the scale reaching $50 a game for experienced referees in the NBA during the early 1950s. (The officials did not go on salary in the NBA until 1969.)

The founders of the Basketball Association of America, who, remember, were mainly hockey promoters, wanted the officials to "let the boys play." If fights broke out, well, that hadn't hurt hockey's appeal, had it? Their successors among the NBA's leaders also leaned toward the slow whistle, but they sometimes vacillated. Chuck Chuckovits, who became a college referee after World War II and also toted a whistle in the NBA, remembered:

> In the NBA we'd have meetings and they'd say, "Look, these players are All-Americans and we're going to play by the collegiate rulebook." Well, Jim Enright and I worked a game at Fort Wayne, and we must have called 80 or a

hundred fouls. The next day we got a telegram from Maurice Podoloff, who said, "If the fans want to see high school ball, they'll pay high school prices, so don't be so technical." The next night we let them play and called about three fouls. It was unbelievable! Then we caught hell because we weren't calling them close enough. It was hard to satisfy them.

Some of the owners and managers had never seen a rulebook before, and they would storm into the locker room and almost knock the door down after they had lost by 20 points. They'd say, "You stole that game from me!" That's why Jim and I left after four years. We were getting $40 a game in the NBA and the Big Ten was paying $75, and that's where we went and stayed.

By the nature of his calling, a referee can expect criticism and abuse from the crowd. But in the early years of the NBA he could expect it from coaches and owners, too. They seemed to have no compunction about fouling their own nest. How could the NBA be major league when the league's leaders were constantly berating the men to whom they had given responsibility for the conduct of their games?

President Podoloff addressed the problem in a bulletin to the owners in December 1952. (During the championship playoffs of the previous season, he and referee Chuck Solodare had needed police protection to leave Boston Garden after a Celtics loss to the Knicks.) Podoloff wrote: ". . . the conclusion is inevitable that unless something is done to stop the criticism of the men, we will not only never be able to develop a staff of officials, but may end up not even having some of the men who are still willing to run the gauntlet of vituperation and abuse of a nature to which no decent self-respecting human being should be subjected. After a recent game, one of our Governors, in a voice that could be heard all over his building, told all and sundry what he thought of the officiating. How he can expect to inspire confidence in the officials on the part of the spectators is beyond me."

In one of the era's uglier incidents, Sid Borgia and John P. Nucatola, both respected, veteran officials, were working a game in Syracuse between the Nats and the New York Knicks during the 1953–54 season. With seconds left in a close game, Nucatola called an offensive charging foul on Dolph Schayes of the Nats and nullified Schayes's field goal. Nats coach Al Cervi and club officer Danny Biasone raced onto the court, and the crowd began showering trash on the officials.

Nucatola recalled the aftermath:

At the end of the game, it took 15 or 20 cops to get us off the court. We went through the crowd, and they had programs and newspapers and handbags and were slapping Borgia on the head—and I had made the call! Not a one touched me! They finally got us into the Knicks' dressing room.

Then they evacuated the building until maybe 75 people were left. They got us out of the Knicks' dressing room, and the crowd that was left was whacking again as we went to our dressing room. A fellow who had refereed college ball for me [Nucatola was supervisor of officials for the Eastern College Athletic Association as well as an NBA official], who was on the Syracuse Police Department, got us out of there with a drawn gun. He passed around the word that we were flying out of Syracuse, and instead we were going by train. He took us by back streets to the railroad station and stayed with us until the train left.

A few weeks later, at a luncheon meeting of the New York Metropolitan Basketball Writers Association, John Nucatola blasted the NBA for its treatment of officials. "I told them it was still a bush league," he said. "I made a number of suggestions on what should be done—which have all come to pass—but basically I said, the referees represent the integrity of the game. Bawl them out, criticize them, but you've got to support them. If you don't support the referees, this will always be a bush league."

Nucatola said he had recommended $1000 fines against Cervi and Biasone and nothing had happened. When he got no game assignments for several weeks after his talk to the writers, Nucatola resigned. (In 1969, all was forgiven and John Nucatola returned to the NBA as supervisor of officials, serving until 1977. By that time he was the author of *Officiating Basketball* and had conducted clinics for referees all over the world.)

The National Basketball Association had other worries besides the continual complaints about officials. The spectators wanted to see the world's greatest players perform wonders in shooting, passing, dribbling, and rebounding. What they often saw was a series of wrestling matches among behemoths near the basket, or, in a close game, the clever backcourt men freeze the ball for several minutes to protect a lead. Only the most avid fans would come back after such a game, and even they would be grumbling if their team lost the wrestling tourney or the game of keepaway.

It was still perfectly within the rules for a team to dribble and pass the ball for as long as possible, but it was not the kind of entertainment that kept spectators on the edge of their seats. The ultimate in stalling tactics occurred on November 22, 1950, in Minneapolis when the Fort Wayne Zollner Pistons stalled through an entire game and nipped the Lakers, 19–18, on a last-second basket by Larry Foust. In the final quarter, exactly four points were scored—Foust's field goal and a free throw by each team.

Laker coach John Kundla said the Fort Wayne tactics "gave pro basketball a great big black eye . . . Many more games like that and we can shut up shop." But Pistons' general manager Carl Bennett retorted, "There is no rule against stalling and if the Minneapolis management wishes to belittle our coach (Murray Mendenhall, a legend in Indiana basketball) and his strategy we shall offer a protest because of the one league rule that was violated—that prohibiting zone defense . . . The Lakers, in refusing to come out and meet our men, were certainly employing that type of game." Within days the NBA instituted a rule calling for a technical foul for obvious stalling, thus making the 19–18 game safe in the record books for all time as the lowest game score in the NBA.

NBA games suffered even more from fouling than stalling. It was not uncommon to have 50 or 60 personal fouls called in a 48-minute game. If a game was close, fouls were traded in the closing minutes; the trailing team was willing to give a free throw for one point to have a chance for two points—but so was the leading team. Frequently the game became a march between foul lines, and it would take 12 or 15 minutes to play the last three as fouls were traded. To deal with that problem, the NBA ruled that for the 1950–51 season there would be a jump ball at center court after a successful foul shot in the last three minutes of a game; this, it was thought, would lessen the attractiveness of fouling because now the offending team could not be sure of getting the ball. It helped, but not much.

Part of the roughness problem was due to the inordinate size of many of the new stars. The Minneapolis Lakers were the prime example—and the most consistently successful team. With 6-10, 240-pound George Mikan, 6-7, 230-pound Vern Mikkelsen, and 6-4 Jim Pollard on their front line, the Lakers got the lion's share of rebounds at both ends of the court and could play a slow, deliberate game, taking full advantage of Mikan's strengths. It was an invitation for the other team to foul in attempts to get the ball or to block shots.

The NBA took away some of the big man's advantage in the 1951–52 season by widening the six-foot foul lane to 12 feet. This helped to open up the middle; now Mikan and the other giant pivots had to set up farther from the basket to avoid a three-second lane violation and loss of the ball. Widening the lane was not without controversy. Carl Bennett of Fort Wayne had proposed a 15-foot lane in 1948 during the last year of the Basketball Association of America, but nothing came of it then. When it was again suggested in 1950, the Minneapolis Lakers, believing (correctly) that it was aimed primarily at George Mikan, mounted a public-relations offensive. The Lakers solicited letters deploring the idea from several prominent college coaches, including the venerable Phog Allen of the University of Kansas, H. R. (Hank) Iba of Oklahoma A&M, Ray Meyer of DePaul, and Everett Dean of Stanford. Nevertheless, the NBA approved the new rule; so, later, did its target, Mikan, who said, "It's the best thing that's happened to basketball since the elimination of the center jump."

Eddie Gottlieb, the most original thinker among the NBA's leaders, had some novel ideas for speeding up the game, if not reducing the number of fouls. Gottlieb suggested that fouls should be penalized by free throws only if they occurred within an "attacking zone" 25 feet out from the backboard. Furthermore, during the first three quarters of a game, all free throws would be taken at the end of the quarter, not immediately after the foul. Only in the last quarter would the free throw follow the foul. And further still, no free throws would be given for fouls in the center of the court between the "attacking zones," although they would count as personals against the offenders. Another Gottlieb suggestion was to play the game by "innings," with Team A having the ball for two minutes, then Team B for two minutes, and so on through the game.

The NBA did not try Gottlieb's ideas but the rule-makers continued to tinker, in hopes of curbing fouls and enticing more fans. Nothing helped, and by the 1953–54 season the NBA's big-league pretensions were hanging by a thread. As Fort Wayne sportswriter Ben Tenny saw it, in a column deploring constant fouling: "The NBA is playing ostrich if it continues to hide its head in the sands of victory alone and forgets the men and women who pay the freight. There won't be enough fans to warrant an NBA unless they wake up to the dangers around them. And by they I mean players, coaches, officials, club owners, etc."

On April 23, 1954, the NBA's Board of Governors, meeting at the Hotel Roosevelt in New York, faced up to their game's problems and, in the view of many sportswriters, saved the league. In the process they ushered in professional basketball's modern era.

Two rules changes aimed at strategic fouling and stalling were adopted. The first called for limiting each *team* to six personal fouls per quarter. For the seventh and all subsequent fouls, an additional free throw would be given (two free throws for a foul that ordinarily was worth one, and three chances to make two points for fouling a shooter). No longer would it make sense to foul deliberately since there was an excellent chance that it would mean two points for the opponents.

The second rule change was just as drastic: "A team in control of the ball must make an attempt to score within 24 seconds after gaining possession of the ball." No longer could a team freeze the ball and run out the clock in a tight game; action would continue for 48 minutes instead of the 40 or 45 that had become all too common.

The idea for a time limit on possession of the ball was not new. Old players and managers recall that it had been discussed earlier as a possibility, but the limit generally mentioned was 30 seconds instead of 24. Danny Biasone, the volatile operator of the Syracuse Nationals, has been credited with suggesting 24 seconds. His rationale was explained by Leonard Koppett in 24 Seconds to Shoot: "Biasone had arrived at 24 seconds as the time limit by the simple method of dividing the number of shots taken in typical games into time played. Twenty-four seconds meant 120 shots per game—60 per team. In the season just completed, each team had averaged 75–80 shots per game. Obviously, the new rule would not be too restrictive."

It is not too much to say that the new rules revolutionized professional basketball. Now a fan could be assured that when he went to an NBA game he would see continuous action, with honest attempts to score at least every 20 or so seconds, and not merely a parade of giants from foul line to foul line.

In 1954–55, the first season with the new rules, team scores jumped by 13.6 points per game—from 79.5 to 93.1. For the first time a professional team averaged more than 100 points a game; it was the Boston Celtics, who scored 101.4—but gave up 101.5 while finishing third in the Eastern Division. The NBA's championship playoffs were exciting and action-filled. In the finals, which went to seven games, Biasone's Syracuse Nationals defeated the Fort Wayne Zollner Pistons.

At long last professional basketball was on its way to full acceptance as a major sport. Success did not come all at once, of course. There were still some rocky times ahead, but the corner had been turned.

The game on the court remained a far cry from today's NBA. Two-hand set shooters still predominated, but jump shooters Paul Arizin, Jim Pollard, and Bob Pettit were pointing the way to the future. Slam dunks were sometimes performed in pre-game warm-ups to thrill the crowd, but they were rare after the tip-off. Fast breaks became much more common, and the deliberate style of play typified by the Minneapolis Lakers languished; with only 24 seconds to shoot there was no longer time enough for a leisurely pace. Even the ball had changed. The old sewn ball had given way to a completely molded ball in the 1952–53 season.

Over the next decade, Bill Russell would bring new dimensions to rebounding, starting the fast break, and shot-blocking. Wilt Chamberlain would shatter scoring marks by previously inconceivable margins. They were charting the path for Kareem Abdul-Jabbar, Michael Jordan, Larry Bird, Magic Johnson, Charles Barkley, Mark Eaton, and scores of other NBA stars whose feats astonish oldtime players no less than today's fans.

These men are the heirs of Fred Cooper and Al Bratton of the Trenton Basketball Team, of Ed Wachter and Harry Hough, of Nat Holman and the Original Celtics, Benny Borgmann, the Renaissance Big Five, Cowboy Edwards and the Oshkosh All-Stars, and of Bobby McDermott, George Mikan, and Bob Cousy. They are following the trail blazed by a line of men who played for peanuts at a time when their game ranked somewhere between dog shows and handball in the national consciousness. It has been a long and often halting journey to today's NBA.

Five of the current 27 NBA franchises had their origins in the old National Basketball League. The oldest is the Detroit Pistons, which started life in 1941 as the Fort Wayne Zollner Pistons. The Sacramento Kings can trace their lineage to the Rochester Royals, and the Los Angeles Lakers to the Detroit Gems. The Philadelphia 76ers were born in Syracuse as the Nationals, and the old Tri-Cities Blackhawks wandered to Milwaukee and St. Louis before winding up as the Atlanta Hawks.

Two of the charter members of the Basketball Association of America, the Boston Celtics and New York Knicks, have been in continuous residence in their cities since 1946. A third, the Philadelphia Warriors, went west in 1962 to become the Golden State Warriors.

It seems fitting to end this book with one more quote from an old player. I ended most of my interview with players and managers by asking, "Was it fun? If you could do it all over again, would you?" To a man, they said yes. For my last word, I have chosen the response of Nat Militzok.

After playing with the New York Knickerbockers in the first season of the Basketball Association of America, Militzok concentrated on his career in accounting and attended law school. Meanwhile, he was playing for Cohoes in the revived New York State League and for the champion Scranton Miners in the twilight years of the American Basketball League. The Miners had Pop Gates, Dolly King, and Eddie Younger, all veteran black players, Hank Rosenstein, another former Knick, Vinnie Verdeschi, and Ed Kassler. The coach was Red Sarachek, who also coached at Yeshiva University and was a legend in New York City basketball circles.

With that background, here is Nat Militzok's reply to the question "If you could do it all over again, would you?"

> Yes, of course. I loved every minute of it and made great, great friends—friends that I maintain to this day. When I still lived in New York, I got a call every day of the week from Red Sarachek. I got a call once a week from Eddie Younger. Hank Rosenstein and I are friends to this day.
>
> There is really, really love between teammates on a successful, happy team. We were one big family. There were no blacks, no Jews, no Italians—they were just our friends. And we loved to be together. I wouldn't trade that experience for anything in the world.
>
> Only a person who has gone through it knows the feeling you have for your teammates. I don't believe it can be felt by someone who hasn't experienced it. I made friends that I keep to this day, and they are very important to me.
>
> I don't think you can ask for more than that out of life.

Appendix A

NOTES ON BASKETBALL'S ORIGINS

No other sport has such a well-documented creation as basketball. Or so it would seem.

But over the years there have been several claims that basketball had been played before December 1891 when, according to James Naismith, he invented the game to amuse his gym students at the YMCA's training school in Springfield, Mass. In most cases the claimants seem to have misplaced the year. They credit Naismith with devising the game but put it in 1890 or early 1891. At that time James Naismith was a student, not an instructor, at the training school and had no need for a new game to keep students happy.

In one case, though, the claim is, in effect, that James Naismith stole the idea for basketball. Given the fact that James Naismith was a Presbyterian divine and led an otherwise upright life, it is hard to believe that he could have been a thief. The story is even harder to credit because the man who is supposed to have introduced Naismith to basketball was a friend of his.

The claim is that the game was first played at the Holyoke, Mass., YMCA in a year variously given as 1885 and 1890. Its inventor was Dr. George Gabler, a physician and YMCA physical training instructor, and/or two other YMCA leaders. (One of them was William Morgan, who did, in fact, invent volleyball in 1895.) Bill Keating, sports editor of the *Holyoke Daily Transcript,* campaigned in his column on behalf of the story that Dr. Gabler brought Naismith to Holyoke in 1890 to see basketball being played. Keating said that before Dr. Gabler's death in 1943 he had told him the story in confidence. The sports editor quoted Gabler as saying, "I don't want you to use this story until after I have passed on. I don't want to hurt my good friend . . . Naismith."

The Holyoke YMCA's records were destroyed by fire in 1943 and Keating has since died, so there is no way to check the story that basketball was born in Holyoke. In the opinion of the author, it is improbable.

There is less certainty about the first professional basketball game than about the game's origin. Most authorities point to the Trenton Basketball Team of 1896–97 as the first professionals, but Frank J. Basloe, a pioneer promoter, wrote that the first play-for-pay game was in his hometown, Herkimer, N.Y., in January or February of 1893. The game, he said, was played with a rugby ball before 150 spectators in Herkimer's Fox Opera House. Total receipts were $30, and after paying the hall rental and the expenses of the visiting team from Utica, N.Y., the Herkimer players took home a small, but unspecified, amount of money. The story could be true, but there is no documentation.

Appendix B

MAJOR PROFESSIONAL LEAGUE
STANDINGS YEAR-BY-YEAR
1898–1954

Compiled by William F. Himmelman
Copyright © 1990 by William F. Himmelman

NATIONAL BASKETBALL
LEAGUE

1898–99
Trenton, N.J. Nationals (18–2–1)*
Millville, N.J. (14–6–2)
Camden, N.J. Electrics (7–13–1)
Philadelphia Clover Wheelmen (5–14–1)#
Germantown, Pa. Nationals (1–4)#
Hancock A.A. (Philadelphia) (0–6–1)#

* Play-off winner—defeated Millville.
# Dropped out.

1899–1900
First Half:
Trenton Trentons (8–0)
New York (3–2)
Camden Electrics (4–4)
West Philadelphia Penn Bikers (4–4)
Bristol, Pa. (3–6)
Chester, Pa. (0–6)*

Second Half:
Trenton Trentons (16–5–1)
Millville Glassblowers (15–6–1)
New York (13–7–1)
Camden Electrics (11–9)
Bristol (6–14–1)

West Philadelphia Penn Bikers (0–20)
* Dropped out.

1900–1901
First Half:
Camden Skeeters (10–4)
Trenton Trentons (10–5)
Millville (7–6)
Bristol Pile Drivers (9–8)
Penn Bikers (Philadelphia) (8–8)
New York Wanderers (6–7)
Burlington, N.J. (0–12)#

Second Half:
New York Wanderers (16–2–3)*
Millville (11–8)
Trenton Trentons (9–7–1)
Bristol Pile Drivers (8–7–1)
Camden Skeeters (7–12–1)
Penn Bikers (Philadelphia) (1–16)

* Play-off winner—defeated Trenton.
# Dropped out.

1901–02
Bristol (28–12)
Camden (25–15)
Trenton Nationals (23–17)
Millville (21–19)
New York Wanderers (18–21)

Philadelphia Phillies (4–35)

1902–03
First Half:
Camden Electrics (15–2)
New York Wanderers (11–2)
Bristol Pile Drivers (12–5)*
Philadelphia Phillies (10–7)#
Trenton Potters (6–9)
Conshohocken, Pa. (4–11)
Burlington (2–12)§
Wilmington, Del. (2–14)§

Second Half:
Camden Electrics (21–7)
Burlington Shoe Pegs (16–11)
Wilmington Peaches (14–12)
Trenton Potters (14–15)
New York Wanderers (11–14)
Conshohocken (4–21)

* Transferred to Burlington.
# Transferred to Wilmington.
§ Dropped out.
The NBL began play in 1903–04 but suspended
   in December with Camden in the lead.

PHILADELPHIA BASKETBALL
LEAGUE

1902–03
Columbia F.C. (22–5)
East Falls, Pa. (20–8)
Jasper A.C. (14–14)
St. John (12–14)
Greystock (12–15)
St. Simeon (12–16)
Xavier (10–17)
Convenant Nationals (6–19)

1903–04
Jasper A.C. (24–4)
Columbia F.C. (18–8)
St. John (18–10)
East Falls (14–14)
Germantown, Pa.*-North Philadelphia (12–16)
Conshohocken, Pa. Giants (10–17)
St. Simeon (9–18)
Xavier (5–23)

* Transferred to North Philadelphia.

1904–05
Conshohocken Giants (31–8)
North Philadelphia Phillies (28–13)
Jasper A.C. (26–15)
DeNeri (22–17)
East Falls (18–22)
St. Simeon (13–26)
Manayunk, Pa. (11–29)
Gray's Ferry, Pa. (7–26)

1905–06
DeNeri (24–6)
Manayunk (22–8)
St. Simeon (18–10)
East Falls (17–11)
North Philadelphia Phillies (15–13)
Jasper A.C. (9–19)
Beacon, Pa. (5–23)
Bridesburg, Pa.*-Trenton, N.J.#-Baldwin, Pa.
   (4–24)

* Transferred to Trenton.
# Transferred to Baldwin.

1906–07
Conshohocken Iron Men (22–8)
Manayunk (19–11)
East Falls (15–15)
St. Simeon (14–16)
DeNeri (11–19)
North Philadelphia Phillies (9–21)

1907–08
Germantown (21–7)
St. Simeon (17–11)
DeNeri (15–10)
Conshohocken*-North Wales, Pa. (16–11)
Manayunk (13–11)
Philadelphia Strattons (13–13)
East Falls (8–8)#
North Philadelphia (6–18)
St. Luke (3–23)

* Transferred to North Wales.
# Dropped out.

1908–09
Germantown (11–2)*
North Philadelphia (7–5)*
St. Simeon (7–6)*
Philadelphia Strattons (5–6)
DeNeri (4–8)
North Wales (2–9)*

* Dropped out.

NEW ENGLAND
BASKETBALL LEAGUE

1903–04
First Half:
Manchester, Mass. (9–1)
Concord, Mass. (7–4)
Lowell, Mass. (6–5)
Haverhill, Mass. (4–7)
Nashua, N.H. (2–8)#
Chelsea, Mass. (0–3)#

Second Half:
Lynn, Mass.§-South Framingham, Mass.
   (24–8)*
Natick, Mass. (21–16)

Lowell (35–30)
Hudson, Mass. (7–8)#
Haverhill (32–35)
Manchester (28–38)
Concord¶-Lawrence, Mass. (19–26)
Pawtucketville A.C. (Lowell) (0–5)#

* Playoff winner—defeated Natick 2 games to 1.
# Dropped out.
§ Transferred to South Framingham.
¶ Transferred to Lawrence.

WESTERN MASSACHUSETTS BASKETBALL LEAGUE

1903–04

First Half:
Pittsfield*-Chicopee (16–3)#
Chicopee§-Pittsfield (12–5)¶
Springfield (14–6)+
Holyoke (13–7)
Westfield (8–10)
Ware (7–12)
Northampton (4–13)
Thompsonville, Conn. (0–18)+

Second Half:
Springfield (28–13)
Chicopee (12–12)+
Northampton (20–21)
Westfield (20–23)
Ware (18–21)
Holyoke (16–24)+

* Transferred to Chicopee.
# Transferred to Springfield.
§ Transferred to Pittsfield.
¶ Transferred to Chicopee.
+ Dropped out.

NEW ENGLAND BASKETBALL ASSOCIATION

1904–05

First Half:
Haverhill, Mass. (28–8)
Natick, Mass. (21–11)
Lowell, Mass. (16–17)
New Bedford, Mass.#-Amesbury, Mass. (19–23)
Newburyport, Mass. (13–19)
Fall River, Mass. (2–9)§

Second Half:
Natick (17–4)*
Haverhill (16–8)
Lowell (11–12)
Portsmouth, N.H. (8–13)

Newburyport (7–15)
Amesbury, Mass. (7–16)

* Playoff winner—defeated Haverhill 5 games to 2.
# Transferred to Amesbury.
§ Dropped out.

WESTERN PENNSYLVANIA BASKETBALL LEAGUE

1903–04
Pittsburgh South Side (20–0)
Manchester (12–8)
Olympics (Pittsburgh) (11–9)
Pittsburgh A.C. (9–11)
Allegheny (5–15)
Duquesne A.C. (3–17)

1912–13
Pittsburgh South Side (24–5)
Braddock (19–9)
Crafton Stags (18–11)
McKeesport Majestics (12–17)
Zion Council (Pittsburgh) (8–19)
Pittsburgh Lyceum*-Beechview (4–26)

* Transferred to Beechview.

1914–15
Mount Washington Lafayettes (21–2)
Pittsburgh South Side (13–11)
Crafton Volunteers (13–14)
Jeannette Rubber Works (12–17)
Charleroi (6–21)

CENTRAL BASKETBALL LEAGUE

1906–07
First Half:
East Liverpool, Ohio Potters (22–8)*
Greensburg, Pa. Tubers (17–13)
Pittsburgh South Side (17–13)
Homestead, Pa. Young Americans (15–14)#
Butler, Pa. (11–19)
McKeesport, Pa. Majestics (7–22)

Second Half:
Pittsburgh South Side (16–3)*
East Liverpool Potters (12–7)
McKeesport Tubers (11–7)
Butler (9–11)
Greensburg Tubers (8–12)
Canton, Ohio (1–17)

* Co-champions—East Liverpool refused to play Pittsburgh in a play-off.
# Dropped out.

1907–08
East Liverpool Potters (53–19)
Pittsburgh South Side (42–28)
Homestead Young Americans (32–38)
Greensburg Tubers (28–42)
McKeesport Majestics (21–49)

1908–09
Homestead Young Americans (49–23)
McKeesport Majestics (46–26)
Pittsburgh South Side (43–28)
Greensburg Tubers (41–31)
Johnstown, Pa. Johnnies (38–33)
Uniontown, Pa. (30–43)
East Liverpool (4–57)*
Alliance, Ohio (0–10)

* Tranferred to Alliance.

1909–10
McKeesport Majestics (49–21)
Johnstown Johnnies (46–24)
Greensburg Tubers (41–29)
Homestead (37–33)
Pittsburgh South Side (24–46)
Uniontown (13–57)

1910–11
McKeesport Majestics (49–21)
Pittsburgh South Side (48–22)
Johnstown Johnnies (40–30)
Connellsville, Pa. (31–39)
Homestead Steeltowners (22–48)*
Uniontown (20–50)

* Dropped out forfeiting last ten games.

1911–12
Johnstown Johnnies (48–18)
Uniontown (45–21)
Connellsville (35–31)
Charleroi, Pa. (26–40)
Pittsburgh South Side (20–34)*
Washington, Pa. (0–30)*

* Dropped out.

EASTERN LEAGUE

1909–10
Reading, Pa. (20–10)
Trenton, N.J. (20–10)*
Jasper (Kensington, Pa.) (18–12)
DeNeri (Philadelphia) (15–15)
Germantown, Pa. (11–19)
Elizabeth, N.J. (0–7)#
Paterson, N.J.§-Princeton, N.J., Tigers (6–17)

*Play-off winner—defeated Reading 3 games
  to 0.
Transferred to Paterson.
§ Transferred to Princeton.

1910–11
DeNeri (Southwark, Pa.) (28–12)
Jasper (23–17)
Greystock (Philadelphia) (22–18)
Reading, Pa. (21–19)
Camden, N.J. Alphas (14–26)
Trenton Potters (12–28)

1911–12
Jasper (29–11)
Trenton (29–11)*
Greystock (20–20)
DeNeri (18–22)
Camden Alphas (13–27)
Reading (11–29)

* Play-off winner—defeated Jasper 2 games to 1.

1912–13
Reading Bears (30–10)
DeNeri (South Philadelphia) (29–11)
Trenton (21–19)
Jasper (20–20)
Camden Alphas (11–29)
Greystock (9–31)

1913–14
Camden Alphas (23–17)
Jasper Jewels (23–17)*
Trenton (23–17)
Reading (22–18)
DeNeri (20–20)
Greystock (9–31)

* Play-off winner—defeated Camden and
  Trenton in round robin series.

1914–15
Camden Alphas (25–15)*
Reading Bears (25–15)*
Trenton (20–20)
Greystock Greys (18–22)
DeNeri (17–23)
Jasper Jewels (15–25)

* Co-champions—Camden and Reading each
  won one game in play-offs with third game
  being cancelled.

1915–16
Greystock Greys (27–13)
Reading (23–17)
Camden Alphas (21–19)
DeNeri (20–20)
Jasper Jewels (17–23)
Trenton (12–28)

1916–17
First Half:
Jasper Jewels (14–6)
Greystock Greys (12–8)
Reading Coal Barons (12–8)
Camden Alphas (11–9)
Trenton (10–10)

DeNeri (1–19)

Second Half:
Greystock Greys (14–6)*
Camden Alphas (10–10)
Jasper Jewels (10–10)
Reading Coal Barons (10–10)
Trenton (10–10)
DeNeri (6–14)

* Play-off winner—defeated (Kensington, Pa.)
    Jasper 2 games to 1.

1917–18
Jasper Jewels (4–2)
DeNeri (5–3)
Greystock (4–3)
Trenton (4–3)
Camden (2–4)
Reading Bears (2–6)

Note: League suspended operations for duration
    of World War I.

1919–20
First Half:
Camden Skeeters (15–5)
Germantown G's (11–9)
DeNeri (10–10)
Trenton Potters (9–10)
Reading Bears (8–12)
North Philadelphia Phillies (6–13)*

Second Half:
Camden Skeeters (15–4)
Reading Bears (10–8)
Trenton Potters (11–9)
Germantown G's (10–10)
DeNeri (7–11)
Bridgeport, Conn. Blue Ribbons (4–15)

* Dropped out.

1920–21
First Half:
Reading Bears (16–5)
Trenton Bengals (15–6)
Camden Skeeters (14–6)
Philadelphia (7–13)
Germantown (5–15)
Newark, N.J. (0–5)#
Coatesville, Pa. (4–11)

Second Half:
Germantown (16–4)*
Camden Skeeters (15–5)
Reading Bears (11–9)
Trenton Bengals (11–9)
Philadelphia (5–15)
Coatesville (4–16)

* Play-off winner—defeated Reading 2 games
    to 0.
Transferred to Coatesville.

1921–22
First Half:
Trenton Royal Bengals (24–3)
Camden Skeeters (20–7)
Scranton, Pa. (11–11)#
Wilkes-Barre, Pa. (10–13)
Reading Bears (10–14)
Coatesville Coats (8–14)
Philadelphia (5–15)#
Harrisburg, Pa.§-New York Whirlwinds¶-New
    York Giants (2–14)+
New York Celtics (3–2)

Second Half:
New York Celtics (16–4)*
Camden Skeeters (15–5)
Trenton Royal Bengals (15–5)
Coatesville Coats (5–14)
Wilkes-Barre (3–13)
Reading Bears (2–15)

* Play-off winner—defeated Trenton 2 games
    to 1.
Dropped out.
§ Transferred to New York Whirlwinds.
¶ Transferred to New York Giants.
+ Transferred to New York Celtics.

1922–23
First Half:
Trenton Bengals (16–3)
Camden Skeeters (16–4)
Coatesville Coats (9–11)
Atlantic City Sandpipers (2–4)#
Atlantic City Celtics (5–6)*
Philadelphia Jasper Jewels (5–13)
Reading Bears (3–15)*

Second Half:
Trenton Bengals (3–0)
Camden Skeeters (2–1)
Coatesville Coats (2–2)
Philadelphia Jasper Jewels (0–2)

* Dropped out.
# Transferred to Atlantic City Celtics.
Note: League suspended operations.

1931–32
First Half:
Philadelphia Moose (15–5)
Philadelphia Sphas (15–5)
Wilmington (8–8)
Bridgeton, N.J. (8–10)
Camden (4–12)
Philadelphia Jaspers (4–14)

Second Half:
Philadelphia Sphas (14–4)*
Bridgeton (10–5)
Philadelphia Moose (10–9)
Philadelphia Jaspers (7–10)
Wilmington (7–10)

Camden (0–10)

* Play-off winner—defeated Philadelphia
  Moose 3 games to 1.

1932–33

First Half:
Philadelphia Sphas (12–6)
Trenton Moose (10–7)
Philadelphia Moose (9–7)
Bridgeton (10–8)
Philadelphia Jasper Jewels (7–10)
Wilmington Cats (2–4)#
Philadelphia W.P.E.N. Broadcasters (1–9)

Second Half:
Trenton Moose (14–1)*
Philadelphia Moose (10–4)
Philadelphia Sphas (8–7)
Bridgeton (5–5)
Philadelphia Jasper Jewels (3–10)
Philadelphia W.P.E.N. Broadcasters (1–14)

* Play-off winner—defeated Philadelphia Sphas
  3 games to 1.
Dropped out.

HUDSON RIVER LEAGUE

1909–10

Troy, N.Y. Trojans (24–4)
Paterson, N.J. Crescents (23–5)
Kingston, N.Y. Wild Cats (14–13)
Catskill, N.Y. Mystics (14–14)
Yonkers, N.Y. Fourth Separates (13–14)
Hudson, N.Y. Mixers (12–14)
Poughkeepsie, N.Y. Bridge Jumpers (6–18)
Newburgh, N.Y. Rose Buds (2–26)

1910–11

Troy Trojans (29–10)
Paterson Crescents (26–11)
Kingston Colonials (26–14)
Yonkers (18–17)
Newburgh Company E (16–23)
Hudson (13–21)
Catskill N.Y. Beare-Cats (12–26)
Poughkeepsie (0–6)*
Schenectady, N.Y. Indians (2–14)

* Transferred to Schenectady.

1911–12

Kingston Company M (14–8)
Newburgh Bizzy Izzies (14–9)
Paterson Crescents (13–9)
White Plains, N.Y. Lambs (8–8)*
Trenton, N.J. (3–5)*
Yonkers (3–16)*

* Dropped out.

NEW YORK STATE LEAGUE

1911–12

Troy Trojans (36–12)
Hudson (28–25)
Schenectady*-Kingston (24–26)
Catskill (23–27)
Cohoes (21–32)
Utica (14–29)

* Transferred to Kingston.

1912–13

Troy Trojans (35–13)
Gloversville (28–22)
Kingston (27–23)
Catskill*-Albany (18–27)
Utica (19–30)
Cohoes (18–30)

* Transferred to Albany.

1913–14

Utica Indians (46–17)
Troy Trojans (45–18)
Cohoes (34–30)
Gloversville (30–30)
Paterson, N.J. Crescents (29–37)
Kingston (23–41)
Newburgh (16–17)*-Syracuse (2–19)¶
Poughkeepsie (1–4)#-Brooklyn Dodgers (9–
   21)§-Newark, N.J. (1–2)¶

* Transferred to Syracuse.
# Transferred to Brooklyn.
§ Transferred to Newark.
¶ Dropped out.

1914–15

Troy Trojans (19–8)
Utica Utes (15–11)
Gloversville (12–13)
Cohoes (13–15)
Kingston Colonials (9–13–1)
Paterson Crescents (7–15–1)

Note: League suspended operations.

1916–17

Schenectady (15–7)
Mohawk (15–8)
Hudson (13–9)
Utica (12–12)
Cohoes (5–13)
Saratoga (0–8)*-Glens Falls (3–6)

* Transferred to Glens Falls.
Suspended operations for duration of World
  War I.

1919–20

First Half:
Albany (17–1)*

Troy (14–3)
Mohawk (13–5)
Schenectady (13–5)
Adams, Mass. (9–7)
Pittsfield, Mass. (6–12)#
Utica (5–10)
Gloversville (5–13)
Cohoes (3–13)§
Amsterdam (1–17)

Second Half:
Troy (27–5)*
Albany (25–9)
Utica (18–13)
Adams (14–11)
Mohawk (18–15)
Amsterdam (16–17)
Schenectady (13–14)
Gloversville (14–17)
Pittsfield (8–16)
Hudson (0–36)

* Co-champions—Albany and Troy could not
  agree on a play-off.
Transferred to Hudson.
§ Transferred to Pittsfield.

1920–21

First Half:
Albany Senators (22–6)
Schenectady (15–12)
Cohoes (15–13)
Gloversville (13–14)
Mohawk (12–15–1)
Utica Utes (12–16)
Pittsfield (11–17)
Amsterdam (10–17–1)

Second Half:
Albany Senators (13–4)
Utica Utes (12–5)
Gloversville (11–5)
Schenectady (9–5)
Cohoes (6–6)
Pittsfield (6–10)*
Amsterdam (3–9)
Mohawk (2–8)
Glens Falls (3–13)

* Dropped out.

1921–22

First Half:
Schenectady (19–7)#
Gloversville (20–9)
Cohoes (17–13)
Utica Utes (13–13)
Kingston (14–15)
Amsterdam (13–15)
Troy (4–8)
Glens Falls (7–16)#
Mohawk Indians (7–18)

Second Half:
Cohoes (11–2)*

Albany (8–4)
Amsterdam (9–5)
Mohawk Indians (5–5)
Troy (5–5)
Kingston (4–6)
Utica Utes (2–8)
Gloversville (0–9)

* Champions—Gloversville refused to meet in a
  play-off.
Dropped out.

1922–23

First Half:
Kingston (20–4)
Albany Senators (11–9)
Troy (10–9)
Cohoes (9–12)
Schenectady (6–12)
Amsterdam (6–16)

Second Half:
Kingston (13–5)
Albany Senators (8–5)
Amsterdam (9–6)
Cohoes (6–9)
Schenectady (4–9)
Troy (3–9)

PENNSYLVANIA STATE LEAGUE

1914–15

Pittston (18–2)
Freeland (11–9)
Nanticoke (9–11)
Wilkes-Barre (9–11)
Hazleton (8–12)
Tamaqua (5–15)

1915–16

Wilkes-Barre (29–13)
Freeland (25–17)
Carbondale Pioneers (24–18)
Nanticoke Nannies (24–18)
Scranton Miners (22–20)
Pittston (18–24)
Hazleton (17–25)
Plymouth (9–33)

1916–17

Carbondale Pioneers (33–7)
Wilkes-Barre Barons (28–12)
Nanticoke (26–14)
Pittston (24–17)
Hazleton (17–23)
Plymouth Shawnees (15–25)
Scranton (9–32)
Freeland (4–26)

1917–18

First Half:
Pittston (22–6)*
Providence (19–8)#
Plymouth Shawnees (18–10)
Wilkes-Barre Barons (12–14)
Scranton (11–15)
Carbondale Pioneers (11–17)
Nanticoke Nans (9–18)
Hazleton Mountaineers (7–21)

Second Half:
Hazleton Mountaineers (15–5)
Nanticoke Nans (14–6)
Wilkes-Barre Barons (10–9)
Pittston (7–11)
Plymouth Shawnees (7–12)
Scranton (4–9)#
Carbondale Pioneers (4–9)#

* Play-off winner—defeated Hazleton 3 games
  to 1.
Dropped out.
League suspended operations for the duration of
  World War I.

1919–20

First Half:
Scranton Miners (18–6)
Nanticoke Nans (16–8)
Pittston (13–11)
Wilkes-Barre Barons (7–17)
Plymouth (6–18)

Second Half:
Nanticoke Nans (16–7)*
Scranton Miners (14–10)
Pittston (14–10)
Wilkes-Barre Barons (12–11)
Plymouth (3–21)

* Play-off winner—defeated Scranton 3 games
  to 1.

1920–21

First Half:
Pittston (14–10)
Wilkes-Barre Coal Barons (14–10)
Scranton Miners (13–11)
Nanticoke Nans (10–14)
Paterson, N.J. Crescents (3–9)#

Second Half:
Scranton Miners (12–5)*
Nanticoke Nans (11–6)
Wilkes-Barre Coal Barons (8–6)
Pittston (6–8)
Plymouth (0–12)

* Play-off winner—defeated Pittston 2 games
  to 0.
Dropped out.

INTERSTATE LEAGUE

1915–16

First Half:
Kingston, N.Y. Pathfinders#-Elizabeth, N.J.
  Bessies (14–5)§
Jersey City, N.J. Skeeters (13–6)
Stamford, Conn. (11–7)
Paterson, N.J. Crescents (11–10)
Brooklyn Trolley Dodgers (6–12)
Elizabeth, N.J.¶-North Hudson, N.J. (2–17)+

Second Half:
Paterson Crescents (13–4)*
Jersey City Skeeters (12–6)
Stamford (7–9)
North Hudson (6–9)
Brooklyn Trolley Dodgers (5–11)
Elizabeth (3–7)

* Play-off winner—defeated North Hudson 3
  games to 2.
Transferred to Elizabeth.
§ Transferred to North Hudson.
¶ Transferred to North Hudson.
+ Transferred to Elizabeth.

1916–17

First Half:
Bridgeport, Conn., Blue Ribbons (15–4)*#
Danbury, Conn., Hatters (14–5)#
Stamford (8–8)#
Paterson Crescents (8–10)
Jersey City (8–11)
New York Cathedral Separate Five (1–16)

Second Half:
Paterson Crescents (16–5)
Newark, N.J. Turners (15–6)
Jersey City (13–7)
Hoboken, N.J. (7–12)
Newark National Turners (6–13)
New York Cathedral Separate Five (2–16)

* Play-off winner—defeated Paterson 2 games
  to 0.
Dropped out.
League suspended operations for duration of
  World War I.

1919–20

New York Treat 'em Roughs (2–3)*
Paterson Silk Sox (8–3)
Jersey City Skeeters (7–5)#
Brooklyn Dodgers (2–2)
Bridgeport Blue Ribbons (8–8)
Ansonia, Conn., Wrightlets (7–8)
Passaic, N.J., A.A. (6–9)
Newark Nationals (0–2)§

* Transferred to Paterson.
# Transferred to Brooklyn.
§ Dropped out.
Note: League suspended operations.

CONNECTICUT STATE LEAGUE

1917–18
Ansonia Wrightlets (14–9)
Bridgeport Blue Ribbons (14–10)
Norwalk (9–12)
Danbury Hatters (5–3)*
Jersey City, N.J., Skeeters (3–11)

* Transferred to Jersey City.

1918–19
League suspended operations for duration of World War I.

1920–21
Stamford (5–0)
Bridgeport (2–2)
Ansonia (0–1)
Norwalk (0–4)

Note: League suspended operations.

METROPOLITAN BASKETBALL LEAGUE

1921–22
Brooklyn Dodgers (12–8)*
New York MacDowell Lyceum (Macs) (12–8)
Brooklyn Prospect Big Five (Pros) (11–9)
Brooklyn Visitations (9–11)
Greenpoint Knights of St. Anthony (9–11)
Paterson, N.J., Powers Bros. Five (7–13)

* Play-off winners—New York players went on strike for play-offs.

1922–23
First Half:
New York Celtics (12–0)#
Elizabeth, N.J. (9–3)
Greenpoint Knights of St. Anthony (7–5)
Brooklyn Visitations (8–6)
Brooklyn Pros (4–7)
New York MacDowell Lyceum (Macs) (5–10)
Paterson Legionnaires (4–8)
Brooklyn Dodgers (2–12)

Second Half:
Paterson Legionnaires (20–11)*
Brooklyn Pros (19–12)
Greenpoint Knights of St. Anthony (16–12)
Yonkers, N.Y., Chippewas (15–13)
Brooklyn Visitations (14–13)
Elizabeth, N.J. (9–14)
Brooklyn Dodgers (10–16)
New York MacDowell Lyceum (Macs) (7–19)

* Play-off winner—defeated Elizabeth 2 games to 1.
# Dropped out.

1923–24
First Half:
Brooklyn Visitations (13–7)
Kingston, N.Y., Colonials (12–8)
Trenton, N.J., Royal Bengals (11–9)
Paterson Legionnaires (10–10)
Greenpoint Knights of St. Anthony (7–13)
Yonkers (7–13)

Second Half:
Brooklyn Visitations (13–7)
Paterson Legionnaires (12–8)
Trenton Royal Bengals (10–10)
Greenpoint Knights of St. Anthony (9–11)
Kingston Colonials (9–11)
Yonkers (7–13)

1924–25
First Half:
Passaic, N.J.,#-Kingston Colonials (13–7)
Greenpoint Knights of St. Anthony (12–8)
Brooklyn Visitations (10–10)
Yonkers (8–10)
Trenton (8–11)
Paterson Legionnaires (7–12)

Second Half:
Brooklyn Visitations (14–5)*
Paterson Legionnaires (11–7)
Greenpoint Knights of St. Anthony (9–8)
Kingston Colonials (8–9)
Trenton (5–11)
Yonkers (4–11)

* Play-off winner—defeated Kingston 2 games to 1.
# Transferred to Kingston.

1925–26
First Half:
Yonkers Indians (15–6)
Paterson Legionnaires (14–7)
New York Pros (5–4)§
Greenpoint Knights (11–10)
Perth Amboy, N.J. (8–11)#
Brooklyn Visitations (8–13)
Newark Bears (4–14)

Second Half:
Greenpoint Knights (10–1)*
Brooklyn Visitations (8–3)
Yonkers Indians (4–5)
Paterson Legionnaires (4–6)
Newark Bears (1–7)
Passaic, N.J., Mets (0–5)

* Play-off winner—defeated Yonkers 2 games to 1.
# Transferred to Passaic.
§ Dropped out.

1926–27
First Half:
Brooklyn Visitations (8–2)*

West Brooklyn Assumption Triangles (7–3)
Paterson Crescents (6–4)
Yonkers Indians (4–6)
Greenpoint Knights (2–5)#
Kingston Colonials (0–7)

Second Half:
Paterson Crescents (7–0)
Brooklyn Visitations (3–3)
West Brooklyn Assumption Triangles (0–2)#
Yonkers Indians (0–2)#
Kingston Colonials (0–3)

* Play-off winner—defeated Paterson 3 games
   to 0.
Dropped out.

1927–28
Kingston Colonials (13–4)
Catskill (11–5)
Brooklyn Visitations (9–6)
Hudson, N.Y. (7–9)
Albany, N.Y. (3–8)
Troy, N.Y. (1–11)
Paterson Pats (0–1)*

* Dropped out.

1928–31
League suspended operations.

1931–32
Brooklyn Visitations (10–2)*
Brooklyn Jewels (10–2)
Union City, N.J. Reds (8–4)
Hoboken, N.J., Lisas (6–6)
Brooklyn Jewish Center (4–8)
Long Island Pros (3–9)
Jamaica, N.Y., St. Monicas (1–11)

* Play-off winner—defeated Brooklyn Jewels 2
   games to 1.

1932–33
First Half:
Brooklyn Jewels (13–3)*
Hoboken Lisas (11–4)
Brooklyn Visitations (9–6)
Union City Reds (9–7)
Long Island Pros (8–7)#
Yonkers Knights (8–8)
Paterson Continentals (3–9)#
Jamaica St. Monicas (3–11)#
Brooklyn Americans (1–10)§
Brooklyn Hillhouse (2–2)¶

Second Half:
Union City Reds (17–6)
Brooklyn Jewels (16–7)
Brooklyn Visitations (12–8)
Hoboken Lisas (12–9)
Brooklyn Americans (2–7)+
Bronx St. Martins (5–6)
Yonkers Knights (4–16)
Jersey City Diamonds (1–10)

* Play-off winner—defeated Union City 2 games
   to 0.
Dropped out.
§ Transferred to Brooklyn Hillhouse.
¶ Transferred back to Brooklyn Americans.
+ Transferred to Bronx.

AMERICAN BASKETBALL LEAGUE

1925–26
First Half:
Brooklyn Arcadians (12–4)
Washington Palace Five (11–5)
Cleveland Rosenblums (10–6)
Rochester Centrals (9–7)
Fort Wayne, Ind., K.C.'s (7–9)
Boston Whirlwinds (6–10)#
Chicago Bruins (6–10)
Detroit Pulaski Post (6–10)
Buffalo Bisons (5–11)

Second Half:
Cleveland Rosenblums (13–1)*
Washington Palace Five (11–3)
Rochester Centrals (9–5)
Brooklyn Arcadians (7–7)
Fort Wayne K.C.'s (6–8)
Buffalo Bisons (5–9)
Chicago Bruins (3–11)
Detroit Pulaski Post (2–12)

* Play-off winner—defeated Brooklyn 3 games to
   0.
Dropped out.

1926–27
First Half:
Cleveland Rosenblums (17–4)
Washington Palace Five (16–5)
Philadelphia Quakers (14–7)
Brooklyn Arcadians (0–5)§
Brooklyn Celtics (13–3)
Fort Wayne Hoosiers (8–13)
Rochester Centrals (8–13)
Chicago Bruins (7–14)
Baltimore Orioles (1–20)
Detroit Pulaski Post (0–6)#

Second Half:
Brooklyn Celtics (19–2)*
Fort Wayne Hoosiers (15–6)
Washington Palace Five (14–7)
Philadelphia Warriors (10–11)
Cleveland Rosenblums (9–12)
Chicago Bruins (6–15)
Rochester Centrals (6–15)
Baltimore Orioles (5–16)

* Play-off winner—defeated Cleveland 3 games
   to 0.
Dropped out.
§ Transferred to Brooklyn Celtics.

1927–28

Eastern Division:
New York Celtics (40–9)*
Philadelphia Warriors (30–21)
Washington Palace Five (7–15)§
Brooklyn Visitations (18–11)
Rochester Centrals (24–28)

Western Division:
Fort Wayne Hoosiers (27–24)
Cleveland Rosenblums (22–29)
Detroit Cardinals (5–13)#
Chicago Bruins (13–36)

* Play-off winner—defeated Fort Wayne 3
   games to 1.
Dropped out.
§ Transferred to Brooklyn.

1928–29

First Half:
Cleveland Rosenblums (19–9)*
Fort Wayne Hoosiers (18–10)
Brooklyn Visitations (15–12)
Chicago Bruins (15–12)
New York Hakoahs (13–16)
Trenton, N.J., Royal Bengals (12–16)
Rochester Centrals (11–15)
Paterson, N.J., Whirlwinds (6–19)

Second Half:
Fort Wayne Hoosiers (11–3)
Brooklyn Visitations (10–4)
Cleveland Rosenblums (10–4)
Rochester Centrals (7–7)
New York Hakoahs (5–9)
Trenton Royal Bengals (4–8)
Chicago Bruins (4–10)
Paterson Whirlwinds (3–9)

* Play-off winner—defeated For Wayne 4 games
   to 0.

1929–30

First Half:
Cleveland Rosenblums (18–8)*
Brooklyn Visitations (15–9)
Rochester Centrals (14–10)
Chicago Bruins (12–12)
Fort Wayne Hoosiers (12–12)
Paterson Crescents (10–14)
New York Celtics (5–5)#
Syracuse All-Americans (4–20)§

Second Half:
Rochester Centrals (19–11)
Cleveland Rosenblums (18–12)
Chicago Bruins (17–13)
Brooklyn Visitations (15–15)
Fort Wayne Hoosiers (13–17)
Paterson Crescents (8–22)

* Play-off winner—defeated Rochester 4 games
   to 1.

Dropped out.
§ Dropped out, forfeiting last four games.

1930–31

First Half:
Brooklyn Visitations (14–7)*
Fort Wayne Hoosiers (13–9)
Rochester Centrals (10–9)
Paterson Crescents (9–9)#
Cleveland Rosenblums (6–6)#
Toledo Redmen (8–13)
Chicago Bruins (7–14)

Second Half:
Fort Wayne Hoosiers (13–5)
Chicago Bruins (11–7)
Brooklyn Visitations (8–8)
Rochester Centrals (5–10)
Toledo Redmen (4–11)

* Play-off winner—defeated Fort Wayne 4
   games to 2.
Dropped out.
League suspended operations in 1931 and was
   reorganized as an eastern regional league in
   1933.

1933–34

First Half:
Trenton Moose (24–6)
Brooklyn Jewels (22–8)
Philadelphia Hebrews (15–12)
Brooklyn Visitations (12–12)
Bronx Americans (10–15)
Union City, N.J., Reds (10–18)
Newark, N.J., Bears (9–17)
Hoboken, N.J., Thourots (0–2)#
Camden, N.J., Athletics (2–8)§
New Britain, Conn., Palaces (3–9)

Second Half:
Philadelphia Hebrews (14–0)*
New Britain Palaces (7–5)
Brooklyn Jewels (4–4)
Trenton Moose (6–7)
Newark Bears (4–5)
Union City Reds (4–7)
Bronx Americans (2–6)
Brooklyn Visitations (1–8)

* Play-off winner—defeated Trenton 4 games to
   2.
Transferred to Camden.
§ Transferred to New Britain.

1934–35

First Half:
New York Jewels (16–6)
Philadelphia Hebrews (13–10)
Brooklyn Visitations (13–11)
Newark Mules (12–11)#
Boston Trojans (10–11)

Jersey Reds (7–14)
New Britain Jackaways (6–14)§

Second Half:
Brooklyn Visitations (14–8)*
Philadelphia Hebrews (13–9)
New Britain Mules (9–9)
Jersey Reds (9–9)
New York Jewels (8–10)
Boston Trojans (4–12)

* Play-off winner—defeated New York 3 games
  to 2.
Transferred to New Britain.
§ Dropped out.

1935–36
First Half:
Philadelphia Hebrews (14–5)*
New York Jewels (11–8)
Brooklyn Visitations (10–10)
Jersey Reds (9–9)
Kingston Colonials (7–12)
Paterson Panthers (4–6)#
Trenton Bengals (0–5)§

Second Half:
Brooklyn Visitations (12–8)
Jersey Reds (11–9)
New York Jewels (10–10)
Kingston Colonials (9–10)
Philadelphia Hebrews (9–11)
Passaic, N.J., Red Devils (8–11)

* Play-off winner—defeated Brooklyn 4 games
  to 3.
Transferred to Trenton.
§ Transferred to Passaic.

1936–37
First Half:
Jersey Reds (14–4)
Philadelphia Hebrews (12–6)
Kingston Colonials (11–6)
New York Jewels (7–10)§
Paterson Visitations (0–1)¶
Brooklyn Visitations (4–11)
Atlantic City, N.J. Sand Snipers (0–10)#

Second Half:
Philadelphia Hebrews (14–6)*
Jersey Reds (12–8)
Brooklyn Visitations (10–9)
New York Original Celtics (10–10)
Kingston Colonials (9–11)
Brooklyn Jewels (4–15)

* Play-off winner—defeated Jersey 4 games to 3.
# Dropped out.
§ Transferred to Brooklyn.
¶ Transferred to Brooklyn.

1937–38
First Half:
Jersey Reds (16–6)*

New Haven, Conn. Jewels (4–2)§
New York Jewels (8–6)
Brooklyn Visitations (13–10)
Philadelphia Sphas (12–10)
New York Original Celtics (11–10)
Kingston Colonials (5–15)
New York Yankees (1–11)#

Second Half:
New York Jewels (15–5)
Jersey Reds (13–7)
Philadelphia Sphas (11–9)
Kingston Colonials (9–10)
New York Original Celtics (7–11)
Brooklyn Visitations (2–15)

* Play-off winner—defeated New York Jewels 4
  games to 2.
Dropped out.
§ Transferred to New York.

1938–39
Kingston Colonials (28–7)
Philadelphia Sphas (24–9)
Jersey Reds (19–14)
New York Jewels (19–15)*
Wilkes-Barre, Pa., Barons (14–22)
Troy, N.Y., Haymakers (12–21)
Brooklyn Visitations (7–20)
Washington Brewers (7–22)

* Play-off winner—defeated Jersey 3 games to 0.

1939–40
Kingston Colonials (8–4)#
Philadelphia Sphas (20–13)*
Washington Brewers (19–14)
Troy Haymakers (3–9)#
Troy Celtics (16–6)
New York Jewels #1 (11–10)§
New York Jewels #2 (4–5)
Baltimore Clippers (15–16)
Jersey Reds (7–14)§
Wilkes-Barre Barons (5–17)¶

* Play-off winner—defeated Washington, Troy,
  New York, and Baltimore in round robin
  series.
Kingston and Troy Haymakers merged to form
  Troy Celtics while continuing with the Troy
  Haymakers won/lost record.
§ New York Jewels and Jersey Reds merged to
  form a new New York Jewels while continu-
  ing with the first New York Jewels won/lost
  record.
¶ Dropped out.

1940–41
First Half:
Philadelphia Sphas (11–4)*
New York Jewels (9–5)
Washington Brewers (7–7)
Troy Celtics#-Brooklyn Celtics (4–7)
Baltimore Clippers (3–11)

Second Half:
Brooklyn Celtics (11–4)
New York Jewels (8–8)
Washington Brewers (7–8)
Philadelphia Sphas (7–9)
Baltimore Clippers (6–10)

* Play-off winner—defeated Brooklyn 3 games
  to 1.
Transferred to Brooklyn.

1941–42
First Half:
Wilmington Blue Bombers (10–3)
Philadelphia Sphas (8–6)
Washington Brewers (5–6)
Trenton Tigers (5–8)
New York Jewels (1–6)*

Second Half:
Wilmington Blue Bombers (8–4)
Trenton Tigers (6–6)
Philadelphia Sphas (5–7)
Washington Brewers (5–7)

* Dropped out.

1942–43
Trenton Tigers (11–2)
Philadelphia Sphas (8–6)*
Camden, N.J., Indians (2–1)#
Brooklyn Indians (1–4)
Harrisburg, Pa., Senators (4–8)
New York Jewels (1–6)

* Play-off winner—defeated Trenton 4 games
  to 3.
Transferred to Brooklyn.

1943–44
First Half:
Wilmington Blue Bombers (12–4)*
New York Americans (9–6)
Trenton Tigers (8–6)
Philadelphia Sphas (4–9)
Brooklyn Indians (2–9)#

Second Half:
Philadelphia Sphas (8–4)
Trenton Tigers (7–5)
Wilmington Blue Bombers (5–5)
New York Americans (2–8)

* Play-off winner—defeated Philadelphia 4
  games to 3.
Dropped out.

1944–45
Philadelphia Sphas (22–8)*
Trenton Tigers (21–9)
Wilmington Bombers (14–14)
Baltimore Bullets (14–16)
New York Westchesters#-New York Gothams
  (11–15)
Washington Capitols (2–8)§

Paterson Crescents (1–15)

* Play-off winner—defeated Baltimore 2 games
  to 1.
Transferred to New York Gothams.
§ Transferred to Paterson.

1945–46
Baltimore Bullets (22–13)*
Philadelphia Sphas (21–14)
New York Gothams (18–16)
Wilmington Bombers (15–19)
Trenton Tigers (14–20)
Paterson Crescents (13–21)

* Play-off winner—defeated Philadelphia 3
  games to 1.

NATIONAL BASKETBALL LEAGUE

1926–27
New York-Arcola, N.J., Original Celtics (14–3)#
Brooklyn Visitations (18–7)*
Greenpoint, N.Y.-Trenton, N.J., Knights§-Greenpoint Knights (11–11)#
Paterson, N.J.-Kingston, N.Y., Raiders (8–13)
Ridgewood, N.Y.-Orange, N.J. (2–9)#
Newburgh, N.Y.-Jersey City, N.J., Skeeters (1–9)¶
Newburgh-Ridgewood (1–3)

* Champions.
# Dropped out.
§ Transferred to Greenpoint.
¶ Transferred to Newburgh-Ridgewood.
Note: League suspended operations.

NATIONAL BASKETBALL LEAGUE

1929–30
First Half:
Toledo, Ohio, Redmen (9–1)*
Detroit (7–3)#
Canton, Ohio, Generals (4–6)
Columbus, Ohio, Robert Lee's (4–6)
Pontiac, Mich. (4–6)§
Dayton, Ohio, Kelly's (2–8)

Second Half:
Dayton Kelly's,
Toledo Redmen,
Jackson, Mich., Elks,
Canton Generals,
Columbus Robert Lee's,

Detroit Tool-Shops
Won-lost records are unavailable.

*Play-off winner—defeated Dayton 4 games to
  2.
#Transferred to Jackson.
§Transferred to Detroit.

NATIONAL BASKETBALL LEAGUE

1932–33
Akron Firestones (10–1)
Toledo Crimson Coaches (NA)
Indianapolis Kautskys (NA)
Fort Wayne Chiefs (NA)
Kokomo, Ind., Kelts (2–3)
Akron Goodyears (1–4)
South Bend, Ind., Guardsmen (1–5)
Muncie, Ind., Whys (NA)
Lorain, Ohio, Fisher Foods (0–1)*

*Dropped out.
NA—record not available.

MIDWEST BASKETBALL CONFERENCE

1935–36
East Division:
Akron Firestone Non-Skids (11–7)
Pittsburgh Y.M.H.A.s (10–7)
Buffalo Bisons (7–8)
Dayton Metropolitans (4–6)

West Division:
Indianapolis Kautskys (9–3)
Chicago Duffy Florals (3–2)*
Detroit Hed-Aids (9–7)
Indianapolis U.S. Tires (5–9)
Windsor, Ont., Cooper Buses (2–11)

*Play-off winner—defeated Indianapolis
  Kautskys, Akron, and Pittsburgh in round
  robin series.

1936–37
Eastern Division:
Akron Goodyear Wingfoots (16–2)*
Akron Firestone Non-Skids (13–5)
Warren, Pa., Hyvis Oilers (8–6)
Columbus, Ohio, Athletic Supply (6–5)
Detroit Altes Lagers (2–8)
Pittsburgh Y.M.H.A.s (2–9)

Western Division:
Dayton London Bobbys (8–6)
Fort Wayne General Electrics (6–6)

Whiting, Ind., Ciesar All-Americans (3–5)
Chicago Duffy Florals (4–7)
Indianapolis Kautskys (2–5)
Indianapolis U.S. Tires (3–9)

*Champion.

NATIONAL BASKETBALL LEAGUE

1937–38
Eastern Division:
Akron Firestone Non-Skids (14–4)
Akron Goodyear Wingfoots (13–5)*
Pittsburgh Pirates (8–5)
Buffalo Bisons (3–6)
Warren, Pa., Penns (3–9)
Columbus, Ohio, Athletic Supply (1–12)

Western Division:
Oshkosh, Wis., All-Stars (12–2)
Whiting, Ind., Ciesar All-Americans (12–3)
Fort Wayne, Ind., General Electrics (13–7)
Indianapolis Kautskys (4–9)
Richmond, Ind., King Clothiers (1–2)#
Cincinnati Comellos (2–5)
Kankakee, Ill., Gallagher Trojans (3–11)
Dayton, Ohio, Metropolitans (2–11)

*Play-off winner—defeated Oshkosh 2 games
  to 1.
#Transferred to Cincinnati.

1938–39
Eastern Division:
Akron Firestone Non-Skids (24–3)*
Akron Goodyear Wingfoots (14–14)
Warren Penns (9–10)#
Cleveland White Horses (5–4)
Pittsburgh Pirates (13–14)

Western Division:
Oshkosh All-Stars (17–11)
Indianapolis Kautskys (13–13)
Sheboygan, Wis., Redskins (11–17)
Hammond, Ind., Ciesar All-Americans (4–24)

*Play-off winner—defeated Oshkosh 3 games
  to 2.
#Transferred to Cleveland.

1939–40
Eastern Division:
Akron Firestone Non-Skids (18–9)*
Detroit Eagles (17–10)
Akron Goodyear Wingfoots (14–14)
Indianapolis Kautskys (9–19)

Western Division:
Oshkosh All-Stars (15–13)
Sheboygan Redskins (15–13)
Chicago Bruins (14–14)

Hammond Ciesar All-Americans (9–19)

* Play-off winner—defeated Oshkosh 3 games to 2.

1940–41
Oshkosh All-Stars (18–6)*
Akron Firestone Non-Skids (13–11)
Sheboygan Redskins (13–11)
Detroit Eagles (12–12)
Akron Goodyear Wingfoots (11–13)
Chicago Bruins (11–13)
Hammond Ciesar All-Americans (6–18)

* Play-off winner—defeated Sheboygan 3 games to 0.

1941–42
Oshkosh All-Stars (20–4)*
Akron Goodyear Wingfoots (15–9)
Forty Wayne Zollner Pistons (15–9)
Indianapolis Kautskys (12–11)
Sheboygan Redskins (10–14)
Chicago Bruins (8–15)
Toledo Jim White Chevrolets (3–21)

* Play-off winner—defeated Fort Wayne 2 games to 1.

1942–43
Fort Wayne Zollner Pistons (17–6)
Sheboygan Redskins (12–11)*
Oshkosh All-Stars (11–12)
Chicago Studebakers (8–15)
Toledo Jim White Chevrolets (0–4)#

* Play-off winner—defeated Fort Wayne 2 games to 1.
# Dropped out.

1943–44
Fort Wayne Zollner Pistons (18–4)*
Sheboygan Redskins (14–8)
Oshkosh All-Stars (7–15)
Cleveland Chase Brassmen (3–15)

* Play-off winner—defeated Sheboygan 3 games to 0.

1944–45
Eastern Division:
Fort Wayne Zollner Pistons (25–5)*
Cleveland Allmen Transfers (13–17)
Pittsburgh Raiders (7–23)

Western Division:
Sheboygan Redskins (19–11)
Chicago American Gears (14–16)
Oshkosh All-Stars (12–18)

* Play-off winner—defeated Sheboygan 3 games to 2.

1945–46
Eastern Division:
Fort Wayne Zollner Pistons (26–8)
Rochester Royals (24–10)*

Youngstown Bears (13–20)
Cleveland Allmen Transfers (4–29)

Western Division:
Sheboygan Redskins (21–13)
Oshkosh All-Stars (19–15)
Chicago American Gears (17–17)
Indianapolis Kautskys (10–22)

* Play-off winner—defeated Sheboygan 3 games to 0.

1946–47
Eastern Division:
Rochester Royals (31–13)
Fort Wayne Zollner Pistons (25–19)
Syracuse Nationals (21–23)
Toledo Jeeps (21–23)
Buffalo Bisons (5–8)#
Tri-Cities Blackhawks (14–17)
Youngstown Bears (12–32)

Western Division:
Oshkosh All-Stars (28–16)
Indianapolis Kautskys (27–17)
Chicago American Gears (26–18)*
Sheboygan Redskins (26–18)
Anderson Duffey Packers (24–20)
Detroit Gems (4–40)

* Play-off winner—defeated Rochester 3 games to 1.
# Transferred to Tri-Cities.

1947–48
Eastern Division:
Rochester Royals (44–16)
Anderson Duffey Packers (42–18)
Fort Wayne Zollner Pistons (40–20)
Syracuse Nationals (24–36)
Toledo Jeeps (22–37)
Flint, Mich., Midland, Mich. Dow A.C.s (8–52)

Western Division:
Minneapolis Lakers (43–17)*
Tri-Cities Blackhawks (30–30)
Oshkosh All-Stars (29–31)
Indianapolis Kautskys (24–35)
Sheboygan Redskins (23–37)

* Play-off winner—defeated Rochester 3 games to 1.

1948–49
Eastern Division:
Anderson Duffey Packers (49–15)*
Syracuse Nationals (40–23)
Hammond Calumet Buccaneers (21–41)
Detroit Vagabond Kings (2–17)#
Dayton Rens (14–26)

Western Division:
Oshkosh All-Stars (37–27)
Tri-Cities Blackhawks (36–28)
Sheboygan Redskins (35–29)

Waterloo, Iowa, Hawks (30–32)
Denver Nuggets (18–44)

* Play-off winner—defeated Oshkosh 3 games
  to 0.
Transferred to Dayton.

BASKETBALL ASSOCIATION OF AMERICA

1946–47

Eastern Division:
Washington Capitols (49–11)
Philadelphia Warriors (35–25)*
New York Knickerbockers (33–27)
Providence Steamrollers (28–32)
Boston Celtics (22–38)
Toronto Huskies (22–38)

Western Division:
Chicago Stags (39–22)
St. Louis Bombers (38–23)
Cleveland Rebels (30–30)
Detroit Falcons (20–40)
Pittsburgh Ironmen (15–45)

* Play-off winner—defeated Chicago 4 games
  to 1.

1947–48

Eastern Division:
Philadelphia Warriors (27–21)
New York Knickerbockers (26–22)
Boston Celtics (20–28)
Providence Steamrollers (6–42)

Western Division:
St. Louis Bombers (29–19)
Baltimore Bullets (29–20)*
Chicago Stags (29–21)
Washington Capitols (28–21)

* Play-off winner—defeated Philadelphia 4
  games to 2.

1948–49

Eastern Division:
Washington Capitols (38–22)
New York Knickerbockers (32–28)
Baltimore Bullets (29–31)
Philadelphia Warriors (28–32)
Boston Celtics (25–35)
Providence Steamrollers (12–48)

Western Division:
Rochester Royals (45–15)
Minneapolis Lakers (44–16)*
Chicago Stags (38–22)
St. Louis Bombers (29–31)
Fort Wayne Pistons (22–38)
Indianapolis Jets (18–42)

* Play-off winner—defeated Washington 4
  games to 2.

PROFESSIONAL BASKETBALL LEAGUE OF AMERICA

1947–48

Northern Division:
Chicago Gears (8–0)
St. Paul Saints (6–3)
Grand Rapids, Mich., Rangers (3–3)
Louisville, Ky., Colonels (2–4)
Omaha, Neb., Tomahawks (2–4)
Kansas City Blues (1–5)
Waterloo, Iowa, Pro-Hawks (1–5)
St. Joseph, Mo., Outlaws (1–6)

Southern Division:
Houston Mavericks (2–0)
Atlanta Crackers (7–1)
Birmingham Skyhawks (5–2)
Tulsa Ranchers (7–3)
Chattanooga Majors (3–3)
Oklahoma City Drillers (2–3)
New Orleans Hurricanes (3–5)
Springfield, Mo., Squires (1–7)

Note: League disbanded early in the season.

NATIONAL BASKETBALL ASSOCIATION

1949–50

Eastern Division:
Syracuse Nationals (51–13)
New York Knickerbockers (40–28)
Washington Capitols (32–36)
Philadelphia Warriors (26–42)
Baltimore Bullets (25–43)
Boston Celtics (22–46)

Central Division:
Minneapolis Lakers (52–17)*
Rochester Royals (51–18)
Fort Wayne Pistons (41–28)
Chicago Stags (40–29)
St. Louis Bombers (26–42)

Western Division:
Indianapolis Olympians (39–25)
Anderson Duffey Packers (37–27)
Tri-Cities Blackhawks (39–35)
Sheboygan Redskins (22–40)
Waterloo Hawks (19–43)
Denver Nuggets (11–51)

* Play-off winner—defeated Syracuse 4 games
  to 2.

1950–51

Eastern Division:
Philadelphia Warriors (40–26)
Boston Celtics (39–30)
New York Knickerbockers (36–30)

Syracuse Nationals (32–34)
Baltimore Bullets (24–42)
Washington Capitols (10–25)#

Western Division:
Minneapolis Lakers (44–24)
Rochester Royals (41–27)*
Fort Wayne Pistons (32–36)
Indianapolis Olympians (31–37)
Tri-Cities Blackhawks (25–43)

* Play-off winner—defeated New York 4 games
  to 3.
Dropped out.

1951–52

Eastern Division:
Syracuse Nationals (40–26)
Boston Celtics (39–27)
New York Knickerbockers (37–29)
Philadelphia Warriors (33–33)
Baltimore Bullets (20–46)

Western Division:
Rochester Royals (41–25)
Minneapolis Lakers (40–26)*
Indianapolis Olympians (34–32)
Fort Wayne Pistons (29–37)
Milwaukee Hawks (17–49)

* Play-off winner—defeated New York 4 games
  to 3.

1952–53

Eastern Division:
New York Knickerbockers (47–23)
Syracuse Nationals (47–24)
Boston Celtics (46–25)
Baltimore Bullets (16–54)
Philadelphia Warriors (12–57)

Western Division:
Minneapolis Lakers (48–22)*
Rochester Royals (44–26)
Fort Wayne Pistons (36–33)
Indianapolis Olympians (28–43)
Milwaukee Hawks (27–44)

* Play-off winner—defeated New York 4 games
  to 1.

1953–54

Eastern Division:
New York Knickerbockers (44–28)
Boston Celtics (42–30)
Syracuse Nationals (42–30)
Philadelphia Warriors (29–43)
Baltimore Bullets (16–56)

Western Division:
Minneapolis Lakers (46–26)*
Rochester Royals (44–28)
Fort Wayne Pistons (40–32)
Milwaukee Hawks (21–51)

* Play-off winner—defeated Syracuse 4 games
  to 3.
The NBA has remained in continuous operation
  since that season.

NATIONAL PROFESSIONAL BASKETBALL LEAGUE

1950–51

Eastern Division:
Sheboygan Redskins (29–16)*
Louisville Alumnites (18–17)#
Anderson Packers (22–22)
Grand Rapids Hornets (6–13)#

Western Division:
Waterloo Hawks (32–24)*
St. Paul Lights (12–8)#
Denver Refiners (18–16)§
Evansville, Ind., Agogans (0–6)
Kansas City Hi-Spots (4–19)#

* Sheboygan and Waterloo both claimed championship.
# Dropped out.
§ Transferred to Evansville.

Appendix C

WORLD TOURNAMENTS

During the 1940s, several cities hosted tournaments for professional teams. The one with the greatest cachet was the World Professional Basketball Tournament played in Chicago Stadium each year from 1939 to 1948 under the sponsorship of the Chicago *Herald-American*. Professional players acknowledged the winner of that tourney to be world champion. The results follow.

Compiled by William F. Himmelman
Copyright © 1990 by William F. Himmelman

1939

FIRST ROUND:
Harlem Globetrotters 41,
Fort Wayne Harvesters 33;
New York Yankees 40,
Benton Harbor, Mich., House of David 32;
Sheboygan Redskins 47,
Illinois Grads (Champaign) 29;
Oshkosh All-Stars 40,
Clarksburg, W.Va., Oilers 33;
New York Rens—bye;
Chicago Harmons—bye;
New York Celtics—bye

QUARTER-FINAL ROUND:
New York Rens 30,
New York Yankees 21;
Harlem Globetrotters 31,
Chicago Harmons 25;
Sheboygan Redskins 36,
New York Celtics 29;
Oshkosh All-Stars—bye

SEMI-FINAL ROUND:
New York Rens 27,

Harlem Globetrotters 23;
Oshkosh All-Stars 40,
Sheboygan Redskins 23

THIRD-PLACE GAME:
Harlem Globetrotters 36,
Sheboygan Redskins 33

CHAMPIONSHIP GAME:

New York Rens 34

	FG	FT	TP
Pop Gates f	4	4	12
Tarzan Cooper f	1	3	5
Willie Smith c	2	2	6
Puggy Bell g	1	2	4
Bruiser Saitch g	1	0	2
Zack Clayton g	0	0	0
Johnny Isaacs g	2	1	5
	11	12	34

Oshkosh All-Stars 25

	FG	FT	TP
Ray Adams f	0	0	0
Pete Preboski f	1	1	3
Ed McGroaty f	0	0	0

Scotty Armstrong f	2	3	7
Al Cafone f	0	0	0
Cowboy Edwards c	3	6	12
Frank Linskey g	1	1	3
Herm Witasek g	0	0	0
Ed Mullen g	0	0	0
	7	11	25

1940

FIRST ROUND:
Chicago Bruins 45,
Fort Wayne Harvesters 27;
Sheboygan Redskins 44,
Rochester Seagrams 32;
Harlem Globetrotters 50,
Kenosha, Wis., Royals 26;
New York Rens 42,
Canton, Ohio, Bulldogs 21;
Oshkosh All-Stars 42,
Benton Harbor, Mich., House of David 22;
Waterloo, Ohio, Wonders 41,
Clarksburg, W.Va., Oilers 32;
Syracuse Reds—bye;
Washington Heurich Brewers—bye

QUARTER-FINAL ROUND:
Syracuse Reds 39,
Sheboygan Redskins 30;
Washington Heurich Brewers 35,
Waterloo Wonders 23;
Chicago Bruins 40,
Oshkosh All-Stars 38;
Harlem Globetrotters 37,
New York Rens 36

SEMI-FINAL ROUND:
Harlem Globetrotters 34,
Syracuse Reds 25;
Chicago Bruins 46,
Washington Heurich Brewers 38

THIRD-PLACE GAME:
Washington Heurich Brewers 41,
Syracuse Reds 30

CHAMPIONSHIP GAME:

Harlem Globetrotters 31	FG	FT	TP
Bernie Price f	2	0	4
Sonny Boswell f	5	2	12
Ted Strong c	1	1	3
Duke Cumberland g	2	2	6
Inman Jackson g	0	0	0
Al Fawks g	1	0	2
Babe Pressley g	2	0	4
	13	5	31

Chicago Bruins 29	FG	FT	TP
Elmer Johnson f	1	2	4
Wibs Kautz f	2	1	5

Mike Novak c	3	1	7
Stan Zadel c	1	1	3
Ed Oram g	1	2	4
Bob MacLeod g	1	0	2
Willie Phillips g	1	2	4
	10	9	29

1941

FIRST ROUND:
Chicago Bruins 53,
Davenport, Iowa, Central Turner Rockets 17;
Detroit Eagles 58,
Indianapolis Kautskys 43;
Harlem Globetrotters 38,
Newark, N.Y., Elks 29;
Oshkosh All-Stars 47,
Fort Wayne Zollner Pistons 41;
New York Rens 43,
Dayton Sucher Wonders 20;
Kenosha, Wis., Royals 40,
Rochester Seagrams 36;
Toledo White Huts 36,
Sheboygan Redskins 28;
Philadelphia Sphas 48,
Bismarck, N.D., Phantoms 30

QUARTER-FINAL ROUND:
Toledo White Huts 43,
Chicago Bruins 33;
New York Rens 43,
Kenosha Royals 15;
Detroit Eagles 37,
Harlem Globetrotters 36;
Oshkosh All-Stars 38,
Philadelphia Sphas 31

SEMI-FINAL ROUND:
Oshkosh All-Stars 40,
Toledo White Huts 37;
Detroit Eagles 43,
New York Rens 42

THIRD PLACE GAME:
New York Rens 57,
Toledo White Huts 42

CHAMPIONSHIP GAME:

Detroit Eagles 39	FG	FT	TP
Bob Calihan f	3	2	8
Jimmy Brown f	0	0	0
Buddy Jeannette f	3	2	8
Ed Sadowski c	3	5	11
Jake Ahearn g	3	3	9
Jerry Bush g	1	1	3
	13	13	39

Oshkosh All-Stars 37	FG	FT	TP
Bob Carpenter f	1	6	8
Lou Barle f	2	0	4
Scoop Putnam f	0	0	0

Cowboy Edwards c	1	3	5
Charley Shipp g	1	1	3
Erv Prasse g	2	0	4
Herm Witasek g	3	0	6
Connie Berry g	3	1	7
	13	11	37

1942

FIRST ROUND:
Chicago Bruins 56,
Detroit A.A.A. 46;
Sheboygan Redskins 34,
Columbus, Ohio, Bobb Chevrolets 26;
New York Rens 55,
Northern Indiana Steelers (Michigan City) 37;
Oshkosh All-Stars 44,
Davenport, Iowa, Central Turner Rockets 29;
Detroit Eagles 46,
Toledo White Huts 29;
Harlem Globetrotters 40,
Hagerstown, Pa., Conoco Oilers 33;
Long Island Grumman Flyers 54,
Indianapolis Kautskys 332;
Aberdeen, Md., Army Ordnance Training Center 56,
Fort Wayne Zollner Pistons 42

QUARTER-FINAL ROUND:
Detroit Eagles 40,
Aberdeen Army Ordnance Training Center 32;
Harlem Globetrotters 37,
Sheboygan Redskins 32;
Long Island Grumman Flyers 48,
Chicago Bruins 38;
Oshkosh All-Stars 44,
New York Rens 38

SEMI-FINAL ROUND:
Detroit Eagles 44,
Long Island Grumman Flyers 43;
Oshkosh All-Stars 48,
Harlem Globetrotters 41

THIRD-PLACE GAME:
Long Island Grumman Flyers 43,
Harlem Globetrotters 41

CHAMPIONSHIP GAME:

Oshkosh All-Stars 43

	FG	FT	TP
Lou Barle f	2	1	5
Bill Komenich f	0	0	0
Erv Prasse f	0	0	0
Cowboy Edwards c	2	1	5
Gene Englund c	7	3	17
Eddie Riska g	3	3	9
Tom Nisbet g	0	0	0
Charley Shipp g	3	1	7
	17	9	43

Detroit Eagles 41

	FG	FT	TP
Ed Parry f	1	0	2
Buddy Jeannette f	5	4	14
Lou Kasperik f	1	0	2
Jake Pelkington c	1	2	4
Jake Ahearn g	5	1	11
Jerry Bush g	3	2	8
	16	9	41

1943

FIRST ROUND:
Detroit Eagles 33,
Akron Collegians 31;
Fort Wayne Zollner Pistons 56,
Indianapolis Pure Oils 52;
Dayton Dive Bombers 46,
Chicago Ramblers 41;
Minneapolis Sparklers 45,
South Bend Studebaker Champions 44;
Oshkosh All-Stars—bye;
Sheboygan Redskins—bye;
Harlem Globetrotters—bye;
Washington Bears—bye

QUARTER-FINAL ROUND:
Oshkosh All-Stars 65,
Detroit Eagles 36;
Fort Wayne Zollner Pistons 48,
Sheboygan Redskins 40;
Dayton Dive Bombers 44,
Harlem Globetrotters 34;
Washington Bears 48,
Minneapolis Sparklers 21

SEMI-FINAL ROUND:
Washington Bears 38,
Dayton Dive Bombers 30;
Oshkosh All-Stars 40,
Fort Wayne Zollner Pistons 39

THIRD PLACE GAME:
Fort Wayne Zollner Pistons 58,
Dayton Dive Bombers 52

CHAMPIONSHIP GAME:

Washington Bears 43

	FG	FT	TP
Pop Gates f	3	3	9
Puggy Bell f	2	0	4
Sonny Wood f	1	1	3
Dolly King c	1	1	3
Charley Isles c	2	3	7
Tarzan Cooper g	0	1	1
Zack Clayton g	1	3	5
Johnny Isaacs g	5	1	11
	15	13	43

Oshkosh All-Stars 31

	FG	FT	TP
Connie Berry f	0	0	0
Bill Crossett f	0	0	0

Bob Carpenter f	0	2	2
Gene Englund c	1	1	3
Cowboy Edwards c	1	5	7
Tom Nisbet g	2	0	4
Ralph Vaughn g	3	0	6
Charley Shipp g	1	1	3
Dave Quabius g	2	0	4
Fred Rehm g	1	0	2
	11	9	31

1944

FIRST ROUND:
Dayton Aviators 52,
Akron Collegians 38;
Brooklyn Eagles 55,
Camp Campbell, Ky., Tankmen 41;
New York Rens 39,
Detroit Suffrins 33;
Cleveland Chase Brassmen 55,
Indianapolis Pure Oils 52;
Oshkosh All-Stars 51,
Rochester Wings 40;
Harlem Globetrotters 41,
Pittsburgh Corbetts 40;
Fort Wayne Zollner Pistons—bye;
Sheboygan Redskins—bye

QUARTER FINAL ROUND:
Fort Wayne Zollner Pistons 59,
Dayton Aviators 34:
New York Rens 62,
Cleveland Chase Brassmen 38;
Brooklyn Eagles 49,
Sheboygan Redskins 43;
Harlem Globetrotters 41,
Oshkosh All-Stars 31

SEMI-FINAL ROUND:
Brooklyn Eagles 63,
Harlem Globetrotters 41;
Fort Wayne Zollner Pistons 42,
New York Rens 38

THIRD PLACE GAME:
Harlem Globetrotters 37,
New York Rens 29

CHAMPIONSHIP GAME:

Fort Wayne Zollner Pistons 50

	FG	FT	TP
Blackie Towery f	3	0	6
Jerry Bush f	2	0	4
Jake Pelkington c	8	3	19
Chick Reiser g	2	1	5
Dale Hamilton g	0	0	0
Bobby McDermott g	7	0	14
Paul Birch g	1	0	2
	23	4	50

Brooklyn Eagles 33

	FG	FT	TP
Bob Tough f	3	5	11

Bernie Opper f	5	1	11
Danny Christie f	0	0	0
Chuck Connors c	1	0	2
Dutch Garfinkle g	2	2	6
Mickey Rottner g	1	1	3
Joe Bellis g	0	0	0
	12	9	33

1945

FIRST ROUND:
Chicago American Gears 58,
Hartford, Conn., Nutmegs 47;
Oshkosh All-Stars 60,
Detroit Mansfields 56;
New York Rens 67,
Indianapolis Oilers 59;
Midland, Mich., Dow Chemicals 61,
Cleveland Allmen Transfers 46;
Pittsburgh Raiders 53,
Newark, N.J. C-O Twos 50;
Dayton Acmes 43,
Long Island Grumman Hellcats 27;
Fort Wayne Zollner Pistons—bye;
Harlem Globetrotters—bye

QUARTER-FINAL ROUND:
Fort Wayne Zollner Pistons 63,
Oshkosh All-Stars 52;
New York Rens 61,
Pittsburgh Raiders 52;
Dayton Acmes 52,
Midland Dow Chemicals 50;
Chicago American Gears 53,
Harlem Globetrotters 49

SEMI-FINAL ROUND:
Dayton Acmes 80,
Chicago American Gears 51;
Fort Wayne Zollner Pistons 68,
New York Rens 45

THIRD-PLACE GAME:
Chicago American Gears 64,
New York Rens 55

CHAMPIONSHIP GAME:

Fort Wayne Zollner Pistons 78

	FG	FT	TP
Jerry Bush f	3	3	9
Paul Birch f	0	0	0
Buddy Jeannette f	7	4	18
Bobby Synnott f	2	0	4
Jake Pelkington c	4	4	12
Ed Sadowski c	3	3	9
Chick Reiser g	3	3	9
Herm Schaefer g	0	0	0
Bobby McDermott g	6	3	15
Charley Shipp g	1	0	2
	29	20	78

Dayton Acmes 52

	FG	FT	TP
Bruce Hale f	5	5	15

Rex Gardecki f	1	0	2
Bobby Colburn f	0	0	0
John Mahnken c	7	2	16
Chris Hansen g	4	3	11
John Schick g	1	0	2
Al Negratti g	2	2	6
	20	12	52

1946
FIRST ROUND:
Chicago American Gears 69,
Pittsburgh Raiders 58;
Anderson, Ind., Chiefs 59,
Cleveland Allmen Transfers 46;
Midland, Mich., Dows 72,
Indianapolis Kautskys 59;
Oshkosh All-Stars 60,
Detroit Mansfields 32;
New York Rens 82,
Toledo Whites 39;
Baltimore Bullets 61,
Dayton Mickeys 58;
Sheboygan Redskins—bye;
Fort Wayne Zollner Pistons—bye

QUARTER-FINAL ROUND:
Oshkosh All-Stars 50,
New York Rens 44;
Chicago American Gears 52,
Sheboygan Redskins 51;
Fort Wayne Zollner Pistons 65,
Midland Dows 62;
Baltimore Bullets 67,
Anderson Chiefs 65

SEMI-FINAL ROUND:
Fort Wayne Zollner Pistons 50,
Baltimore Bullets 49;
Oshkosh All-Stars 72,
Chicago American Gears 66

THIRD PLACE SERIES:
Chicago American Gears 59,
Baltimore Bullets 54;
Chicago American Gears 65,
Baltimore Bullets 50

CHAMPIONSHIP SERIES:
Oshkosh All-Stars 61,
Fort Wayne Zollner Pistons 59;
Fort Wayne Zollner Pistons 56,
Oshkosh All-Stars 47

CHAMPIONSHIP GAME:

Fort Wayne Zollner Pistons 73

	FG	FT	TP
Jake Pelkington f	2	6	10
Bob Tough f	5	0	10
Ed Sadowski c	7	0	14
Bob Kinney c	1	1	3
Chick Reiser g	3	2	8
Bobby McDermott g	8	4	20

Jerry Bush g	3	0	6
Charley Shipp g	0	0	0
Buddy Jeannette g	0	2	2
Curly Armstrong g	0	0	0
	29	15	73

Oshkosh All-Stars 57

	FG	FT	TP
Bob Carpenter f	1	1	3
Clint Wager f	3	0	6
Gene Englund f	1	0	2
Cowboy Edwards c	9	6	24
Erv Prasse g	0	1	1
Bob Feerick g	5	3	13
Fred Rehm g	1	2	4
Eddie Riska g	0	3	3
Bud Engdahl g	0	1	1
	20	17	57

1947
FIRST ROUND:
Oshkosh All-Stars 60,
Herkimer, N.Y. Mohawk Redskins 54;
Anderson Duffey Packers 59,
Pittsburgh Pirates 38;
Midland, Mich., Dows 71,
Syracuse Nationals 39;
Sheboygan Redskins 62,
Portland Indians 48;
Toledo Jeeps 62,
New York Rens 59;
Tri-Cities Blackhawks 57,
Baltimore Bullets 46;
Fort Wayne Zollner Pistons—bye;
Indianapolis Kautskys—bye

QUARTER-FINAL ROUND:
Oshkosh All-Stars 53,
Sheboygan Redskins 44;
Indianapolis Kautskys 65,
Tri-Cities Blackhawks 56;
Fort Wayne Zollner Pistons 52,
Anderson Duffey Packers 40;
Toledo Jeeps 59,
Midland Dows 55

SEMI-FINAL ROUND:
Indianapolis Kautskys 57,
Oshkosh All-Stars 38;
Toledo Jeeps 61,
Fort Wayne Zollner Pistons 56

THIRD PLACE GAME:
Fort Wayne Zollner Pistons 86,
Oshkosh All-Stars 67

CHAMPIONSHIP GAME:

Indianapolis Kautskys 62

	FG	FT	TP
Leo Klier f	6	0	12
Gus Doerner f	4	1	9
Bill Closs f	5	0	10

Woody Norris f	1	0	2
Arnie Risen c	3	0	6
Bob Dietz g	2	0	4
Roy Pugh g	0	1	1
Herm Schaefer g	3	1	7
Ernie Andres g	4	3	11
	28	6	62

Toledo Jeeps 47

	FG	FT	TP
Hal Tidrick f	3	1	7
Paul Seymour f	1	0	2
Bernie Mehen f	1	1	3
George Sobek f	7	6	20
John Schick f	1	3	5
Bob Gerber c	5	0	10
Joe Patanelli c	0	0	0
Jules Rivlin g	0	0	0
Dale Hamilton g	0	0	0
Frank Gilhooley g	0	0	0
	18	11	47

1948

QUARTER-FINAL ROUND:
New York Rens 67,
Bridgeport, Conn., Newfield Steelers 51;

Tri-Cities Blackhawks 57,
Fort Wayne Zollner Pistons 50;

Anderson Duffey Packers 59,
Indianapolis Kautskys 53;

Minneapolis Lakers 98,
Wilkes-Barre, Pa., Barons 48

SEMI-FINAL ROUND:
Minneapolis Lakers 59,
Anderson Duffey Packers 56;
New York Rens 59,
Tri-Cities Blackhawks 55

THIRD PLACE GAME:
Anderson Duffey Packers 66,
Tri-Cities Blackhawks 44

CHAMPIONSHIP GAME:

Minneapolis Lakers 75

	FG	FT	TP
Jim Pollard f	6	2	14
Tony Jaros f	0	0	0
Jack Dwan f	1	0	2
John Jorgensen f	1	1	3
George Mikan c	14	12	40
Herm Schaefer g	3	3	9
Don Smith g	1	1	3
Paul Napolitano g	2	0	4
	28	19	75

New York Rens 71

	FG	FT	TP
George Crowe f	6	0	12
Duke Cumberland f	5	4	14
Sweetwater Clifton c	8	8	24
Jim Usry c	1	1	3
Dolly King c	0	0	0
Sonny Wood g	1	0	2
Pop Gates g	7	2	16
Eddie Younger g	0	0	0
	28	15	71

Notes on Sources

For the beginnings of basketball, the best source is the horse's mouth—James Naismith himself. In his book, *Basketball: Its Origin and Development,* which was published two years after his death by the YMCA's Association Press, Naismith gave a detailed account of why and how he invented basketball. Although it was written long after the event, Naismith's book is the authoritative story of the game's genesis.

Basketball's first few years, when the game was still being controlled and fostered by the YMCA, are well covered by several YMCA publications of the period. The publications are indexed in the archives of the YMCA of the USA, making it easy to locate references to basketball.

I depended primarily on two sources for information about the earliest professionals. One was the *Daily True American* of Trenton, N.J., which covered the names of the Trenton Basketball Team in the 1896–97 season. The other was a series of forty newspaper columns by Marvin A. Riley which appeared semiweekly in Trenton's *State Gazette* in the fall and winter of 1922–23. Riley, a sportswriter and basketball referee, wrote in exhaustive and loving detail about early professional teams and players. Some of his assessments have to be taken with more than a grain of salt because he was a Trentonian first, last, and always; he chose five Trenton men as the best players in the first quarter-century of professional basketball. But his reminiscences provide an invaluable look at the embryo professional game, especially around the turn of the century.

Easily the most useful publication for the 1901–26 period is the annual *Reach Official Basket Ball Guide.* It was edited by William J. Scheffer, a Philadelphia newspaperman, and published by the A. J. Reach Company, a Philadelphia sporting-goods manufacturer. The *Guide* covered amateur, high school, and collegiate basketball, as well as professional teams and leagues. Most of the articles and statistics were furnished by officers of leagues and teams, and so the reader must keep his skeptical faculty in gear. Nevertheless, the factual material, and especially William Scheffer's commentary on the previous season and the state of basketball in general, make the *Reach Guide* essential for the researcher. Some useful information is also found in the *Converse Basketball Year Book,* which was published annually beginning in 1922 by the Converse Rubber Shoe Company of Malden Mass., manufacturers of basketball footwear.

After 1926, when the *Reach Guide* ceased publication, the trail is muddied because for the next twenty years there are few sources of contemporary reporting about professional leagues and players. The researcher must depend on newspapers and the few magazine articles on pro basketball for on-the-scene reporting about the game. Several of the men I interviewed contributed their recollections for the 1920s and the Depression period.

Magazine stories about the professional game were rare until the 1940s. The *Literary Digest* published a handful of articles before its demise in the mid-1930s, but other magazines ignored the professionals. Beginning about 1939, such major publications as *Life, Time, Saturday Evening Post, Collier's, Look, True,* and *Argosy* ran an occasional piece about a professional player or team. So did *Sport, Sport Folio,* and *Sport Life.*

Two basketball encyclopedias, *The Sports Encyclopedia: Pro Basketball* and the *Ronald Encyclopedia of Basketball,* have fairly detailed coverage of the first "big league"—the American Basketball League—from 1925 through 1931; the *Sports Encyclopedia*'s coverage is more complete. The *Ronald Encyclopedia* gives standings and scoring leaders for the ABL for the years following its rebirth as a regional league in 1933. For coverage of the National Basketball League during its life from 1937 through 1949, the *Sports Encyclopedia* is best. It carries a summary of each year, the standings, playoff results, and team rosters. Neither encyclopedia, of course, has much about how the game was played; for that I relied mostly on my interviews and scattered magazine and newspaper articles.

The story of the Basketball Association of America and its merger with the National League to form the National Basketball Association is told in several books and all encyclopedias. For season-by-season reports, including standings, playoffs, and rosters, the most complete is *The Sports Encyclopedia: Pro Basketball.* But the best recounting of the BAA's years and the infancy of the NBA is *24 Seconds to Shoot,* by Leonard Koppett (1968).

Much of my background material on the BAA and NBA came from the minutes of their Boards of Governors meetings and the bulletins issued periodically to team owners by Maurice Podoloff, the president of both leagues. The minutes are kept in the office of the NBA's counsel. Fortunately, Podoloff's bulletins were preserved and given to the Basketball Hall of Fame library in Springfield, Mass., by William G. Mokray, who was in the front office of the Boston Celtics during the BAA's three years and the infancy of the NBA. (Mokray, incidentally, was the author of the *Ronald Encyclopedia of Basketball.*)

Some information about the BAA and early years of the NBA can be found in three magazines: *Basketball Illustrated* (1945–49); *Basketball Magazine* (November 1946–February 1947); and *Basketball,* an annual put out by Dell Publishing Company beginning in 1950.

The Basketball Hall of Fame library has a complete collection of books on the game. It also has files on many professional players, teams, and leagues, but they are spotty. The researcher will chance upon such gems as a letter by John Wendelken reminiscing about the turn-of-the century New York Wanderers and the minutes of the American Basketball League's directors' meetings. Surprisingly, though, the files on the Original Celtics and Renaissance are quite slim, and there is no file at all for Olson's Terrible Swedes, another well-known barnstorming team of the 1920s and '30s. The National Basketball League's file is skinny too but contains one prize—a league yearbook called *Pro Magazine* which was issued for the NBL's final season after four of its strongest clubs had jumped to the Basketball Association of America.

Hundreds of books have been published about basketball. Most are instructional guides, biographies of famous players, stories of championship teams, and roundups of "greatest teams" and "greatest players." Probably 90 percent of them have been published since 1950 and in most the early professional players, teams, and leagues are given short shrift. The following books, however, contain useful information about the professional game:

Auerbach, Arnold (Red), *Basketball for the Player, the Fan and the Coach.* New York: Simon and Schuster, 1952.

———— and Sann, Paul, *Winning the Hard Way.* Boston: Little, Brown and Co., 1966.

———— with Joe Fitzgerald, *On and Off the Court.* New York: Macmillan, 1985.

Basloe, Frank J., *I Grew Up with Basketball,* in collaboration with D. Gordon Rohman. New York: Greenberg, 1952. An entertaining story of the life and times of a pioneer manager and promoter.

Bole, Robert D., and Alfred C. Lawrence, *From Peachbaskets to Slam Dunks.* Canaan, N.H.: B & L Publishers, 1987. A review of the whole period of professional basketball with emphasis on the Eastern League from 1920 through its collapse in 1923.

Brown, Gene, editor, *The Complete Book of Basketball.* New York Times Company, 1980. A scrapbook of newspaper clips on college and professional basketball from *The New York Times.*

Cousy, Bob, *Basketball Is My Life,* as told to Al Hirshberg. Englewood Cliffs, N.J.: Prentice-Hall, 1958.

Devaney, John, *The Story of Basketball.* New York: Random House, 1976. Well-written account, including information about pioneer players and teams.

Chalk, Ocania, *Pioneers of Black Sport.* New York: Dodd, Mead, 1976. Informative about early black players and teams.

Dickey, Glenn, *The History of Professional Basketball Since 1896.* New York: Stein and Day, 1982.

Frank, Stanley B., *The Jew in Sports*. New York: Miles Publishing Company, 1936.

Hebron, George T., editor, *How to Play Basket Ball*. New York: American Publishing, 1904. The earliest book on basketball. It is an instructional guide, including photos, for players, managers, and officials; professionalism is not mentioned.

Hirshberg, Al, *Basketball's Greatest Teams*. New York: G. P. Putnam's Sons, 1965.

Hollander, Zander, editor, *The NBA's Encyclopedia of Pro Basketball*. New York: New American Library, 1981.

————, *The Modern Encyclopedia of Basketball*. New York: Four Winds Press, 1973. Both have useful season-by-season reviews beginning with the Basketball Association of America.

Hobson, Howard A., *Basketball Illustrated*. New York: A. S. Barnes & Co., 1948.

Holman, Nat, *Scientific Basketball*. New York: Incra Publishing Co., 1922.

————, *Winning Basketball*. New York: Charles Scribner's Sons, 1934. Primarily instructional guides, with some mention of professional techniques.

Jares, Joe, *Basketball: The American Game*. Chicago: Follett Publishing Co., 1971. Very good historical review, including some material about early teams and players.

Koppett, Leonard, *24 Seconds to Shoot*. New York: Macmillan, 1968.

————, *The Essence of the Game Is Deception*. Boston: Little, Brown and Company, 1973.

Lapchick, Joe, *50 Years of Basketball*. Englewood Cliffs, N.J.: Prentice-Hall, 1968.

Mendell, Ronald L., *Who's Who in Basketball*. New Rochelle, N.Y.: Arlington House, 1973.

Menville, Chuck, *The Harlem Globetrotters*. New York: David McKay Co., 1978.

Messer, Guerdon N., *How to Play Basket Ball*. New York: American Sports Library, 1911.

Mikan, George, *Mr. Basketball: George Mikan's Own Story*, as told to Bill Carlson. New York: Greenberg, 1952.

Mokray, William G., *Ronald Encyclopedia of Basketball*. New York: Ronald Press, 1963.

Naismith, James, *Basketball: Its Origin and Development*. New York: Association Press, 1941.

Neft, David S., Roland T. Johnson, Richard M. Cohen, and Jordan A. Deutsch, editors, *The Sports Encyclopedia: Pro Basketball*. New York: Grosset and Dunlap, 1975.

Rumlow, Wayne O., *The Oshkosh All-Stars and the National Basketball League*. Oshkosh, Wis.: Steinert Printing Co., 1979.

Russell, John D., *Between Games, Between Halves*. Washington and San Francisco: Dryad Press, 1986. Good biography of Honey Russell by his son, with insights into the early game and its players.

Salzberg, Charles, *From Set Shot to Slam Dunk*. New York: E. P. Dutton, 1987. Oral history by players from the 1930s to the '70s.

Scheffer, William J., editor, *The Reach Official Basket Ball Guide*, annual from 1901 to 1926. Philadelphia: A. J. Reach Company.

Weyand, Alexander M., *The Cavalcade of Basketball*. New York: Macmillan, 1960.

Index

(Photos are indicated by page numbers in *italics*.)

215